THE
OUTDOOR COMPANION

THE
OUTDOOR COMPANION

An environmental handbook for surviving and enjoying the outdoors

**QUENTIN CHESTER
and JONATHAN CHESTER**

SIMON & SCHUSTER
AUSTRALIA

DEDICATION

To George and Carmel Adams

THE OUTDOOR COMPANION

First published in Australasia in 1991 by
Simon & Schuster Australia
20 Barcoo Street, East Roseville NSW 2069

A Paramount Communications Company
Sydney   New York   London   Toronto   Tokyo   Singapore

©1991 Quentin Chester and Jonathan Chester

All rights reserved. No part of this publication may be reproduced, stored in a retrieval system, or transmitted, in any form or by any means, electronic, mechanical, photocopying, recording or otherwise, without the prior permission of the publisher in writing.

National Library of Australia
Cataloguing in Publication data

Chester, Quentin.
    The outdoor companion: a handbook for surviving and enjoying the outdoors.

    Bibliography.
    Includes index.
    ISBN 0 7318 0166 0.

    1. Outdoor life. I. Chester, Jonathan.
    II. Title.

796.5

Designed by Michelle Havenstein

Illustrations by Leslye Cole

Typeset in Helvetica and Novarese Book in Australia
by The Type Group Pty Ltd

Printed in Singapore by Kim Hup Lee Printing Co Pte Ltd

CONTENTS

Authors' Note *viii*
Acknowledgments *viii*
Introduction *ix*

PART 1
OUTDOOR SKILLS AND ESSENTIALS

1 GETTING READY *3*
Where to Start *3*
Trip Planning *5*
Physical Preparation *8*
Gear Preparation *8*
Getting There *10*

2 OUT THERE *11*
Heading Off *11*
Choosing a Campsite *12*
Setting Up Camp *13*
Hygiene *15*
Moving On *16*

3 WEATHER *18*
Reading the Signs *18*
Cloud Formations *19*
Rain *20*
Cold *21*
Snow *22*
Heat *23*
Thunderstorms *23*

4 NAVIGATION *25*
Map-reading *25*
Using a Compass *27*

Alternative Navigation *31*
Being Lost *32*

5 FOOD *33*
Basic Requirements *33*
Food Types *34*
Menu Planning *34*
Buying Food *35*
Packaging and Food Carrying *36*
Breakfast *36*
Lunch *37*
Dinner *37*
Drinks *38*
Snacks *39*
Cooking *39*

6 ENJOYING THE OUTDOORS *41*
Botany *41*
Birdwatching *42*
Other Wildlife *42*
Geology *43*
The Night Sky *43*
Photography *44*
Reading *48*
Diaries *48*
History *49*

7 FIRST AID AND SURVIVAL *50*
First Aid *51*
Personal First Aid Kit Checklist *51*
Emergencies *51*
Trauma and Injuries *55*
Minor Ailments *57*

Nature's Annoyances 59
Accidents and Survival
    Skills 59
Survival Kit Checklist 62

PART 2
OUTDOOR ACTIVITIES

8 BUSHWALKING 65
Setting the Pace 65
Rest Stops 66
Ups and Downs 66
Treading Lightly 67
Pack Carrying 67
Route Finding 68
Challenging Terrain 69
Day Walk Checklist 73
The Path Ahead 74

**9 CROSS-COUNTRY
    SKIING** 75
The Basic Skills 76
Touring 80
Day Tour Checklist 81
Snowsense 82
Snowcamping 83

**10 CLIMBING AND
    MOUNTAINEERING** 86
Bouldering 88
Soloing 88
Rock Climbing 88
Mountaineering 95

11 TREKKING 99
Options and Planning 99
Cultural Considerations 101
Health Considerations 103
Gear for Trekking 107
Equipment Checklist 107

12 OTHER ACTIVITIES 109
Canoeing 109
Rafting 110
Canyoning 111
Caving 111
Paragliding 112
Mountain Biking 113
Orienteering 114
More Options 115

**13 OUTINGS WITH
    CHILDREN** 117
Preparation 119
Activities 119
Camping Out 120
Gear for Kids 121

PART 3
OUTDOOR EQUIPMENT

Buying Outdoor Gear 125

14 FOOTWEAR 128
Comfort 128
Design and Construction 129
Shoes 131
Lightweight Fabric Boots 132
Leather Boots 133
Accessories 134
Buying Footwear 135
Taking Care of Your Footwear 136
Taking Care of Your Feet 136

15 CLOTHING 137
Functional Layering 137
Fibres and Fabrics 138
Underwear 139
Insulation 140
Rainwear 141
Extremities 144
Buying Clothing 145

General Clothing *146*
Clothing Checklist *147*
Clothing for Trekking *147*

16 SLEEPING BAGS *148*
The Human Element *148*
Intended Uses *149*
Filling *150*
Shape *151*
Construction *152*
Design Details *153*
Materials *154*
Variations and Innovations *154*
Necessary Accessories *155*
Buying a Sleeping Bag *155*
Taking Care of Your Sleeping Bag *156*

17 PACKS *158*
Load Carrying *158*
Materials and Design *159*
Daypacks *160*
Alpine Packs *162*
Rucksacks *162*
Buying a Pack *164*
Travel Packs *165*
Fitting a Pack *166*

18 TENTS *167*
Buying a Tent *168*
Three-Season Tents *169*
Mountain Tents *170*
Lightweight Alternatives *172*
Tents of the Future *173*
Taking Care of Your Tent *173*

19 STOVES AND COOKING EQUIPMENT *175*
Stove Types *176*
Stove Accessories *179*
Lighting a Stove *181*
Cookware and Utensils *181*
Buying a Stove *182*

20 CLIMBING, MOUNTAINEERING AND CROSS-COUNTRY SKI GEAR *184*
Rock Climbing *185*
Buying Rock Climbing Gear *188*
Mountaineering *192*
Buying Mountaineering Gear *197*
Cross-Country Ski Gear *198*
Buying Cross-Country Ski Gear *202*

21 ACCESSORIES *203*
Maps and Compasses *203*
Knives *203*
Lights *204*
Repair Kits *205*
Sunglasses *205*
Toilet Kit *206*
Entertainment *206*

Glossary *207*

Bibliography *209*

Outdoor Clubs and Associations *213*

Adventure Companies *215*

Equipment Suppliers *217*

Index *220*

AUTHORS' NOTE

The products in this book are described according to our experience, research and knowledge. Readers may find they have different experiences. The book is a guide only. If you have any problems or queries, please seek further information on the products described herein from the suppliers and/or retailers who can provide more detailed explanations of the products. Likewise, this book is in no way intended to be used as the only source for those wishing to undertake any of the specialised activities (such as rock climbing, cross-country skiing, canoeing, paragliding etc.) mentioned. Readers should seek personalised instructions from qualified or experienced friends or professional guides.

ACKNOWLEDGMENTS

The authors would like to thank Robert Easther, Peter Stroud, David Wagland and Warren McLaren for their helpful comments on the manuscript. We are indebted to the editorial team at Simon & Schuster for their support, guidance and good humour. We would also like to thank Leslye Cole for the illustrations.

INTRODUCTION

This book is for anyone contemplating going into the outdoors. It's divided into three parts: the skills you need to take care of yourself and others; the activities to pursue; and the gear required to help you make the most of your time in wide-open spaces.

In the same spirit as a walking map or a climbing guide, we have tried to show possible starting points and some directions to follow. The idea is to give the newcomer a grasp of the essentials of outdoor living. At the same time we hope experienced hands will pick up some words of advice.

For this book to work as a map of what the outdoors has to offer, then it is of necessity on a large scale. Small libraries can be found on topics we sketch in a single chapter – this is particularly true of the section dealing with outdoor activities. We describe the scope of what's available and give readers the information they need to take their interest further. We do not pretend that reading this book will make anyone an expert skier, walker, climber or canoeist. There are many excellent manuals that help perform this role and the bibliography signposts some recommended reading.

There are also several classic handbooks on bushcraft. The basic skills – finding your way; seeking food, water and shelter – have not changed, but these fundamentals are being interpreted in new ways. There have been many developments in techniques and equipment. Fresh attitudes prevail on taking care of wild places. Newcomers are entering the outdoors through the recent growth in adventure travel, outdoor education and conservation groups. Most of all, with greater mobility and leisure time, more people are crossing freely from activity to activity. *The Outdoor Companion* attempts to reflect these changes.

Yet, in the face of all the trends, the back-country remains its raw, gritty self. Venturing into the outdoors still means having to rough it – sweat will bead on your forehead, thick scrub can graze your shins, and there will be moments when you curse your load and wonder why you are there.

Our guiding philosophy is to keep it simple – to do more with less. The very aim of heading out to the bush is to 'get away from it all', to experience a world free from urban clutter and clamour. For us, it makes no sense to venture into the wilderness burdened with unnecessary gear, or to design an itinerary which simply recreates the pressures of life in the big city. Aside from any sweet-sounding philosophy, travelling light means less damage to the areas we visit.

Indeed, given the widespread interest in preserving what remains of our environment, it is inevitable that more and more people will want to see these places with their own eyes. We have regarded it as our first duty to encourage everyone to treat the outdoors with the utmost care.

There are countless measures everyone can take to limit depredations on the environment. Far from being just another set of rules to follow, these simple steps once practised are all part of rekindling an empathy with natural surroundings – surely one of the richest rewards of being in the bush.

Preserving wild areas is ultimately not just a matter of good behaviour when we are there. It also requires us to view each journey as a gift and something to be savoured. Long before any authority imposes limits on when and where to travel, we must recognise that trips to the bush are not for squandering.

As vital as these concerns have become, the most likely reason to go outdoors is to have a good time. The bush is where we can give ourselves some free rein and feel a lightness of heart.

If you find self-knowledge or environmental enlightenment along the way, then all the better.

Inevitably a book like this has a cautionary tone and is peppered with a few dos and don'ts. But, in the long run, there is no correct line to follow. Beyond an understanding of some elementary skills, you're on your own. Most of the time the outdoors is fun. Even when it's not, there is pleasure in knowing that it is up to you to turn hardships into achievements, and draw lessons from mistakes. And the wonderful thing is, the opportunities are so open-ended.

Finally, this book reflects the experience of two brothers who shared a blissful childhood exploring the bush in the Adelaide Hills, who then moved on to become keen climbers, walkers and skiers. While we have these common interests and have enjoyed many trips together, there are just as many points of difference between us and how we approach the outdoors. Jonathan likes to be closer to the edge by pushing his personal limits on expeditions and high mountains. Quentin's preference is for communal ski trips, rock-climbing weekends and bushwalks closer to home. We hope this complementary experience has brought balance and variety to the text.

PART 1

OUTDOOR SKILLS AND ESSENTIALS

1
GETTING READY

WHERE TO START

The place to begin is in the outdoors itself. The simplest of journeys – a short walk in familiar parkland or a stroll along a quiet beach – is enough. Settle into a comfortable walking rhythm and open up to your surroundings. Forget about plans and outcomes; look instead for the small things, the textures and shades of colour. Smell the air. Feel the ground underfoot and walk softly.

Such outings require no special training or equipment, and you should not necessarily hurry on to anything more grandiose. It takes time and patience to become attuned to the natural world and your place in it. Gradually you sense why it is that you want to return: whether it be the challenge of the climb or the wonder of the place. No matter what the incentive, you begin to comprehend that the journey is the destination.

When the time comes for new horizons and extended outdoor experiences there are numerous ways forward. If you had endless hours to devote to your outdoor initiation you might go it alone; discover new areas, sketch your own maps, build your equipment – perfect your skills from the ground up. Unfortunately there is no longer room in most lives for this kind of exemplary pioneering, and instead we usually choose to learn our skills and bush-lore through the guidance of others.

Join a club

The most common path to outdoor knowledge is through an organised group. Clubs come in many guises. The bigger ones offer many activities, and roam far and wide to pursue them. Others are localised and focus on a particular interest such as canoe touring or rock climbing. Clubs can thrive in surprising places and as offshoots of larger organisations, such as universities, corporations or community groups. A little research will uncover what's available and how the groups differ in emphasis.

In the better clubs newcomers are made welcome and beginners are given the chance to develop skills. Larger groups usually run a programme of outings and courses which allow you to progress gradually to more challenging trips. The instruction given is often low-key and can even be a little haphazard, but it won't cost you much. The real value of clubs is the chance to share your learning with others, and pick up practical wisdom from the old hands.

The chief drawback of most clubs is

their size and the bureaucracy that usually goes with it. For some people the committee meetings, club rules and busy social atmosphere can be stifling. It all seems too close to the very things that most people go outdoors to get away from. Yet, in an age of fast-diminishing open spaces, clubs play a crucial role in promoting a conservation ethic and fighting for wilderness causes. At a local level a club may be the only way to effectively lobby for land access, wildlife preservation and other freedoms. In this sense there are compelling reasons for supporting clubs, even if you graduate to enjoying the outdoors by more independent means. (See *Outdoor Clubs and Associations*.)

Take a course

Another option is to sign up for a commercially run instructional course or join a professionally led trip into the back-country. These are offered by many adventure travel operators, park services or equipment suppliers.

Though costly, such courses can provide a quick, convenient introduction to the outdoors. They are particularly suited for activities such as skiing, canoeing and climbing which demand both technical skills and specialised equipment. The better instructors are both talented exponents and accomplished teachers, but even so the experience you have is often short-lived. To consolidate on the knowledge gained you need to devote time to practise in the field.

There are also private guides who, for a fee, will take you into many wilderness areas. Guides are especially useful if you want individual instruction in an activity, or for leading a group into unfamiliar territory.

Go with a friend

Perhaps the best possible introduction is through a close friend who is willing to share some hard-won skills. This approach, however, is by no means foolproof. There are plenty of cases of friendships not surviving the transition to the wilds. Your friend may grow weary of shepherding you along and answering your incessant questions. Conversely a normally good-humoured companion may become surly if they've been talked into going on a trip just to make up the numbers. It takes a good measure of discernment on both sides for the arrangement to succeed: beware the self-appointed expert and the overbearing novice. As always, the safest policy is to start out small and build up to the longer trips.

Read a book

In the early stages of learning about the outdoors much can be gleaned from books and magazines. As well as the practical how-to-do-it manuals there are expedition narratives, historical accounts and autobiographies that can make palpable the lure of the wild. If you like reading, there is a rich vein of outdoor literature to be mined.

Magazines too offer a wealth of information on areas to visit, current equipment trends and wilderness concerns. Of course stunning pictorials and gripping yarns are no substitute for first-hand experience, but as you take your first steps it can be comforting to know that others find the outdoors as mysterious and fascinating as you do. (See the *Bibliography* for suggested books and magazines.)

TRIP PLANNING

Trips into the wild never go entirely to plan and nor should they. The very essence of being in the outdoors is to encounter the unexpected: if you are only satisfied when things run like clockwork, then take up watchmaking. The object of planning a trip is not to eliminate the unforeseen, but to be mentally and physically equipped to enjoy it.

Inspiration for a trip may come from a description in a book, an overheard remark, or an intriguing place name on a map. Many a momentous expedition has had its genesis in a huddle of friends poring over a fuzzy snapshot of a peak. Whenever climbers, walkers, skiers and paddlers get together the conversation bubbles with talk of the next trip. As you become part of such networks the question of where to go is rarely a problem.

Gathering information

No matter what the catalyst is for a trip you will need to assemble a little factual information. The primary source for cross-country journeys is a current topographic map of the area. Interpreting the symbols and contours of these maps is an acquired skill, but with practice map-reading has manifold rewards. These maps, however, will not necessarily show established tracks, campsites and water supplies. For such detail you need to seek out additional maps published by the relevant park service or recreation body. These are usually sketch maps and not in themselves precise enough for navigation, but they do mark popular trails and highlights, with specific advice about walking in the area. Many popular walking destinations also have their own guidebooks giving information on routes to follow, sometimes in step-by-step detail.

The options

Once the raw information is gathered, take the opportunity to sift through the alternative routes and highlights. Also, remember that getting there is half the fun, so to create a vision of your backcountry journey, assemble the gear, mull over maps and anticipate the challenges ahead – all are pleasures in themselves.

Timing

As the trip takes shape the obvious question arises: when to go? In the broadest sense spring and autumn offer the right mix of conditions for many temperate areas. By contrast a desert trek is more promising during midwinter, while a hike into the high country is best left until snow has receded in summer. Venturing into an area off-season may seem perverse but, increasingly, this is the only way to appreciate a popular place free from the madding crowd. For the same reason busy holiday weekends are best spent in more remote locations.

The decision about how long to go for is sometimes made for you. Areas of renown have their classic trips – the pass crossings, lake circuits and ridge traverses – that take an acknowledged number of days. Approaching the question from another angle, you can construct your own itinerary around the time you have available. This requires more imagination and a sense of priorities. Do you want a leisurely time with lots of side trips, or a 'gung ho' week of peak bagging?

Plotting the trip

Working with your map, try to plot your trip day by day. A rule of thumb is that most people can walk between 15 and 25 kilometres a day. Bear in mind that this figure may be more than halved in difficult terrain. One common approach to plotting a trip is to devise a loop or circuit that includes the places you want to visit and returns you to your starting point and means of transport. To go out and return on exactly the same track rather limits your horizons, but sometimes this cannot be avoided. Another option is to plan a traverse to another roadhead, and organise a car shuffle by parking a car at each end of the route.

The longer the trip the more care and detail needs to go into the planning. Daily distances, likely campsites, sources of water and the provisions required all need to be finely judged. A two-week exploration of deep wilderness is not something to be blundered into.

Contacts and permits

By definition, wilderness areas are not frequented so word of mouth information is scarce, yet it can be invaluable to talk to someone with local knowledge, be they a fellow walker or park ranger. For the ultimate protection of the area it is imperative that you find out about any permits required, or regulations such as fire bans that may be in force.

> ## LEAVING WORD
>
> Whenever you venture into the bush someone at home should know where you are and what to do if you don't happen to return by an agreed time or date. This applies as much for day trips as for ambitious trips into the wilderness.
>
> Choose your home contact carefully. Ideally they are a friend or relative who knows the area and the likely consequences of being delayed. Nevertheless, it is a good idea to write down the details of your planned route and any possible variations, the names and contact addresses of those in your party, plus details of your expected return time.
>
> This latter information needs to be interpreted carefully. Nominate how much time should be allowed to pass before any alarm is raised. On longer trips some people give themselves as much as 24 or 48 hours leeway. Your home contact should also have the telephone number of the most appropriate authority to call if you are overdue.
>
> In many areas it is necessary to obtain a wilderness permit from the local park office. This usually means leaving detailed information about your plans with the local ranger. Be sure to 'check out' at the end of the trip.

The group

The longer the trip, the more important is the choice of companions. Dealing with personality differences is not usually a great drama on a weekend walk, but the rigours of a month-long adventure can place a strain on the best of relationships. In dire situations you need to have an unspoken confidence in your fellow travellers, and this comes naturally if you start out together on a number of shorter trips.

Settling on the size of the party is mostly a matter of intuition. For any serious excursion there is safety in a group of three to six people. Many more than that makes it difficult to find campsites, cater for meals and stick together on the track, and most importantly, large groups cause a lot of damage to delicate wilderness trails and campsites. Even if you do find a dozen people with compatible interests and abilities, the sheer effort of maintaining consensus on a long trip runs counter to what the outdoors is all about.

Leadership

If you spend enough time in the outdoors with friends, a strong rapport develops and there is little need for a nominal leader or authority figure. Individual strengths and weaknesses are understood and decisions, even in an emergency, are often made with minimal fuss or debate.

Leadership only really becomes an issue when a group is made up of people with varying abilities, interests or experience. In the case of club trips and other organised outings a reliable leader is normally appointed beforehand. On less formal occasions someone usually assumes the role of leader, either by virtue of their work as a planner and organiser, or on account of their greater experience.

No one leadership style suits all occasions. Just as a benevolent dictatorship can drift towards authoritarianism, so a participatory democracy can collapse into tedious argument. The ideal leader is inconspicuous yet ensures that everyone achieves their aims in going bush.

The only guaranteed way to bypass this issue is to go alone. For some people a solo trip is the ultimate wilderness experience. The total freedom to move when and where you please, without the distractions of company, does have its appeal. At another level there is a one-on-one communion with nature, yet the risks attached to these freedoms should not be underestimated. Solo trips are for those who have served a long apprenticeship and those willing to accept the consequences of any misadventure.

Non-planning

When your experience in the outdoors can be measured in years the need for complicated planning diminishes. The doyen of British expeditioners, Bill Tilman, once said that any worthwhile trip could be organised on the back of an envelope. Certainly the more mundane aspects of planning become second nature with experience and there is less reason to dissect how each day will be spent.

Once you have outdoor experience, all you need to do for a weekend away is decide on an area, grab your pack and a good map and go. The best trips thus generate their own shape and momentum in the field. A large dose of spontaneity should be part of every journey; after all, a compelling reason for going bush is to be liberated from everyday regimentation.

PHYSICAL PREPARATION

While being fit adds to the enjoyment of any activity, the outdoors is not solely the preserve of the svelte and supple. Age is no barrier, nor is there any need to break records or outwalk a rival. A trip into the bush can be as gentle or as testing as you want to make it.

General fitness

The key difference between outdoor pursuits and other sports is that typically you are walking or paddling or skiing for most of the day, and sometimes for several days in a row. Assuming you are otherwise healthy the best preparation is to develop your stamina and endurance. For the long haul you need a strong heart and efficient lungs. Any exercise that conditions your cardiovascular system helps, but the perfect training for a walk is to go walking, and this is the case for all outdoor activities. There's no need for a stopwatch or an elaborate schedule, just start out gradually and increase your workload as you get stronger.

Specific training

If you have never paddled a canoe before, by the end of the first day you will discover sore muscles that you didn't even know existed. The same goes for a skiing or climbing trip, and even a day's hiking can make your shoulders sore if you are not accustomed to carrying a pack.

As you become focused on a particular activity it will be worth developing the specific muscle groups involved. Canoeists need power from their arms and shoulders. Skiing puts a strain on knees and thighs. Climbing demands sustained finger strength and a good power-to-weight ratio. The steep climbs and descents on a mountain trek can be a real test of leg muscles and joints.

For all these activities there are exercise programmes that help you prepare for an extended trip. Most pursuits have a competitive dimension, and if you want to reach the top the training required is of a standard and intensity equal to that of any sport you wish to excel at.

GEAR PREPARATION

Getting your gear together at the last minute is a sure way to forget some small, indispensable item.

The business of deciding what to take and then organising everything into a manageable load takes time. This experience will also help you find ways to minimise what you have to carry on your back.

Make a list

Start with a checklist, for example Survival Kit Checklist in Chapter 7, *First Aid and Survival* and make it as comprehensive as you like. The list will be different for each trip but there will be core items that always appear. A list will be more useful if it's logically divided into groups such as clothes, cooking and eating equipment, sleeping gear, first aid and safety, and so on. In time you will learn ways to edit the list to suit the type of trip and your preferences.

Gather gear

Working from the checklist, assemble the gear into its groups. For your initial outings this may take a day or two as you work out what items you have to borrow, buy or improvise. If, halfway through the list, you already have a pile you can't jump over, then cast a sceptical eye over any superfluous luxuries.

Checks and tests

Critical items or gear with moving parts should be checked carefully. Look for signs of wear and tear that may become terminal in the field. Just because the stove worked last time, there is no guarantee that it is still functional. Fire it up to make sure. Likewise, sleeping bags should be checked, tents pitched, torches switched on, first aid kits inspected, etc. This is also the time to seal seams, test zippers, examine stitching and waterproof your boots.

Packing up

Effective packing is more an art than a science. At home it's no trouble to stow everything neatly into a rucksack, but the challenge is to keep it that way when you are constantly delving for odds and ends. The trick is to work out a system that allows for loading and unloading with the least amount of chaos. For this, gear should be grouped in waterproof stuffsacks and then given a familiar home in your pack. Stuffsacks help to protect gear and keep it dry. (See Chapter 3, *Weather*.)

For general walking, heavy items like the food, stove and fuel should be close to the back and closer to the shoulders than the hips. Make sure however that any hard-edged gear such as billies and stoves are carefully positioned so they don't dig into your back or abrade the pack fabric.

Lighter and less dense gear such as your clothing and sleeping bag can be stowed in the base of the pack: indeed many packs have a separate compartment for just such a purpose. Smaller, often-used items like your map, compass, water bottle, camera and pocket knife can be stowed in outside pockets.

HOW TO PACK A RUCKSACK
1. Heaviest items close to the back between the shoulders and hips 2. Less heavy 3. Lighter and less dense 4. Lightest should go at the top and bottom

For skiing, climbing, walking in steep terrain, or any activity requiring balance and stability, the heavier items should be carried lower in the pack.

With experience, organising your gear becomes less of a chore and ultimately it's possible to do away with lists and longwinded packing sessions.

GETTING THERE

The importance of the hours spent travelling before and after a trip should not be overlooked. This time brackets your experience in the wild. Use the approach journey to get into the mood of being away and the spirit of the place you have chosen.

While many fine areas are serviced by public transport many can only be accessed by private vehicle. For weekends it makes sense to take the quickest and easiest route, but when heading into the bush for a week or more what's an extra hour or two when you can enjoy scenic backroads, free from the bedlam of highway traffic?

If you drive to a remote wilderness area the adventure can begin well before you put on your pack. Negotiating punishing outback tracks with bewildering intersections takes time and determination. You and your vehicle need to be prepared for the rigours and any likely emergency. Carry spare fuel and extra food and water. Even when it may seem unnecessary, taking a second vehicle is often good insurance.

After all the planning and anticipation, you've arrived at the beginning of your adventure, and yet the most dangerous part of the journey is probably already over!

2

OUT THERE

HEADING OFF

After what seems like an eternity cooped up in your vehicle or other method of transport, there is a strong temptation to grab the rucksack and cut loose onto your appointed river, rock or range. Unless you are supremely confident, or just plain reckless, it's worth doing a few pre-flight checks.

Local conditions

First be ready to tailor your plans according to what conditions are like when you actually arrive. This means keeping a sharp eye on the local weather. Unseasonal snow, for instance, can turn a planned two day alpine ramble into something akin to a retreat from Moscow. Alternatively, sudden rain may have transformed your sedate canoeing stream into a raging torrent. At the same time, size up what you can see of your objective. A peak that appeared to be a modest afternoon climb from the map may seem to loom overhead. Remember to advise, if possible, the park authorities or your home contact of any revised itinerary.

Final gear check

Before stepping out it's wise to do a final gear check. Depending on the groans emitted as you haul your pack from the car this will usually result in lightening the load by weeding out surplus food or clothing. If travelling with a group this is also the moment to share out communal gear and make sure that everyone's load is roughly in proportion to their carrying ability. If this is your rucksack's maiden voyage you may discover that with a full load a few harness adjustments are in order. (See Chapter 17, *Fitting a pack*.)

Leaving the vehicle

Finally, if leaving a vehicle make sure it is parked in a safe spot, preferably on high ground. Any valuables left in the car should be hidden, and the car securely locked. As a precaution against theft it may also be an idea to remove the rotor arm from the distributor, or something similar which can be easily carried. Whether you take the car keys with you or conceal them on the vehicle is a matter of personal preference. Whatever is decided it is important that everyone in the party knows their whereabouts in case of emergency.

The time has come to move out. Even if you have arrived at your starting point after dark it's often worth making the effort to get a little way into the bush before bunking down for the night. With help from a torch, and some moonlight if you're lucky, you need only to go 100 metres or so to pitch the tent. There are few worse places to wake up than in the middle of a carpark.

Making the transition from the highway to the back-country can take a little time. You are leaving behind the snarl of traffic and the burdens of town life to enter a realm of the senses and to test your mettle, so ease into it.

CHOOSING A CAMPSITE

The perfect campsite is in a grassy clearing by a burbling mountain stream. There is an abundance of dry firewood, soft level ground for your tent and a sandy pool with a waterfall nearby. From the tent door you gaze at a vista of peaks with a dusting of fresh snow. Most important of all, you discover this pristine splendour quite by chance and just at the appointed hour to down packs.

Such nirvanas must exist — the travel brochures are full of them — but in real life campsites are invariably a compromise of the picture postcard ideal. One of the most potent reasons for going bush is the serendipity of the trail, and selecting a spot in which to spend the night can be one of the unexpected pleasures.

Sleep and shelter

The first requirement of any site is to ensure a comfortable night's sleep. This means finding a patch of level, or at least only gently sloping, ground for your tent or swag. In steep or rocky terrain this may not be easy so it pays to be prepared and imaginative.

Consider the weather and the seasons. In summer seek out shade and a site protected from the hot morning sun. A sun-screened clearing in the bottom of the valley will be refreshingly cool and breezy during these months. In winter, however, the same place can become correspondingly bleak and windswept: such spots are known as frosty hollows for good reason. To find warmer air choose a site higher on a hillside and in the company of trees and vegetation.

Shelter from wind and rain is also a priority. Look for natural windbreaks in the form of trees, outcrops or low ridges. Be careful though not to sleep directly beneath any tree with suspicious looking dead branches, or hard up against crumbling rock overhangs.

Water

While the sound of running water may be relaxing for some it pays to site tents well back from any watercourse, no matter how dry or innocuous it might appear. In mountain or gorge areas flash flooding far upstream can cause river levels to rise rapidly without so much as a drop of rain falling in your neighbourhood. Similarly, try to avoid soggy ground or depressions where overnight rain could collect.

At the same time the preferred campsite will have a plentiful supply of fresh running water close by. Alas, nowadays even the most crystal clear flowing creeks can be contaminated by human and animal habitations upstream, so unless absolutely sure of the purity of your supply any water for drinking must be boiled, some say for at least five minutes. (Add a minute for every 300 m (1000 ft) above sea level.) Another solution is to use water purification tablets.

Campfires

A roaring campfire is an emotive and enduring symbol of outdoor life. Sitting around a fire watching the flames dance and the coals glow is perhaps the ultimate atavistic experience. Sadly, many popular areas have been so stripped of suitable firewood that this most primitive of luxuries is no longer practicable. Indeed, the new wilderness ethic rightly exhorts us not to light campfires at all, and to do our cooking on lightweight stoves, and the need for a campsite to have a firewood supply is no longer the prerequisite it once was.

Nevertheless, some outdoor people simply cannot live without a cheery blaze and if there is ample fallen dead timber available they will build a small campfire for communal warmth, and do at least a portion of their cooking on stoves. Whether this compromise is tolerable depends entirely on the area in question. If you do plan to have a campfire make sure it is a small one and always completely under control. (See Chapter 5, *Cooking fires*.) If a fireplace is ready in existence, use it, rather than building another.

All the rules that make a good campsite are there to be broken, except one, and that is to leave the site as you found it, or if possible looking better. Aside from this stipulation it's worth seeking out varied and unusual locations. This may mean forsaking easily accessible water and timber in favour of a high ridgetop or summit camp which gives spectacular views of the country you're passing through, as well as being a place to witness moon and sun rises. Such perches are exposed to the winds and elements so choose your nights carefully.

Plan ahead

No matter what the terrain is like it pays to have a working plan as to where the night will be spent. This means looking for suitable spots well before darkness descends, and being flexible in case delays force a halt to be called earlier. Stumbling on in the gloom, merely to reach an appointed destination, does not make for a relaxed day's end and in bad weather often leads to accidents and cases of hypothermia. Alternatively, if in the early afternoon you happen upon the Garden of Eden your schedule should be pliable enough to allow you to savour such special surroundings.

Finally, if venturing into a popular area commonsense or local park regulations may dictate that you use an existing campsite, and most likely share it with other parties. Such practices limit the human impact on the environment to specific sites. Wherever possible use established sleeping plots and fireplaces, and of course respect the privacy and needs of fellow travellers.

SETTING UP CAMP

You've discovered the campsite of your dreams. At last you can loosen the pack straps and lower your load, and perhaps yourself, to the ground. Take a moment to survey the scene.

In which direction is the prevailing

breeze blowing? What's a good spot for the tent? Where to cook, sit and while away the evening?

Tent pitching

For the sake of sleeping soundly, a few minutes preparing the tent site is time well spent. If the ground is rocky or covered in sticks it may be necessary to do some gentle clearing, and to level out hollows with fallen leaves and the like, though any excavations should be avoided. If there is an inescapable dip in your chosen plot, then it is more comfortable to sleep with your hips in the hollow.

Hopefully this will not be the first time you have pitched your tent. If so, try to remain calm and when all else fails read the instructions. Tents should be orientated so that you sleep with

ROLLING HITCH KNOT
An adjustable sliding knot used for tent guys

BOWLINE KNOT
A non-slip all-purpose knot

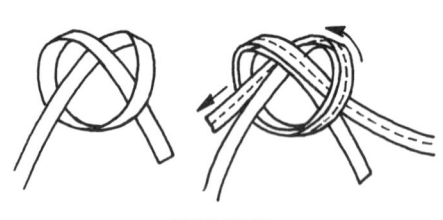

TAPE KNOT
For joining flat webbing

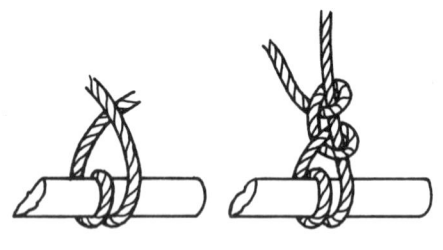

ROUND TURN AND TWO HALF HITCHES
For securing a rope to a tree or another object

FIGURE OF EIGHT KNOT
Widely used for rock climbing, tying into harnesses and anchors

DOUBLE FISHERMAN'S KNOT
Used for tying two rope ends together

your head uphill and at the same time take advantage of views and morning light. Bear in mind too the need for ventilation or shelter from the wind. Whether the best defence comes from turning the tent door into or away from the wind will depend on its design. Aligning the doorway into a steady breeze can inflate the tent and keep it taut. The other way round can mean pointing the sharper, wind-spilling end of the tent into the wind. Only experience will show which is the best arrangement for the tent you are using.

Once the tent is pitched lay out sleeping mats and fluff up sleeping bags so the filling has time to loft. If you are a light sleeper give your allotted sleeping space a quick test run so you can smooth out any remaining lumps or bumps while there is still daylight. It's also worthwhile sorting through clothing and finding a torch before darkness falls. After leaving the tent to watch the sunset, don't forget to zip up all mesh doors and windows to keep out mosquitoes.

Cooking area

Setting up an outdoor kitchen may mean little more than unpacking and lighting the stove, laying out your food, and putting a pot of water on for a brew. If on the other hand you plan to cook on a campfire, gather up an adequate supply of kindling and wood. Fires should be positioned well away from your tent and nearby vegetation, and the surrounding ground should be cleared of dry sticks and leaves. Building elaborate stone fireplaces should be avoided, especially as river stones have a habit of exploding in fires. Remember the first law of campfires is that the smoke will always blow where it is not wanted. (See Chapter 5 for more on campfires for cooking.)

Before the light fades completely collect as much water as is needed for the evening meal and a morning cuppa. Used wine cask inners make excellent campsite water bags. If there is no alternative to standing or dirty water, you can use a lightweight water filter or sterilise the water by adding an iodine solution (see Chapter 7) or improvise a filter out of some fine weave, porous fabric.

The order in which these tasks are carried out will be governed by the weather, remaining daylight and personal preferences. If cooking on an open fire, for instance, get this underway first to allow a good foundation of hot coals to form. Whatever the sequence of events there is rarely any need to rush. Stay in touch with what is happening around you; the changing light and the sights and sounds of the bush. Even humble chores have a grace of their own in such a setting.

HYGIENE

Staying clean

There's nothing like a week spent roughing it in the bush to make you appreciate a hot shower or bath when you get home. While life in the outdoors limits the opportunities for total cleanliness, it doesn't mean you can't enjoy a level of comfort and hygiene.

The first law of washing yourself in the bush is not to pollute rivers and water supplies in doing so. This means curbing any urge to jump into the nearest waterhole with a cake of soap. One alternative is to take a couple of billies of water to a pleasant spot, well away from any water source, and have a 'bird bath'. If camped by a suitable river, an afternoon swim downstream is probably all you need.

On extended outings the feeling of being 'dirty' becomes very subjective. After several days you, your body and your companions seem to adapt to the new order of things. Indeed, aside from attending to basics one begins to wonder whether all that soap and detergent we scrub onto our skin at home is really necessary.

Dishwashing

Cleaning up pots and pans after meals should also be done well away from any primary water supply. The best approach is to heat up water in the largest cooking pot and use a small scourer if necessary. A small amount of biodegradable detergent can help, but it is amazing what you can do to clean dishes with sticks, fibrous bark or a handful of wet sand. (Ideally the meal is so delicious that every plate and pot will be scraped clean.) It's wise to give everything a final rinse with a little boiling water. Leftover dishwater should be disposed of carefully or used to help douse the fire.

Toilet matters

As a friend once observed, this is the subject you never read about in any of the journals of the great explorers and adventurers. How *do* they go to the toilet when hanging off the north face of Mt Everest, or tentbound in a raging Antarctic blizzard?

For those of us who travel in more benign places it is a relatively simple matter. Unless occupying a standing camp, or a busy site where the park service may have installed toilets, the decision about where one answers the call of nature is largely up to you.

Once more the golden rule is not to urinate or defecate anywhere that might cause the fouling of a water supply. This means studiously avoiding any watercourse or obvious catchment area. For defecating in particular choose a place well away and downwind from the campsite or any other visited spot. Using a rock, stick, or small plastic trowel carried for this purpose, dig a small hole. Toilet paper will break down, but only very slowly, so wherever possible the preferred practice is to burn the paper before covering the hole.

All this can be quite an ordeal if you are above the snow line where the weather is often less forgiving. In this situation it is imperative to pick a place as far as possible from any stream or runoff. A deep snow hole is required and the burning of toilet paper essential.

MOVING ON

Leaving a campsite requires at least as much care as choosing it in the first place. The clear aim is to leave absolutely no trace of your tenure. This means ensuring that every last scrap of rubbish, paper, foil and plastic is collected and taken out with you. A sturdy, easily tied rubbish bag should be carried with you for this purpose.

Fires should be completely extinguished using as much water as is required to make the coals cool enough to touch – but be careful about putting this to the test. Accumulated ash can be carefully scattered. Any earth removed to create a fire pit should be used to cover up the residual ash and coals. Campfires are the most conspicuous and lasting scar that campers leave in the bush, so spend time erasing their presence. The exception is a campsite that is obviously well used, and where the fireplace has become a permanent fixture. Better to leave it in place, and as a kindly deed you may also wish to gather a supply of wood for the next group.

Tents should be taken down and if possible aired and dried before packing. (Even in dry conditions some condensation will have gathered under the tent floor.) If the weather is kind it is worth airing sleeping bags as well. Kitchen areas take a lot of punishment so make every effort to restore them to their original state.

After you have packed up check for anything you may have overlooked. It is surprising how many times you will turn up stray tent pegs or paper scraps. Scatter leaf litter and twigs over any cleared or scuffed ground. When the moment comes to shoulder your pack the only thing left should be the memory of a night well spent.

3
WEATHER

One common paradox of the outdoors is that the worse the weather the more memorable is the trip. In fact, many hardy outdoor types secretly relish the rumbling advance of thunderstorm or a blizzard's lashing fury. They revel in the spectacle and caprice of nature at its wildest, safe in the knowledge that they know how to take care of themselves.

For many people, however, dealing with changes and extremes of weather, without four walls and a sturdy roof, can be a little daunting. This is no surprise considering the way in which the artificial climates of city life so completely buffer us from the real elements. It also encourages us to regard even the humblest storm as some kind of aberrant behaviour to be avoided, if not feared. Yet with the right equipment, an open mind and an understanding of weather patterns it is possible to endure and even enjoy the worst that can be thrown at us.

READING THE SIGNS

Weather is the great governer of the outdoors – it can make or break a trip. The ability to prepare for likely conditions, and then adapt to changes, ranks high on a list of outdoor skills. While a working knowledge of meteorology is helpful, vigilance in the field is far more useful and rewarding.

In the preparatory stages of a trip piece together as much information as possible about the prevailing conditions in your chosen area. Good sources are weather bureaux, the park service, guidebooks and, best of all, friends who have first-hand experience of local variations, particularly in mountain country.

Prior to leaving home keep a close eye on the forecasts for the region. Study weather maps and ideally get a version of events from someone on the spot, like a local farmer or park ranger.

A weather map or synoptic chart shows the movement of pressure systems across the continent. The lines drawn on the map are isobars which link points of equal atmospheric pressure. Winds blow parallel to the isobars: anticlockwise in a high, and clockwise in a low. The closer together the isobars, the stronger the wind.

A high pressure system generally means fine, stable weather and lighter winds. Low pressure systems are normally associated with unsettled conditions, rain and lower temperatures. Cold and warm fronts occur where low and high pressure systems meet.

Once in the bush it's feasible to make

your own forecasts by interpreting changes in temperature, wind speed and direction and, most of all, cloud formations. If you are particularly keen you may even want to carry a pocket barometer to monitor rises and falls in atmospheric pressure, which are precursors to weather changes.

CLOUD FORMATIONS

Clouds are formed in two ways. Cumulus clouds are created by rising hot air currents and develop into the familiar fluffy white clouds. They often signal fair weather, but if they grow to a tremendous height they can become a cumulonimbus thunderhead. Stratus cloud forms with the cooling of moist air and appears in vast sheet-like expanses.

Cloud types can be grouped by their altitude. The highest clouds are cirrus, cirrocumulus and cirrostratus which occur between 10,500 m (35,000 ft) and 7500 m (25,000 ft). They consist almost entirely of ice crystals. Cirrus are thin, wispy clouds with formations often called 'mare's-tails'. Next down in the range are cirrocumulus clouds which are commonly described as a 'mackerel sky'. Cirrostratus form a very fine veil of cloud across the sky.

The middle grouping of clouds are the altocumulus and altostratus. Altocumulus are of a whitish-grey colour and occur in puffy rolls or bands. Altostratus form a dark mass of cloud that can lead to steady light rain.

Low cloud includes stratus, nimbostratus, cumulonimbus and stratocumulus. Nimbostratus are dark low cloud masses that produce heavy incessant rain. Stratocumulus clouds are thick and irregular. They may bring light drizzle.

Distinguishing between cloud types will help you predict what weather is in store. Remembering the names is not as important as being able to predict the results. So, for example, cirrus cloud and high winds often precede bad weather. Similarly, stratocumulus may gather and thicken to become nimbostratus and you know it's time to keep your waterproofs near the top of your pack.

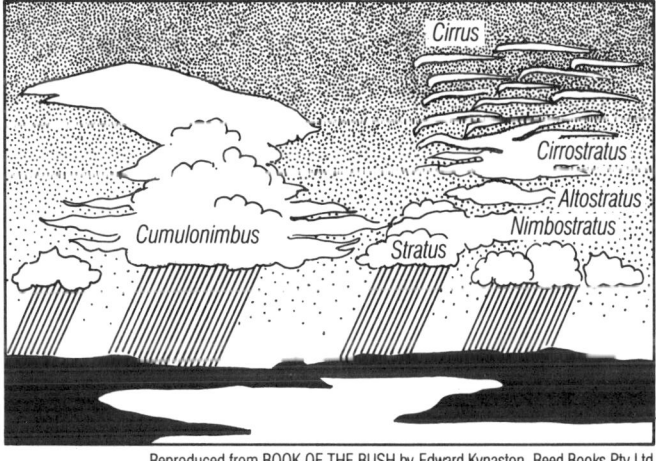

Some cloud types and their positions

Reproduced from BOOK OF THE BUSH by Edward Kynaston, Reed Books Pty Ltd

RAIN

More outings have been sabotaged by rain than by any other agent. It has the power to dampen spirits and incite mutiny.

The truth is that walking in the wet can be one of life's great pleasures. Rain makes the bush come alive before your eyes: everything smells lush; trees and vegetation are suddenly more vividly coloured; rocks glisten; and low, misty clouds soften the view.

To enjoy this revelation you need functional clothing. A quality rain-jacket is essential. For bushwalking in mild climates a calf-length jacket with adjustable hood and cuffs is ideal. When you're on the trail clothing worn underneath your jacket should be kept to a minimum – a light shirt and pair of shorts will normally suffice. Bushwalking in long wet pants is literally a drag. Avoid cotton garments that are slow drying, and opt instead for a layered ensemble of wool or new generation synthetics. Waterproof overpants are only really necessary in alpine conditions or for activities like skiing, climbing and cycling where a long coat is impractical.

In heavy rain keeping your feet dry is virtually impossible, even with all the advances in waterproofing compounds and 'waterproof' boot liners. Wearing gaiters helps but ultimately water will find a way in. Whatever footwear you choose, it should be lightweight and fast-drying.

Anyone who has trekked in the Himalaya around monsoon time will be familiar with the local tradition of walking with an umbrella. This is also worth considering for other styles of wet weather walking although naturally not in dense scrub or high winds. In a similar vein, the classic wide-brimmed stockman's hat is another defence against dripping trees.

Enjoying a day walking in the rain is only really possible if you have somewhere dry to sleep at night. Natural shelter in the form of a dry cave or overhang is often the best. In wind-driven rain, camp on the lee side of a ridge or escarpment. Trees can also offer a margin of shelter, particularly in light misting rain.

Tents should be pitched on a well-drained site, and if possible use an additional groundsheet underneath the tent. The same groundsheet could also function at mealtimes as a fly or tarpaulin to cook under. Hopefully, all the critical seams on your tent have been sealed. Even so, water seems to appear miraculously inside the best of tents, and a small sponge is handy to soak up surface moisture. Keep the tent well-ventilated to reduce condensation. A taut flysheet will shed rain more effectively, so make regular checks on the guy ropes.

The other secret to surviving damp weather is ensuring that the contents of your pack stay as dry as possible. Waterproof stuffsacks with sealed seams should be used for items such as your sleeping bag and spare clothes. You may also want to line your pack with a heavy duty plastic bag or a large proofed nylon rucksack liner. For river journeys or walking in areas with high rainfall and notorious stream crossings the specialised drybags used by canoeists and rafters are invaluable. Waterproof rucksack covers that envelop the pack offer additional protection but are no substitute for the contents being securely stowed in individual stuffsacks. During the day, be prepared to take advantage of any sunny breaks to dry out wet gear.

Despite all these wise precautions there is no doubt that after days of continuous drumming rain the novelty wears off. Wet tents, sodden clothes and 'trench feet' take their toll on morale. This, combined with fatigue and sharp winds, can often lead to cases of hypothermia. At such times shrewd judgement is required to decide whether to press on, turn back, or rest up under cover.

COLD

Venturing into the outdoors in mid-winter may seem a forbidding prospect when the alternative is a cosy armchair, a good book and a glowing fire. Admittedly the days are short and the nights long (so take a good book with you), but there is nothing quite like a winter landscape with its angled light and more sombre moods. Most importantly you will have more of the country to yourself: more of that most essential of outdoor ingredients – solitude.

Chilly weather can, of course, set in no matter what the season. A sudden wind change, rapid altitude gains, a cold front moving through – all can cause the mercury to plummet. Even in the heart of the desert the hours just before sunrise can be bitterly cold.

To deal with low temperatures you need more of everything: more food, more clothing, more fuel, more effective shelter. Most importantly you need more commonsense, as the penalties for ill-considered moves can be severe.

When you are on the move, cold is not a problem. Provided you have adequate clothing the heat you generate through exercise will keep body and soul contented. Resist the temptation to overdress. Too many clothes create as many problems as too few. You become overheated and sweat more than you need to. The result is that you have to replace lost fluids and deal with clammy clothes that can sap vital warmth, especially during long breaks.

Even in decidedly nippy weather it's possible to walk in shorts and a shirt or two. By all means start out rugged-up on a cold morning, but be prepared to peel off layers as soon as you reach a comfortable temperature. Wear several lighter layers rather than cumbersome coats and thick pants. Your extremities are most vulnerable, so good socks, hats and gloves are indispensable. The time-honoured maxim, 'if your feet are cold, put on a hat' still holds true. Anything you wear should be snug but not so tight-fitting as to restrict blood circulation. Cold toes are all too often caused by feet clad in too many pairs of socks, and crammed tight into boots.

On the trail make shorter but more frequent rest stops. Choose places in the sun or at least out of the wind. Cold weather burns up calories, and dry frosty air can give you a mighty thirst so snack away and drink up. A thermos or some form of insulated bottle is handy for a supply of warming drinks during the day.

It's at nightfall, after a character-building day in the wild, that cold really makes its presence felt. The priorities are: some dry warm clothes; food and fluid to warm the cockles of your heart;

and a cosy spot to nestle into your sleeping bag. The latter is the most crucial, for without proper rest a cold weather expedition degenerates into a survival exercise. A high-lofting bag with a hood is only half the answer. You also need an efficient sleeping mat for insulation from the ground and some metabolic activity to generate warmth. A hot drink and energy snack before retiring will do the trick. If you feel the cold consider wearing additional clothing and using a thermal sleeping bag liner at night.

There is cool weather and there is profound, mind-numbing cold that poses another dilemma altogether – surviving this extreme is discussed in Chapter 7. For short spells of bracing temperatures you simply need to make the most of the limited resources you have, conserve the heat you create, and be mindful of the interplay of the elements. There are any number of windchill charts and graphs but here are some facts to remember:

- A strong wind can more than double the severity of the cold you experience.

- Moisture conducts heat away from the body nearly 20 times faster than air.

- You can lose up to one-third of your body heat through your head.

SNOW

Snow is at once the most wonderful and most challenging outdoor medium. It transforms the land, but there is a world of difference between seeking out snow-covered territory for a ski tour, and waking up one morning on a bushwalk to find your tent plastered, and every path home thigh-deep in dense powder. Skiing and snowcamping are discussed in Chapter 9. For now let us consider the response to unexpected snowfall.

It should be said that such a phenomenon is rare in most parts of Australia, but in mountain country it can happen anytime, even in summer. To start with, the air *will* be cold so the preceding paragraphs apply equally here. If your schedule permits, stay put for a day or two and enjoy the spectacle. In doing so you will give the snow time to consolidate and the weather time to clear.

Breaking a trail through deep snow is hard work and the task should be shared by as many members of your party as possible. Set a moderate pace and plan to cover half the distance you would walk in a normal day. If snow is falling, wear your rainjacket or windproofs to deflect as many flakes as possible. A pair of socks function admirably as emergency mittens. Keeping your feet dry and warm in normal footwear is virtually impossible, but if you have warm socks and gaiters wear them. Should you begin to lose feeling in your fingers and toes be ready to stop and rewarm your feet. Serious snow-related ailments such as frostbite, snowblindness and sunburn are a real risk. (See Chapter 7.)

Finding your way in snow-covered terrain often requires precise map and compass work, especially if landmarks are further obscured or obliterated by low cloud. A true 'whiteout' is a vexing experience. Avoid walking on lee slopes where the snow will be at its deepest, and where there may even be a risk of avalanches. Wherever possible use a marked trail rather than breaking through low scrub and springy snow-laden bushes.

All of these hazards will be diminished if you can spare time and have the resources to pitch your tent and sit it out. Unseasonal snow melts and recedes quickly, especially if followed by rain. For tips on snow-camping and travelling in snow country see Chapter 9.

HEAT

With enough inner fuel and outer covering it is possible to enjoy sub-zero temperatures outdoors. Coping with corresponding extremes of heat is not so easy. Once the mercury rises above 30°C (86°F) there is little joy in carrying a pack and being exposed to the fierce sun. Yet with a few precautions and modest aims a summer trip is almost always feasible.

Choose your time and venue with care. The preferred area will have a reliable water supply and abundant shade. Plan for short days and not too many long, strenuous ascents. The high country will be cooler, but above the tree line natural shade is scarce. Wooded gullies and river systems, especially cool canyons, are often the best routes to follow.

Travel in the early morning and the late evening – rest up in the shade during the heat of the day. Seek out refreshing breezes and waterholes. Your clothes should be loose fitting, easily ventilated and light in colour and weight. Shirts should be long-sleeved to help prevent sunburn. A wide-brimmed, well-ventilated hat is mandatory. Bandannas and scarves are handy for mopping brows and dipping into streams. Walking on hot ground is hard on the feet and the arid terrain often found in hot climates is typically rocky and sandy. Take steps to avoid blisters and use rest stops to bathe feet and air socks.

Of paramount concern is the need to drink water, and plenty of it. The body's response to heat is to produce sweat which, as it evaporates, cools the skin surface. On really hot days a person acclimatised to such conditions can lose 1 L (1¾ pt) of water an hour, and replacing this fluid is essential. At 35°C (95°F) you need at least 5 L (9 pt) of water a day just to endure sitting in the shade – start walking and the figure can double.

Dehydration and overexposure to heat may lead to heat exhaustion, a serious rise in core body temperature and heat stroke. (See Chapter 7.)

Water is heavy stuff to carry, but in dry country it's wise for *each person* to have bottles and water bags with a total capacity of about 10 L (18 pt). By way of compensation you will have to carry much less clothing, food and other equipment than you would on a winter trip.

THUNDERSTORMS

Being caught in a violent electrical storm is both frightening and exhilarating. Suddenly one's clothes and tent feel very thin indeed. While the sound and light show is spectacular, and the effects of such storms are mostly short-lived, they do present real risks.

Lightning takes the shortest path to the ground, so it uses elevated points; cliffs, overhangs, isolated tall trees and the like, to reach its goal. All of these places are to be avoided, as the risk is not just of taking the strike, but of being on the receiving end of the charge as it disperses through the nearby ground.

If you hear thunder approaching move swiftly to lower ground, preferably a valley floor. Look for a hollow or depression and *sit* out the storm tucked up on your sleeping mat with your feet together, minimising the number of points of contact (conduction) with the ground. As we all know, metal is a wonderful electrical conductor so stay well clear of anything metallic. This may include pack frames, and particularly any rock-climbing hardware.

4

NAVIGATION

Finding your way in the bush is mostly a matter of careful observation and commonsense – in many areas you can follow well-marked trails. On organised walks there is often somebody who takes responsibility for route finding and map-reading.

However, there will come a time when you want to strike out into untracked country and test your own skills. There is also always the possibility of finding yourself separated from the trail or your companions, in which case a working knowledge of map and compass is essential.

Far from being a chore, navigating is simply an extension of enjoying the bush and being alert to your surroundings. The alternative is to wander mindlessly in the wake of a 'leader' and remain blinkered, not just to the way forward, but to the features of the terrain you are passing through. In most groups navigating is a shared task and the course taken is a consensus decision. Being lost is not necessarily the drama it's made out to be – it happens regularly, and in various degrees of seriousness, to all bush travellers. Thus the art of navigating is to know not simply where you are and what to head for, but equally to know how to re-orientate yourself when the inevitable happens.

Most of the time navigation is no more than good map-reading. Without being able to interpret the information contained on a map a compass by itself has limited use. At key moments, especially in tortuous terrain and bad weather, the marriage of map and compass is the only way out.

MAP-READING

To the outdoor traveller a topographic map has a significance that transcends its basic purpose. What is simply a two-dimensional representation of a piece of land surface is for the bushwalker and skier a wealth of information about routes to follow, obstacles to avoid and possible campsites. For some people maps are their favourite reading material.

For back-country journeys maps with a scale of 1:50,000 are most commonly used. The scale indicates the relationship between the distances on the ground and those represented by the map. So with a 1:50,000 map 1 cm (⅜ in) on the map equals 500 m (1600 ft) on the ground. Maps with a scale of 1:25,000 can show much finer detail and are available for certain areas. In some remote parts only, 1:100,000 maps are obtainable.

Contours are the most important information on a map. These are the brown lines that link points of the same height, and so the three dimensional is rendered in two dimensions. The closer together the contour lines the steeper the terrain. Where contour lines are massed together, this indicates precipitous ground, although major cliffs are usually marked by a separate symbol. The contour interval is the vertical distance between each contour line on the map, so if the contour interval is 10 m (33 ft) then every time you cross a contour line you will gain or lose 10 m (33 ft) in elevation.

Grid lines 1000 m (3300 ft) apart are drawn vertically and horizontally over the map. A grid reference is often given in guidebooks for specific points like huts or waterholes. A grid reference is a six-figure number: the first two numbers refer to the vertical grid line to the left of the point in question. The third number is an estimate in tenths from this grid line to the point. The fourth and fifth numbers refer to the horizontal grid line below the point and the sixth number is an estimate in tenths from the horizontal grid line to the point.

These grid lines are aligned north and south, although there is a marginal difference between true north and the north of the grid lines. This is usually shown diagrammatically as grid north in the margin of the map. For almost all purposes the difference between grid north and true north is not critical. Magnetic north is usually shown in the same diagram and is more relevant for detailed compass work.

Other map symbols are identified in the legend: these include creeks, roads and various types of vegetation. Topographic maps contain a remarkable amount of detail, but you may also need to refer to other more recent sketch maps supplied by parks or other bodies for information about prepared trails, established campsites and water supplies. With any topographic map it's important to be aware of its date of publication in case of changes.

The most important map of all is the one in your mind, which is an amalgam of what you see around you and what's inscribed on a topographic sheet. Map-reading is about relating a simple set of graphic signs to the living landscape. Contour lines give you the shape of the land and its formations: the ridges and valleys, the saddles, summits and spurs. With a little practice, map-reading becomes like a second language: you learn to translate quickly and accurately from

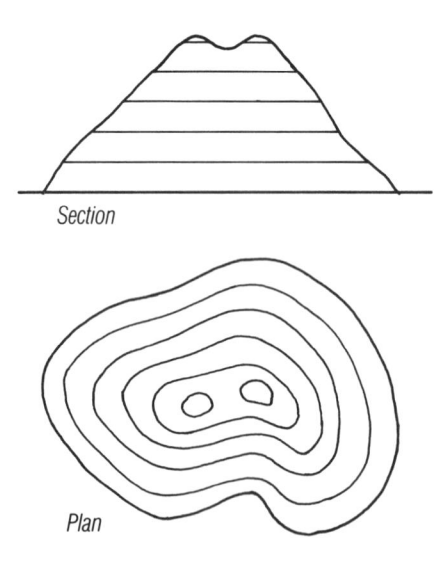

Section

Plan

Contours link points of the same height giving the map-reader important information about the gradient of the terrain

the landscape to the map and back to the landscape.

USING A COMPASS

With a compass you can easily orientate a map, then verify your position and plot a course to follow. It is a blessedly simple instrument, but using a compass is also notoriously difficult to describe in words.

A compass has four universally known cardinal points: north, east, south and west. The points in between can be described, for example, as north-west and south-east, then north by north-west, etc. For accurate direction finding the compass circle is divided into 360^0 with east at 90^0, south at 180^0, west at 270^0 and north at 360^0 (also 0^0). A bearing is simply a direction quoted in degrees.

For wilderness travel the most useful compass is one used for orienteering. The compass needle is mounted on a pivot point and enclosed in a fluid filled housing, so the needle will rotate freely if the compass is held flat. The housing has a dial graduated in degrees and rotates on a rectangular base plate made of clear plastic. This plate has a large direction of travel arrow and is edged with map scales.

The heart of the compass is the magnetised needle which will align itself according to magnetic north. This will vary slightly with the line of magnetic force at a given time in a given place – hence the need for magnetic declination to be marked on maps and taken into account in precise compass navigation. The needle can also go haywire if it comes under the influence of another magnetic field or magnetic metal object. When an accurate reading is required it is therefore important not to use a compass in close proximity to tin buildings, cars, electricity lines or terrous metals in the ground. Even watches, cameras, torches, car keys and pocket knives can create errors.

It is worth emphasising that the bulk of navigation does not demand intricate compass handling. The compass is merely another point of reference which can be used occasionally to check your location and keep you from veering too far off course. Precise details of magnetic variation and the like can reasonably be ignored for most bush travel – provided you have a good idea of your approximate whereabouts.

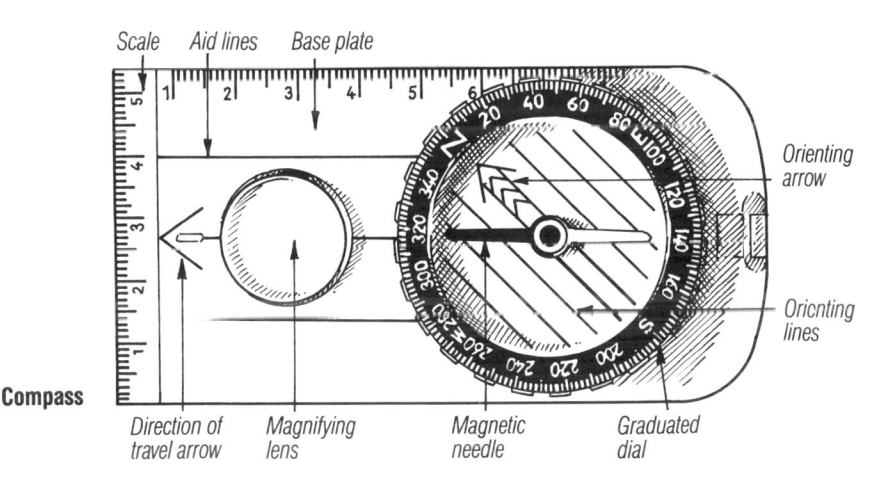

Compass

Labels: Scale, Aid lines, Base plate, Orienting arrow, Orienting lines, Direction of travel arrow, Magnifying lens, Magnetic needle, Graduated dial

1. Approximate magnetic declination for Australia
2. True north, grid north and magnetic north as represented on most maps

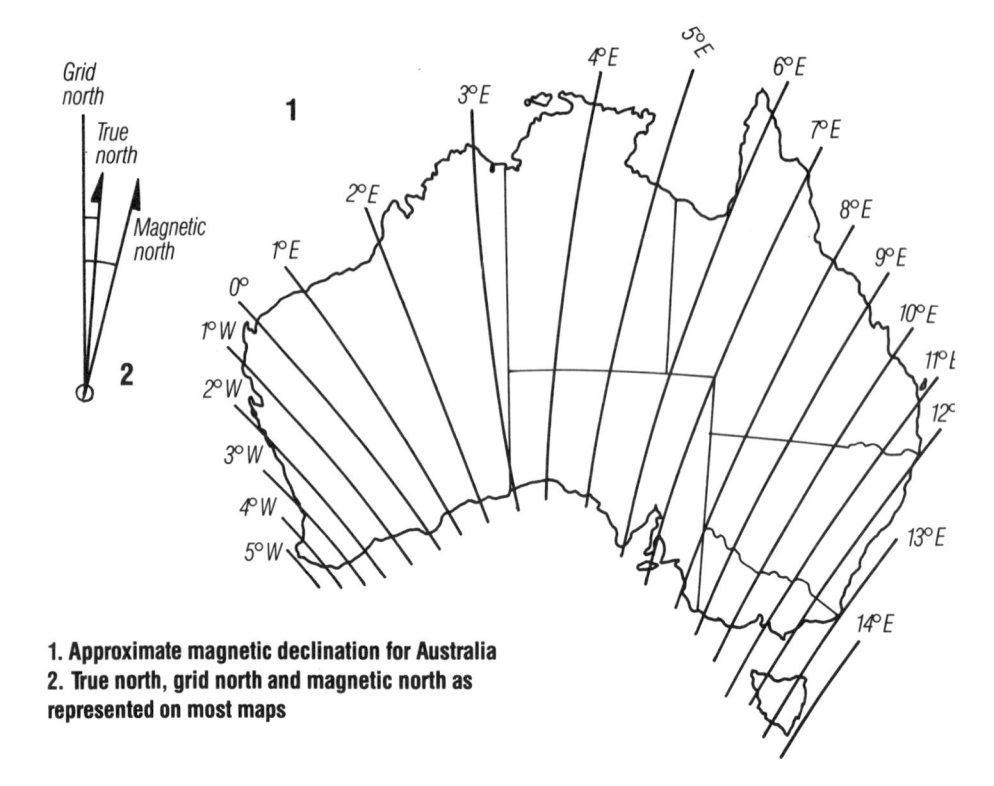

Magnetic declination

Given that a compass needle will, in most places, point slightly to the west or east of true north this difference needs to be included in some calculations. As mentioned, maps carry a diagram which both illustrates the angular difference with arrows, and expresses in degrees or fractions of degrees the extent of the divergence.

For truly accurate readings a compass bearing taken from a landmark needs to be converted to a grid bearing for using the map. Conversely, a bearing based on the map grid needs to be converted to a magnetic bearing for using the compass. For the eastern half of the Australian continent the magnetic declination happens to the east of north, so for practical purposes you need only remember to add the declination when starting from a magnetic bearing and subtract when starting from a grid bearing.

Orienting map and compass

To orient the compass, set the direction of travel arrow along the grid north line and the orienting arrow over the magnetic north arrow. The dial should show the grid magnetic angle in degrees.

Without changing the dial, place the compass along a grid line so that the direction of travel arrow is pointing to grid north. Leaving the compass in position on the map, turn the map until the compass needle points north over the orienting arrow.

Map bearings

If your position is known and you want to ascertain the direction of travel to a feature on land, a map bearing can be used. This is particularly useful if the feature is out of sight or may become obscured once you get underway.

Firstly, place one edge of the compass on the map along the intended line of travel with the travel arrow pointing in the direction of your destination. Then rotate the compass housing so that the orienting arrow points north parallel with the grid lines.

To adjust for grid magnetic north, position the compass over the north arrow diagram on the map. Align the orienting arrow with the grid north line. Keeping the base plate stationary, turn the dial so the orienting arrow points to magnetic north.

Without altering the dial setting, take the compass off the map, hold it flat in your hand and turn the whole compass until the north (usually red) end of the magnetic needle is pointing north over the orienting arrow. The direction of travel arrow will then point to your destination.

Land bearings

These can be used if you know two landmarks and want to establish your position on a map, or if you want to travel to a visible landmark using a bearing. They can also be used to do back bearings.

Face the landmark and hold the compass so that the direction of travel arrow points to the landmark. Without changing the position of the base plate, turn the compass housing until the orienting arrow is in line with the red end of the magnetic needle. The dial now shows the magnetic bearing to your destination.

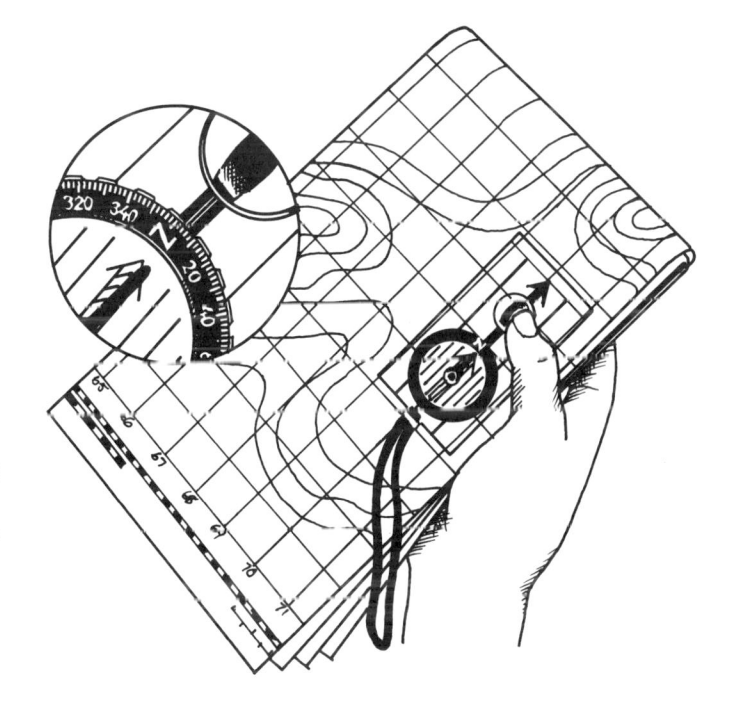

To set a map accurately, ensure that the direction of travel arrow runs along the grid north line and the orienting arrow follows the magnetic north arrow

THE OUTDOOR COMPANION

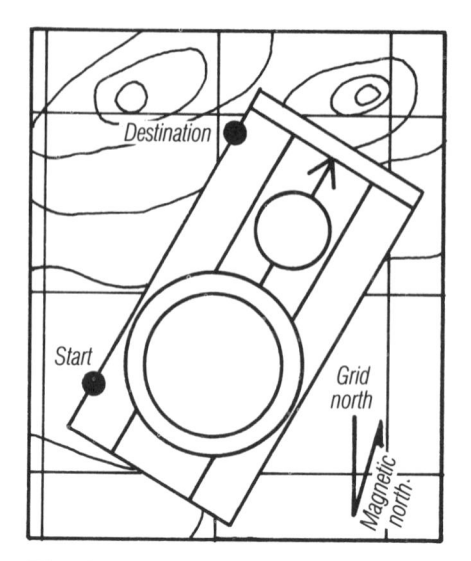

TAKING A BEARING FROM A MAP
1. Place a long edge of the compass along the intended line of travel. The travel arrow should point in the direction of your destination

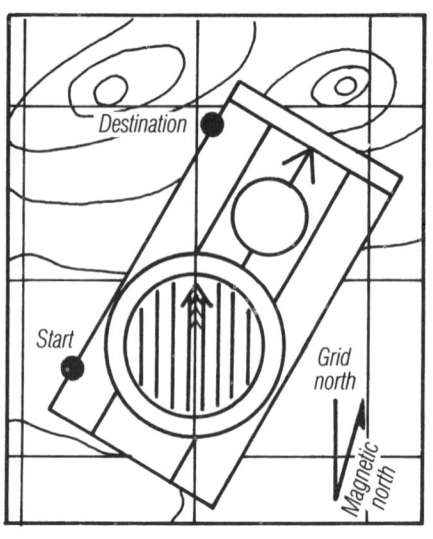

2. Rotate the compass housing so that the orienting arrow is parallel with the grid lines and points to grid north

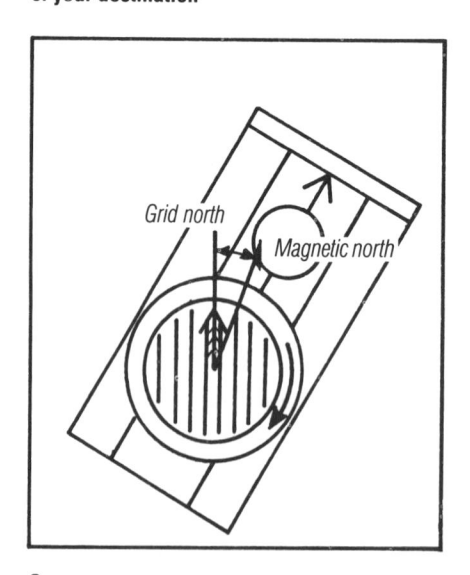

3. Adjust for grid magnetic north by placing the compass on the north arrow diagram on the map. Align the orienting arrow with the grid north line. With the base plate stationary, turn the compass housing so the orienting arrow points to magnetic north

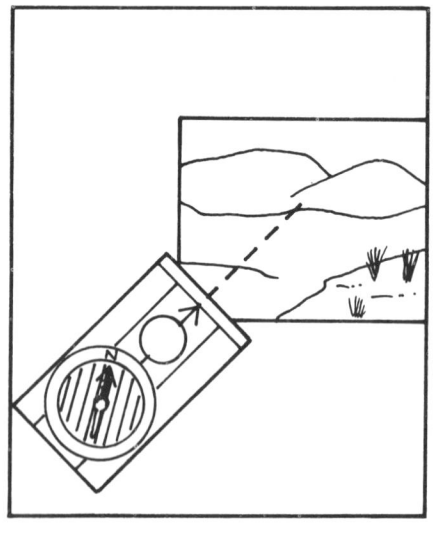

4. Direction of travel is determined by removing the compass from the map (do not alter the dial setting) and, holding it in the palm of your hand, turning it until the north end of the needle aligns over the orienting arrow

To locate your position on the map you need to translate this bearing into a grid bearing by placing the orienting arrow over the magnetic arrow on the north arrow diagram and rotating the housing to the grid north arrow. Then place the compass on the map with one edge on the landmark. Turn the compass so the orienting arrow is parallel with the grid lines pointing north. You then know that you are located on the line from the landmark formed by the edge of the compass.

To pinpoint your position it is necessary to take a bearing from a second landmark using the same method – where the two lines intersect on the map is your position. If you know you are on a creek or road or some other lineal feature in the landscape, a single bearing from a known landmark can be used to determine your position.

Back bearings

These are useful for checking your forward position against prominent landmarks. If the original landmark, from which you took your forward bearing, is still visible then turn around until you're facing this landmark. With the travel arrow pointing back at this landmark the south point on the compass needle should now be over the north point of the compass dial. If not, you need to move sideways to return to your original bearing and so stay on course.

Compass bearings can also be taken from alternative landmarks and are translated into back bearings by adding or subtracting 180 – the back bearing is the point on the compass directly opposite the compass bearing. These can then be plotted on the map and an intersecting point marked to show your current position.

ALTERNATIVE NAVIGATION

For precise navigation there is no substitute for a map and compass. If you are venturing into rugged country every member of the party should be familiar with reading maps and taking bearings with a compass. There are nevertheless some rudimentary methods of establishing direction without a compass. These will not give pinpoint accuracy, but in an emergency they can help.

At night the Southern Cross can be used to locate the South Celestial Pole. One method is to imagine the intersection of a line extended from the long axis of the cross, and a line bisecting the pointers. This intersection identifies the position of the

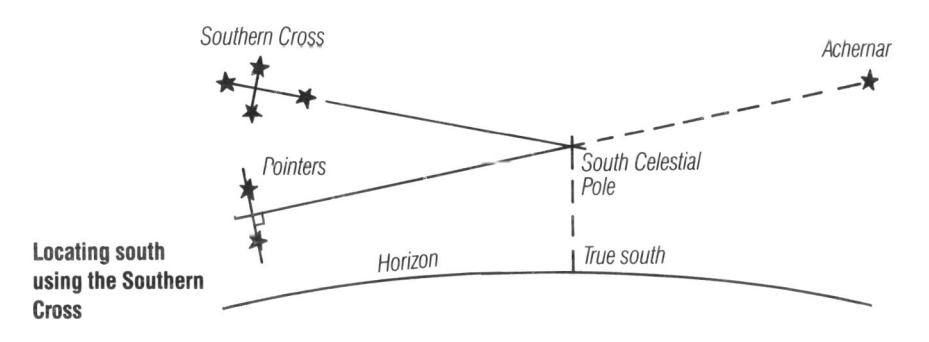

Locating south using the Southern Cross

South Celestial Pole and a vertical line to the horizon will locate due south.

Alternatively, if the long axis of the Southern Cross is extended by 4.5 times it will indicate the South Celestial Pole. One final method is to locate the midpoint of line between the star Achernar and the pointer nearest the cross. A perpendicular line down from this midpoint will be due south.

During daylight hours the sun is your only guide, and not a very reliable one at that. It rises due east and sets due west only at the equinoxes in March and September. Come mid-December it rises and sets roughly south-east and south-west respectively. In mid-June it's traversing the sky from around north-east to north-west.

One technique for getting an approximate direction is to plant a straight stick upright in a patch of level ground and observe the shadow cast by the stick in the hour or so before and after noon. By marking the tip of the shadow on the ground you will end up with a curved line which can be used to establish a rough east–west line.

BEING LOST

Slight errors in navigation happen all the time. It is easy enough to overshoot your destination, miss a turn-off, or arrive at a creek junction that's not supposed to be there. One common problem is to try and make the terrain conform to an assumed location on the map. It's much safer to start from a detailed interpretation of the features around you and then make the map fit the terrain.

If you are baffled by your whereabouts it's time to calmly study the map and work through in your mind the ground you have just covered. In most cases careful reading of terrain and map will be enough to reorientate you. If not, try to retrace your steps to a known feature or higher ground and start again. Pride is often the navigator's worst enemy – to push on with only the expectation of finding a landmark can quickly plunge you into a deeper unknown. Always be prepared to backtrack a little distance to a reliable point of reference.

Whatever the circumstances, it is essential to keep your cool. The moment you feel unsure of the surrounding signs is the moment to have a rest stop, and something to eat and drink. If the light is fading or the weather bad consider making camp or finding shelter nearby. The first step in getting 'unlost' is to take your time and think before making the next move.

5

FOOD

In the outdoors food is elevated to its rightful place. Elsewhere the need to eat is increasingly seen as an inconvenience; food is something to be eaten quickly, and good meals are picked at. But after a hard day in the wilds, eating is never taken for granted. In the absence of other diversions, and with an appetite honed by fresh air and exercise, meals are the natural focus. Some of the best trips become movable feasts!

It is a universal truth that in the bush almost everything tastes better, but this should not be taken to mean that anything will taste good. Although there will be instances when bad weather, exhaustion and raw hunger make you content with big serves of whatever stodge can be hustled into a billy, bush cooking is generally a creative and leisurely exercise. Even with the limitations of carrying food in a pack and working on simple stoves, there is still ample scope to prepare fine meals. As every good cook knows, the secret is in having quality ingredients and handling them with care.

Food is, of course, the fuel you need to keep going. It needs to be nourishing and in good supply if you're carrying a pack and being energetic in the outdoors, but while the need for food will be more keenly felt, that does not mean you have to eat more. Of greater importance is a balanced intake throughout the day. Indeed, many people find they eat less in total than they would at home. One's metabolism seems to make more efficient use of food consumed on the trail, and perhaps, too, the process of carrying and rationing provisions makes us less prone to gluttony.

BASIC REQUIREMENTS

The choice of food is largely dictated by its weight and ease of packing. On extended trips food rations will be the heaviest part of your load, so scrupulous planning pays off. Aside from being lightweight, outdoor food needs to be compact and robust enough to survive the ordeal of being crammed in a pack and shaken about all day. Meal preparation should minimise the need for elaborate utensils and excessive use of fuel or firewood.

With a few modifications it's possible to follow much the same diet as you probably have at home – switching to a regime of unfamiliar foodstuffs can cause more problems than it solves. Assuming you normally enjoy a healthy and balanced diet there is little need to calculate daily kilojoule intakes or precise percentages of food groups. It is sufficient to say that for strenuous or cold weather trips there should be a slight increase in foods with a high energy yield.

Estimating proportions for each meal, and then total quantities for a trip, is not hard. Begin with a menu list, then itemise the ingredients and try to estimate amounts by weight. Almost invariably you start out carrying surplus food, but that's better than going short. After a few trips your judgement and preferences will become clear. As a rough guide, 1 kg (2 lb) of food per person per day will satisfy most needs.

FOOD TYPES

It's tempting to bypass such details and simply buy an armful of prepared packet foods – an impressive choice of freeze-dried meals is now available, at equally impressive prices. While the quality of these dishes is improving and less preservatives are being used, they are best used as a supplement to a more varied diet, or carried as emergency rations.

The more traditional dehydrated meals are not good. With their contrived flavours, nondescript chewy nuggets and heavy doses of monosodium glutamate, their value is highly suspect. Ordinary dehydrated vegetables are by themselves quite palatable and can be very useful for adding to stews.

There is also a great array of dried fruits and meats that are ideal for the outdoors. Another worthwhile option is to dry your own foods.

Tinned food is bulky to pack and heavy to carry around; it also leaves you with the chore of carrying out empty cans. Nevertheless, for shorter trips many people choose to carry a few small tinned delicacies like sardines, pâté or anchovies.

As useful as specialised dried foods are for backpacking, there is nothing like fresh, unadulterated produce. It is surprising how many natural foods can be carried without much increase in weight or bulk. A few well-chosen fresh ingredients and some subtle seasoning can transform a meal. For outings lasting only two or three days almost all the food you carry and eat can be fresh. On longer trips fresh items can be used to pep up the texture and flavour of otherwise bland dishes.

The ultimate fresh food is the bush tucker you may find along the way. Native fruits, seeds, nuts, berries and tubers can supplement your rations, as long as you know what they look like and where to find them. Choose the wrong plant and you might end up with serious side effects. Bush tucker need not be just for the vegetarian – trips by the coast and along mountain streams present the opportunity of catching fish and assorted *fruits de mer*. A meal of fresh trout or native yabbies is truly a bush delight, but it's folly to rely exclusively on such sources. Living off the land also requires sensitivity – try not to disrupt the local ecology.

MENU PLANNING

With a little ingenuity, outdoor cuisine can be as tasty and satisfying as any other. The simplest approach is to start with the meals and foods you know you like, then devise ways of adapting them to the constraints of being in the bush. Some habits might need changing if you're accustomed to skipping meals or having one big feed a day. Three light meals and frequent grazing on snacks are more beneficial for people on the move. It is also common in the bush to crave foods that you may not normally countenance eating at home. These can include salami and smoked meats, tinned fish, sugary drinks and heavy-duty muesli.

Individual catering is the only way to guarantee that your personal food preferences are met, but group purchasing, packing and cooking of food saves time, weight, fuel and money. Members need to be consulted in the planning stages to ensure that menu ideas satisfy the group's tastes, and to avoid specific items that individuals have an aversion or allergy to. One person may elect to do all the providoring, or certain meals or days might be allocated among the group. For trips lasting a week or more it's not worth striving to make every meal entirely different. A simpler solution is to have bulk ingredients for three or so basic menus and create variations using different sauces and seasonings.

Other factors also affect menu planning. Meals on snowcamping trips need to be quick and simple to prepare, especially if you have to melt snow and cook in the confines of a tent. Soups and one-pot stews are ideal. When bushfire restrictions prevent the lighting of stoves or campfires some inspiration is handy for devising stimulating cold meals. Salad ingredients don't generally travel well but there are exceptions, and with a variety of dressings, cured meats and breads your diet need not be monotonous. In arid areas or high camps without water, choose foods that have a high moisture content. Avoid salty dishes and anything that needs lots of cooking water.

BUYING FOOD

Most outdoor food can be purchased in a quick visit to the supermarket. These days an average store carries a range of dried foods and a selection of lightweight, easy-to-cook meals. For some special items you may need to shop at health food stores or grocery shops that carry Asian products. The more exotic freeze-dried dinners and elusive ingredients like dried egg powder are usually sold only through backpacking outlets.

When buying freeze-dried food, go for meals that couldn't otherwise be made with conventional dried ingredients. There is little advantage, for instance, in buying expensive freeze-dried macaroni cheese or spaghetti dishes — better to try some of the more exotic fish or meat dinners that can be introduced for variety in the latter stages of a trip. It also pays to be sceptical about the number of serves a packet will yield.

Special consideration should be given to allowing for emergency rations. If you're heading out for a week or more you should carry at least a couple of extra freeze-dried dinners, some spare packet soups and extra chocolate and fruit bars. These should be packed separately and stowed deep in your rucksack.

With experience, buying and preparing food becomes a smooth operation. In between trips durable foods and condiments can be left in their lightweight containers and storage bags so that all you need to do is buy the necessary fresh ingredients.

PACKAGING AND FOOD CARRYING

There is quite an art to sorting food into logical groups, labelling the packages and then stowing them securely into a rucksack. The plastic, cardboard and paper most food comes in is bulky and ill-suited to the rigours of pack transport. Packaging should be removed, except from items like biscuits which last longer in their packets. Foods in tins and foil pouches are best left in this packaging, as long as you are meticulous about carrying the empty containers out with you.

Bulky, loose items are best carried in strong plastic bags that are clearly labelled with a felt pen and tied in a loose knot (wire twists and rubber bands always go astray). Meats and cheese should be wrapped in paper or cloth bags. Other foods such as margarine, peanut butter, honey and the like should be transferred from glass jars into stout plastic containers with secure lids. Film canisters can be recycled for carrying herbs and condiments.

It's rarely necessary to divide out the ingredients for each separate meal. The most common method is to sort food into breakfasts, lunches and dinners, and pack these items into one large cloth or mesh bag for each meal type. A fourth bag is normally carried for things like spreads, margarine, milk powder and drinks that are common to all meals. These bags can then be distributed among group members for carrying.

BREAKFAST

When facing a full day of load carrying or activity it's vital to take in something substantial before starting out. Muesli or porridge with brown sugar and milk is the foundation of most outdoor breakfasts. Dried fruits and honey are popular additions.

To follow, most people are content to have breads and biscuits with spreads and jams. Bacon is a quickly cooked breakfast and the aroma of it frying in the pan will prise slow starters from their sleeping bags. Bacon is also handy to liven up evening meals and travels well if wrapped in strong paper or cloth.

On overnight trips fresh eggs can be carried as a treat, if carefully wrapped or cracked into a secure container. Alternatively, powdered egg is acceptable if scrambled with milk or made into an omelette. Powdered egg is a useful ingredient for other dishes too – pancakes make sustaining breakfast food and savoury variations are also an option for evening meals.

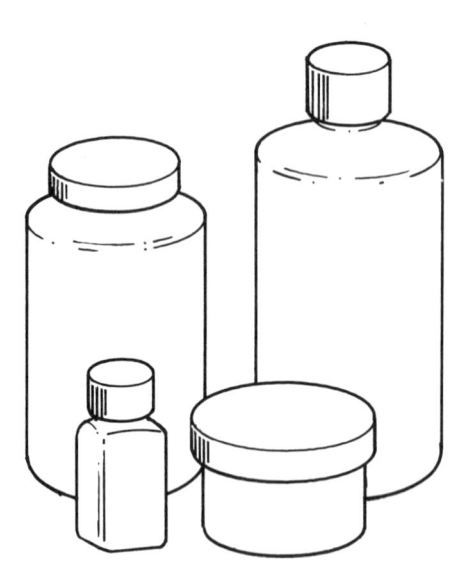

Assorted containers for food storage

On some mornings a leisurely cooked breakfast in pleasant surroundings is more than justified. At other times follow the impulse to pack and go after a muesli bar or a quick bowl of cereal and a hot drink or two. The early part of the day is often a good time to be moving; when the light is still soft, while the snow's fresh or before the heat sets in.

LUNCH

A heavy meal in the middle of the day is not recommended. It takes too long to prepare and leaves you lethargic just when you need to be sharp on your feet. Lunch is better regarded as an extended rest stop where you snack, smorgasbord-style on an array of lighter, easily digested foods.

Good breads and crackers are the basis of lunch. Dark rye breads will keep for several days and can take a rough ride. Some form of the flat pitta bread is a good alternative for the first few lunches of a trip. Plain dry biscuits and rye crispbreads are handy for smaller delicacies. The classic European alternative is pumpernickel bread, which is tasty and long lasting.

There are any number of goodies to be eaten with the bread. Harder vintage cheeses travel well, as do small wax-coated cheeses like edam and gruyère, but bries and camemberts survive only for a day or two. Robust cold meats like salami and metwurst are perfect for the bush and will keep for a week or more. Softer smoked hams and pork are fine for shorter outings. A range of spreads like peanut butter, tahini, jam and honey always go down well. If you're partial to fish, tinned sardines, herring fillets, anchovies and salmon are good in small amounts. For balance take along a few salad vegetables: cucumbers, celery and carrots will endure being stuffed in a pack. With a good container it's also surprisingly easy to make your own sprouts on the trail. Whole fruit is generally too fragile to carry but a few oranges or mandarins go a long way.

Lunches can take on a certain sameness — for variety, pack a selection of condiments. Mustards, pickles, horseradish and chutneys have a special piquancy in the bush. A little salad dressing or some olives are other variations. If you take a stove, soups and hot drinks are invigorating when the wind blows cold. Nibbles like nuts, chocolate and dried fruit round out the meal.

DINNER

Soup is a popular way to start an evening repast. It's easy to make and keeps everyone occupied while other courses are being prepared. The quality of packet soups has improved dramatically and the Asian varieties are particularly tasty. Heartier soups can be created by adding dried vegetables, grains or bacon.

On overnight trips it's no problem to prepare the style of main courses you would have at home. Curries and casseroles can also be made and frozen in advance, then simply reheated. For confirmed carnivores fresh meat, in the form of sausages, kebabs and steak, is an option for the first night or two. Otherwise, most evening meals revolve around staples like rice and pasta with a choice of sauces and additions.

Rice is excellent bush food and can be boiled (the absorption method saves water), served fried or sweetened as a dessert. As well as spaghetti, other pastas like tagliatelle, fettuccine and spiralle are good for a change, and any leftovers can be converted into a pasta salad for lunch the following day. Ravioli and tortellini are also possibilities, especially if vacuum packed. Quick-cooking Chinese noodles are ideal for adding to soups or with stir-fried vegetables. If you have more time, lentils, bulgur wheat and assorted dried beans make a substantial main course. Instant mashed potato is light to carry and is easily redeemed with seasonings.

Vegetables can be boiled, sautéed or baked in foil in a fire. As well as the dried varieties, durable fresh vegetables like onions, carrots, radishes, pumpkin, beetroot and sweet potato all lend themselves to outdoor cooking. Even capsicums and zucchini will survive if packed with care. For meat flavours and textures try adding bacon or some diced salami to the frying pan. Smoked fish and cheese can also be included to give stews a protein base.

The key to making a week of bush dinners palatable is using subtle variations in flavour. For this it's essential to have a bag with ingredients like fresh garlic and ginger (or the dried versions), ground black pepper, dried chillies, curry powder, tomato paste and parmesan cheese. Herbs and spices like dried parsley, basil, oregano, dill, coriander, cinnamon and nutmeg are always handy and take up little room in the pack.

As a change from the normal fare of breads and biscuits consider cooking up pappadums or prawn crackers to accompany the main course. With the right fire or stove it's only a little extra work to make chapatis, flat breads and pancakes. Carrying some flour is always worthwhile for thickening sauces and stews, and trying your hand at more exotic goodies like steamed puddings, bush cakes, damper and biscuits.

After a solid main course many people are satisfied and need only a hot drink and perhaps some chocolate to finish the meal, but for those with a sweet tooth there are several dessert options. Dried fruit such as apples and apricots take on new character when stewed and served warm with custard. Whole apples can be filled with raisins and brown sugar, wrapped in foil and baked in a fire. The ubiquitous pancake can be served with a little sugar and a squeeze of lemon juice, or there are any number of 'instant' jellies, puddings and cheesecakes to choose from, if you don't mind a little artificial flavouring. For something different, cook up some popcorn to nibble when viewing the heavens.

DRINKS

For a serious thirst plain water is best. Fruit powders like lemon barley are good for a dose of sugar, and disguising any water that's less than fresh. On ski trips a hot fruit brew goes down well during the day. Billy tea is the time-honoured bush drink but fruit and herbal teas make a pleasant change. For some reason instant coffee is even less palatable than usual in the wild. Caffeine addicts are far better off tossing fresh coffee grounds into a pot of boiling water, and settling the grounds by adding some eggshell or a little cold water. Hot chocolate is a sustaining nightcap and can be made more sinful by adding a dash of rum or whisky.

SNACKS

The best nibbles are nuts, dark chocolate and dried fruit. As well as the familiar sultanas and apricots most supermarkets also have dried apple, banana, peach, pear and pineapple. Old-fashioned raisins, dates and figs are just as good. Many people also like to have a large supply of glucose sweets. 'Scroggin' is simply your own mixture of these snack foods, and is ideal for munching on as a filler between meals.

COOKING

When it's cold, dark and windy the last thing you may feel like is going ten rounds with a temperamental stove or smoky campfire, yet this is the very time when good food is most important. Without a sheltered cooking spot and reliable heat source the task becomes doubly difficult, so the minutes spent setting up your kitchen are crucial. Experienced cooks work methodically, sorting ingredients and arranging them where they can be found without fuss. A head torch and a strong pair of billy grippers are two essential pieces of equipment for a bush cook.

Most meals require only one or two pots and perhaps a frying pan. Work in sequence so for example the soup billy becomes the stew billy. Meanwhile a second billy can be used for boiling rice, and this is then easily cleaned for the after-dinner drink. Good billies stack, so that one dish can be kept warm over another that's on the stove burner. Likewise a frying pan can be used as a billy lid. Such pot juggling is not easy over a campfire but neither is it as necessary as the heat source is larger.

Cooking fires

The most important thing about campfires is to decide whether in good conscience it's justified to have one at all. So many areas have been denuded of suitable timber and degraded by fire rings that the decision is often made for you. At other times the risk of bushfire is too great to contemplate building any fire, no matter how small.

But traditions die hard. If you must have a fire there are ways to reduce its impact. (See Chapter 2, *Choosing a campsite* and *Setting up camp*.) Where there are no existing fireplaces it's best to carefully dig a shallow pit or trench which can be filled before you depart. This trench should be orientated to the prevailing wind, dug less than a metre long, and narrow enough so the sides help support your cooking pots. Large logs can also be laid on either side of the pit to cradle billies. Though a sometimes precarious arrangement, this is a lot simpler than engineering tripods and forked sticks to hang your pots on.

To light a fire, gather a good handful of dried leaves and grass to make a small pile of tinder in the upwind end of your fireplace. Surround this with a tepee shape of small dry twigs, and have a supply of increasingly larger sticks and wood close by. Light the tinder low down and on the upwind side of the tepee. As it catches alight feed it gradually with thicker sticks until it gains strength. Try not to collapse the tepee in the early stages, but at some point the fire will assume a shape of its own. For meals that require simmering, or baking food in foil, wait until you have a solid foundation of coals giving a consistent heat. Once the meal is underway the fire needs to be carefully tended and fed with new wood.

There is considerable craft in lighting fires in all weathers, breaking thick branches, selecting the right wood species and knowing just where to blow on a fading fire. Campfires have their own rewards. They can also be fiddly to start and hard to maintain — often a stove would be easier all-round.

At the end of a meal make sure all food is stored out of reach of local wildlife. Don't leave food bags lying on the ground or outside in a pack: some animals can gnaw right through the toughest fabrics. Keeping food in the tent or suspending your ration bags from a tree branch will foil most scavengers. Billies and plates should be washed before retiring. At the very least clean one pot ready for the morning brew.

Variety and surprise is the secret of good bush eating, but even with consummate skills this is tricky to achieve on wilderness trips lasting several weeks. Inevitably one develops cravings for things like crunchy green salads, ice-cream and fresh, crusty bread. You return home with a renewed fondness for such foods.

Outdoor meals may be humble, but take heart: in restaurants where the food costs much more they have only five stars. In the bush there's a sky full of them!

6

ENJOYING THE OUTDOORS

For some people just being outdoors is enough. The basic tasks of moving through the bush, finding shelter and preparing meals are satisfying in themselves. There is merit too in experiencing the bush on your terms and seeing it through your eyes, almost as if you are the first to do so.

Going bush can also be a bridge to other pastimes and pleasures. A feeling for landscape and a knowledge of places and place names happens as a matter of course. With the imprint of each new trip this mental mapmaking takes on deeper levels of interest. Natural curiosity often leads to an amateur study of plants and wildlife: activities that can easily be woven into the day's journey. Most people also like to make some record of the trip, be it pencil notes on the margin of a map, a photographic diary or a detailed journal with sketches.

Such diversions are more than just academic. It can be of practical benefit, for example, to know which plants are edible, what snakes are venomous and where you found water on an earlier trip.

BOTANY

An appreciation of native flora involves much more than remembering a lot of scientific names. One of the joys of going bush is to witness plants in their distinctive habitats. As well as the satisfaction of recognising a particular tree or flowering shrub, one can see the balance that exists between different species and the interaction of climate, topography, soils and other living creatures that makes each ecosystem unique.

At first the bush can seem overwhelming in its diversity – there is a mass of colours, shapes and foliage. As you learn to identify various shrubs and flowers the confusion eases. This takes time and it's often only after several trips in different seasons that one accumulates the knowledge to be familiar with a habitat. In areas like rainforests, which are richly endowed with vegetation, it can take a lifetime of observation to confidently recognise even a fraction of the plant types.

The place to start is with an area you know and are likely to visit regularly. Rather than attempting an inventory of every living thing, select trees and flowering plants that you find striking or interesting. There are many practical field guides that help you identify and name plant types based on descriptions and illustrations of their leaves, flowers and other botanical characteristics. As important as such books are, it is much easier in the early stages to be introduced to the bush by someone who already knows the subject and the skills involved.

In addition to the familiar dry eucalypt forests there are many special habitats to be experienced by the outdoor convert. Skiers develop a strong affinity with snow gums, both for the shelter they afford and their example of stoicism before the elements. In the late spring the alpine meadows become blanketed with wildflowers. Canoeists have the ability to experience the vegetation of coastal wetlands and be awed by river red gums. Bushwalking in lush tropical and sub-tropical rainforests is becoming increasingly popular as the importance of these areas is acknowledged and their numbers diminish.

While the grandeur of a beech forest or a stand of King Billy pines is undeniable, there's just as much to admire in less prepossessing landscapes like mallee scrub and coastal heathland. Invariably it's the surprising details that make one's botanical encounters come alive: the tiny orchid making a splash of colour amidst a sprawl of leaf litter, or the cluster of ferns at the end of a flinty desert chasm.

BIRDWATCHING

In a continent where much of the wildlife is nocturnal, sparsely scattered and extremely shy, the birds stand out. With over 700 species, many of them brilliantly coloured and highly vocal, it is impossible to ignore the animating role that birds play in the bush.

To create some order out of the gallery of calls and glimpses of plumage is not too difficult. All you need is a sharp eye, a keen ear and a good pair of compact binoculars with a magnification of around x 7, x 8 or x 9. If you want to become more serious about identifying a particular species you'll need a portable field guide for your region and a notebook and pencil. The idea is not to madly flip through the field guide in search of the bird you're trying to recognise. Instead, take note of its size, shape, colour, conspicuous markings, its action in flight, call or song, and so on. Later you can refer to the field guide at your leisure.

With practice your observations will become more accurate and interesting. Many people note the date and place of important sightings on pages of their field guide. Enthusiastic spotters will be out of their sleeping bags before dawn, ready for the prime viewing time around daybreak, but many birds can be spied in the course of pursuing your outdoor pastime.

Aside from honey-eaters, finches and wrens, there are many brilliant parrots and garrulous cockatoos that are not hard to find. Rock climbers are uniquely placed to observe wedge-tailed eagles, peregrine falcons and other raptors, though care should be taken not to disturb their nesting sites. Similarly, gliding silently along in a canoe is the only way to study most water birds at close quarters. Seeking out rare and elusive species can add a sense of intrigue to a bushwalk — for example, observing a lyrebird is always memorable.

OTHER WILDLIFE

Any kind of methodical study of mammals and reptiles usually goes beyond the ambit of most outdoor trips, but this doesn't mean it isn't worth being on the lookout for them and their tracks. Small nocturnal marsupials aren't often encountered, but in popular camping spots possums are often heard fighting in the treetops or raiding billies in the middle of the night. If you have a torch with a strong focused beam it's possible to pinpoint these visitors, and perhaps the spectacular gliders mid-flight.

Other marsupials like bandicoots, bilbies and quolls can sometimes be spotted in the scrub around campsites but they are coming under increasing competition from feral predators. Koalas are more often heard rather than seen. Their baleful groans are common in certain areas where, with a little luck, they can be spotted dozing on branches in the daylight hours. Wombats are reasonably widespread and their tracks and burrows are often evident around the snowline in the high country. Most wild areas have a substantial population of kangaroos and wallabies. Bushwalkers regularly stumble upon kangaroos grazing in open woodland, or lying up in the shade during the middle of the day. In arid areas euros and rock wallabies are best observed near waterholes and favoured rocky outcrops.

Reptiles include both the more delightful and the most feared creatures in the bush. Goannas, for all their size, are relatively docile and are often seen scavenging around campgrounds — even so, do not attempt to hand feed them. Dragon lizards, with their spiny scales and darting movements, are among the more spectacular reptiles. Skinks and geckos are common although the latter are more nocturnal and less frequently seen.

Snakes have a notoriety way out of proportion to their numbers. Though very few people would contemplate seeking them out, they are impressive creatures in their own right. There is also some insurance in being able to identify snake species in case of a bite that requires antivenene. Suffice it to say that sharp observation and an understanding of habitats are useful for avoiding snakes in the first place.

GEOLOGY

For the outdoor traveller a working knowledge of rock types is an integral part of what distinguishes a habitat for plants and animals. Similarly, an understanding of the larger landforms, and the forces that generated them, is worthwhile particularly if traversing broken or mountainous terrain.

Field guides usually contain background information on the local geology. In areas of prominent sandstone escarpments or deep gorges, knowing the characteristics and weaknesses of rock formations is crucial to route finding. Needless to say, rock climbers develop an instinctive feel for such things.

As well as the drama of large rock structures there is the fascination of fossil remains and the lure of gemstones and precious metals.

THE NIGHT SKY

One of the profound pleasures of the bush is being able to enjoy the night sky. Away from the glow of city lights and the mantle of air pollution the heavens are revealed in their true splendour. Freed from the routine distractions of home life, you have the time to gaze upwards and wonder.

It's not necessary to be a budding astronomer to enjoy the show. Many hours can be passed just watching the sky and ruminating on the biggest picture of them all. A little knowledge of the major stars, however, can add to the entertainment and is also a useful tool for emergency navigation.

In ideal conditions there are some 2500 visible stars so there's plenty to work with, but that's a minute fraction of the billions of stars that share our galaxy. A portable star chart will help immeasurably in your plotting of the heavens. Having located the prominent celestial landmarks you can set to work identifying the constellations, although a vivid imagination helps with the more obscure configurations.

The moon might seem too familiar to be of much interest but it can help you get your bearings, and a lunar eclipse is worth making a special trip into the bush for. Meteors and meteor showers are spectacular and more frequent. Comets are trickier to spot and even the brighter of the species are unpredictable. One of the most eerie experiences is observing the Aurora Australis – the Southern Lights. Though more common in the higher latitudes it can also be visible in the southern parts of the continent.

To read a star chart it's handy to have a small torch, preferably with a red filter so your eyes don't have to re-adjust to the night light. Binoculars for star gazing need to be bright enough for use in low light.

PHOTOGRAPHY

Capturing the magic of the bush on film is the most popular outdoor pastime of them all. In addition to being a convenient way of documenting a trip, photography is also a good discipline. Creating memorable images often means seeking out special light, finding better angles and patiently stalking wildlife and floral beauty. There's no doubt that such close-grained observation heightens one's perception of the natural world.

Photography can easily become an end in itself, in which case marrying equipment needs with your chosen area and outdoor pastime is a specialised business. Recent years have seen an explosion of interest in wilderness photography which is reflected in the pages of innumerable magazines, diaries and calendars. Images of the highest standard are more often produced by solitary, painstaking artisans, but being in the right place at the right time can yield spectacular results for the lucky snap-shooter.

Cameras

For almost all outdoor photography a reliable 35 mm camera is ideal. No matter what brand you choose it should be lightweight, robust and easy to operate. A model capable of taking wide angle, close-up and telephoto images is preferable, and no longer are single lens reflex (SLR) cameras the only models with this flexibility.

Many companies now also have compact autofocus models with a mid-range zoom, (tele-wide) lens, a rangefinder viewing system and built-in flash. For quick easy shooting these cameras are unsurpassed, but an SLR camera is still the most versatile option. If only one lens is to be carried with an SLR, a zoom lens with a range from wide angle (35 mm) to medium telephoto (105 mm or 135 mm) is best. Should you prefer two fixed focal length lenses, a combination of a 28 mm lens and a 100 mm lens for portraits should cover most needs.

Disposable 'quick-snap' type cameras are another alternative – some of these models are waterproof and have a built-in flash, but all come preloaded with print film. They are limited to good light situations and if you plan on shooting more than one roll of film a more conventional 35 mm compact camera is more efficient.

Film

When deciding on which type of film to use think carefully about what you plan to do with the images. Colour print film is ideal if you want a convenient record of a trip in the form of snapshots or a photo album to browse through at any time. Colour transparencies (slide film) are ideal if you hope to have images published, or want to give slide shows. Prints can be made from slide film using a cibachrome-type process, although this can be expensive. It is more difficult, though not impossible, to have transparencies made from prints.

Both colour and black and white print film is also called negative film. Black-and-white film is recommended if you wish to produce fine art prints or sell images to newspapers. With negative film there is much more latitude to compensate for over- or underexposed images at the stage that the print is made. Negative film is also more able to handle low-light situations.

Experienced photographers use film brands that they know and like. The following suggestions are good starting points, but they are far from the only possibilities. For colour transparencies Kodachrome 64 ASA is still the best option for general shooting. If a faster film is needed, Kodachrome 200 ASA is excellent. Kodak Gold 100 ASA and 200 ASA are reliable colour print films. Depending on your needs, Ilford FP4, Kodak Tri X, TMax 100 ASA or 400 ASA are all useful black-and-white films.

Whatever film you choose, take plenty of it. Film does not weigh much and there is rarely any opportunity to buy more once you're into your journey. For a detailed record of your trip, or specialised photography of activities or wildlife, extra film is needed. A good rule of thumb is a ration of one roll of film per day. Professionals can use five to ten rolls a day, but this is an expensive and weighty habit to keep up in the wilds.

Accessories

A sturdy, lightweight tripod is invaluable when shooting self-portraits and for taking photographs at night, in low light, or where a big depth of field is required. There are many conventional tripods that are light enough for the backpacker and they can be made more stable by suspending a stuffsack, filled with something heavy, from the tripod head. Take care when leaving a camera on a lightweight tripod as wind gusts can easily topple the lot.

Other alternatives include a range of tabletop tripods with various c-clamps, brackets and vice grips. The sturdiest tabletop model is made by Leitz and has legs that swing together to make a compact package. The Ultrapod brand has two weights and comes in two versions – both have velcro straps so they can be fastened to a ski pole, ice-axe or tree branch. With the legs folded out they can also be mounted on a boulder or the ground. Mountaineers have an even simpler solution: a compact connector that clamps onto the adze of an ice-axe. Similar units are also available for attaching cameras to skis.

For SLRs a cable release is worthwhile, although the self-timer can also be used to trip the shutter.

Any lens you use should have a skylight or UV filter to protect the front element from becoming scratched. A polarising filter is handy for cutting down on reflections from water, and giving more saturated colours in blue skies where there are some clouds. It's not a good practice to leave a polarising filter on permanently as it cuts down the amount of light reaching the film by at least one stop.

Other extras to consider are a separate flash unit and a collection of lens brushes, cloths and tissues to help wage the war on dust and moisture.

Equipment care

Outdoor photography is punishing on cameras. Aside from the ravages of dust, moisture, heat and cold there are the constant knocks and bumps of life in the bush. The answer is to use one of the excellent weatherproof, padded camera bags or waist packs now available. Film too should be protected from extremes of heat and cold.

Cameras should be kept warm to minimise the drain on batteries caused by the cold. A cold camera taken back into a warmer environment can also lead to condensation forming on the cold surfaces. This will evaporate eventually, but if you want to shoot straight away the lens will need to be dried with a photographic lens tissue. Likewise, when taking photographs in light rain or falling snow there are lens hoods that can be used but ultimately one ends up using a pocket full of tissues.

In extremely cold, dry air be sure to wind film on slowly as it becomes brittle at low temperatures and static discharges can occur that appear as clear blue specks or streaks on exposed film.

Spare camera batteries are worth taking and should be kept warm inside your jacket in cold temperatures. Some fully electronic cameras have battery powered shutter mechanisms – if your batteries are dead these will not work. Some models have a manually operated back-up speed, in which case you may need to guess the exposure – take note of the speed and choose an appropriate aperture.

Camera bags

Timing is often 90 per cent of what makes a good outdoor photograph. To capture the light, the action or the special moment, you need a camera that's close at hand, but protected, not one that's submerged in the pack.

For small autofocus or compact cameras a pouch that can be belt-mounted is ideal. Heavier SLR cameras ride better in pouches that suspend around the neck and have straps that restrain side-to-side movement. These come in a variety of sizes to accommodate different camera/lens combinations, and the better versions also have room for spare film and lens tissues.

For more serious photography a larger waist pack or bum bag has extra capacity for toting additional lenses, flash units, film and filters. Though most comfortable worn on the back, they can also be carried up front when wearing a full rucksack. Lowe Pro and Camera Care Systems are among the better known brands. Lowe Pro and Tamrac also make large daypacks with foam cut-outs and padded velcro dividers specifically designed for photographic gear.

Taking photographs

Despite the claims of many camera manufacturers no amount of technology can create good images. A lot of thought, imagination and sheer effort goes into producing the best pictures.

Landscapes and scenery are the most popular outdoor subjects and among the easiest to shoot. The secret is having a feel for natural light and an eye for composition. This is a matter of taste, but simple rules can help — like having the horizon in the bottom or top third of the image rather than the centre. The best moments to shoot landscapes are early on clear mornings or in the late afternoons when the light is warmer and there is less contrast. In the middle of a sunny summer's day the light is harsh and there is little detail in the shadows, but in winter, with the sun at a lower angle, shadows can add interest to your shots. Overcast conditions are ideal for portraits, but landscapes with too much grey are best avoided at these times.

Photographing flora and fauna is a fine art. For wildlife an SLR camera with a long telephoto lens is essential, and a flash is often necessary to capture images of nocturnal species. A close-up or macro lens is best for shooting small subjects like flowers or insects.

Documentary photography that records events as they happen is no less challenging. Taking a shot of a campsite is one thing, but trying to photograph at the same time as pitching a tent in a 60 knot wind is altogether more difficult. There is a world of difference between group shots at rest stops and capturing the action on the move as a group crosses a footbridge or descends a ski slope. The effort involved in getting into position is worthwhile. Good action images have a dynamism and spirit that is always memorable. The secret is having the camera ready and anticipating events.

While the opportunities are boundless, there are many pitfalls for the outdoor photographer. For example, shooting snow scenes using an automatic camera without compensating for the additional reflected light will leave you with underexposed images. For correct exposure you will have to set the camera on manual and open up one or two f stops. With automatic cameras that have no manual mode this adjustment can also be made by shifting the film speed (ASA or Din) dial. Some cameras have special compensation steps marked on the same dial.

A hand-held light meter that records

incident light – the light falling on a subject rather than that reflected by it – will give more accurate exposure overall. A camera meter reading off the back of one's hand will also more closely approximate the correct exposure in most instances. Bracket exposures around this reading to ensure that you don't miss the shot.

The key to outdoor photography is to be totally familiar with your camera before you go. On the trail you need to be sensitive to the needs of others in the group who may become tired of constant breaks to take shots. Some people can also find photography intrusive and distracting, so use your judgement. Having said that, if the mood is right and the scene is perfect don't stint on film while you're out there – great times in the wild are unrepeatable.

READING

Few people seem to go bush without taking something to read. Even though many a book has returned home unread, it's guaranteed that the time you decide to go without a book you'll be incarcerated in the tent by a two-day storm with only soup packets to read.

Some people find the outdoors conducive to reading the great novels they never have time for at home, but if space in your pack is critical something reliably engaging is best. Any book that involves the area or activity you've chosen is obviously worth considering. There are nature writers whose vision of landscape and living things can create resonances with your own experience. Stirring expedition accounts may inspire but they can also be too close for comfort, especially if the outcome is marred by accident.

Ultimately, reading is a personal matter. Perhaps a slim volume of poetry would appeal for the weight-to-content ratio, or you may prefer the contrast between sylvan innocence and the seedy world of detective fiction. On long trips the only proviso is that members of the party consult each other before making their selection so that books can be shared.

DIARIES

Keeping a simple record of daily events – distances covered, weather, water supplies, campsites, etc – is helpful when planning future trips, but a diary has the power to be much more than a bland travelogue.

There is a great tradition of journals which document expedition triumphs and tribulations, but finding the time to pen a detailed record of your progress is difficult without retinue of helpers to free you from other tasks. The best that most people can hope for is a few minutes during the lunch break and an hour or so in the evenings. Aside from random entries one approach is to focus on a particular incident or highlight of each day.

Beyond impressions of landscape and descriptions of incidents a diary can be an opportunity for more reflective writing. For some people their diary is an outlet for private emotions about the trip, or other aspects of their life, which are cast in a new light by being in the bush. Given the need to work closely with others in the outdoors a diary is a valuable way of releasing tensions that are perhaps best not expressed openly.

Any kind of stout notebook will do, as long as it fits easily into the pocket of your jacket or rucksack. For river and rainforest trips consider a notebook with waterproof paper. Everyone has their preferred writing instrument but the humble pencil has many advantages: it won't leak, it is easy to sharpen, and is better for sketching and marking on maps. The graphite can also be used to help zippers run smoothly, and in dire moments a pencil may be the driest wood you can find!

HISTORY

By their very nature wilderness areas can seem like places without a human past. There is little if any sign of habitation and what contact there has been is largely unrecorded in the traditional histories.

Yet, as our knowledge of Aboriginal culture widens, it's clear that even the most remote and inhospitable areas have supported a way of life that's steeped with history and mythology. It may seem presumptuous for outsiders to imagine that they can understand what a place meant to the Aborigines of the area, but of all people bushwalkers living close to the land must bear some of the strongest hopes for bridging the gaps.

Sadly in most areas the opportunities to share the Aboriginal culture first-hand are lost forever. There are, nevertheless, some helpful written histories and many parks have Aboriginal rangers who introduce visitors to their lands. No-one who travels in bushland which contains Aboriginal rock art, engravings, middens and artefacts can remain indifferent to their suggestive power.

Against this background the history of white exploration and settlement appears both slight and tragic in its legacy, but there is no denying the fascination that people have for the era when much of our bush folklore was forged. Reading the accounts of the early explorers and outback travellers can enrich one's experience of the outdoors. Equally, there are an increasing number of excellent books that chart the efforts to preserve our natural lands. As this struggle goes on anyone who enjoys wilderness areas must heed the most recent lessons of history.

Ultimately, there is nothing wrong with your trips being a quest for the perfect photograph, rare wildlife species or some deeper contact with the past. Side interests need not, however, rule your time in the outdoors. It's a pity if the bush is reduced to being just another compartment in a busy life. There is a lot to be said for experiencing the wild as it is and enjoying the moment, without props or prompts.

7

FIRST AID AND SURVIVAL

Heading off into the outdoors will invariably take you away from easy access to doctors, ambulances and hospitals. The wilder and more remote the territory the greater also is the possibility of becoming geographically embarrassed – a polite euphemism for being 'lost'. When venturing into rugged terrain, or participating in activities with less margin for error such as rock climbing, para-sailing or rafting, there is also the possibility of accidents. In many situations in the outdoors minor complaints, that elsewhere would not be serious, can occasionally turn out to be life-threatening. It is therefore sensible for all those venturing into the wilds to have some survival training and first aid skills, and to carry a useful first aid kit. Where the activity or destination is prone to a particular type of accident or medical problem, then more specific preparations should also be included. For example, if mountaineering or trekking in the Himalaya, where there is every likelihood of experiencing altitude or mountain sickness, the causes, signs, symptoms and treatment should be researched.

Preparations for first aid and survival should, understandably, be in proportion to the seriousness of the objective, and the degree of skills and experience of your party. Major expeditions, for example, include a doctor as an essential part of their team. On an extended bushwalk or trek with a group, it is advisable that one or more members of the party have some first aid or paramedical training. A comprehensive group first aid kit should be carried. Individuals should also take their own basic first aid and survival kits, plus any special medications that are necessary. If travelling on your own in the outdoors your preparation needs to be exceptionally thorough, including learning first aid and carrying an extensive first aid kit.

Regardless of the group size and destination certain first aid and survival books are well worth studying before you go, and some can be carried with you. *Medicine for Mountaineers* is an excellent self-help manual for groups travelling in remote areas without a doctor in their party. While this is perhaps too bulky to carry if you are on your own, *Mountaineering First Aid and Accident Response* will readily fit into your first aid kit.

There is every likelihood that on a long hike, expedition or trek someone will get sick at some stage. Blisters, strains, sunburn, chest, throat or stomach complaints are among the most likely maladies, but the real problems arise if there is an accident or emergency.

FIRST AID

First aid in the outdoors may have to be administered in a myriad of circumstances – especially in the case of accidents, drowning, burns, bites, stings, sprains, shock, hypothermia or illness. In the course of this chapter it is only possible to skim the surface of basic first aid procedures. Individuals contemplating spending time in the outdoors or undertaking serious adventure activities should complete a first aid course to enable them to cope with accidents and serious emergencies. At the same time, the most common complaints that are encountered on the trail or track will be relatively minor, and with some experience, commonsense and the help of a few simple medicines, bandages and procedures, people can usually treat themselves.

Weight and space are the obvious limitations to what can be carried in an outdoors first aid kit. Commercially available kits are rarely either well-equipped or good value for money. Specially made nylon fabric organisers with many pockets and zippered pouches are now available, and the appropriate contents can be bought from a chemist to suit specific requirements. A plastic lunchbox is another good first aid kit container, and has the advantage of protecting the contents from being crushed. The following checklist forms the core of a basic kit.

EMERGENCIES

Most accidents are preventable. With a little care, weather knowledge, and proper equipment and clothing, many problems can be avoided. Knowing your limits and having an understanding of the bush are essential for accident prevention. If an accident does occur, commonsense is the most important attribute, but having a good

PERSONAL FIRST AID KIT CHECKLIST

- Adhesive dressings
- Anti-diarrhoea tablets
- Antacid tablets
- Antibiotic (broad spectrum)
- Antifungal powder (for the feet)
- Antiseptic cream
- Bandage
- Codeine
- Cough mixture
- Crepe bandage (for sprains)
- Decongestant
- Diamox (for altitude sickness)
- First aid handbook
- Insect repellent or cream
- Iodine
- Laxative
- Lipscreen
- Mercurochrome
- Moleskin (for blisters)
- Nasal spray or drops
- Soluble aspirin or Paracetomol
- Sterile non-stick dressing
- Sunscreen
- Tampons
- Toilet paper
- Throat lozenges
- Water purification tablets

first aid kit will often help you to deal with the situation, or at least help minimise the pain, discomfort and potential for complications.

There are a number of environmental extremes that have to be faced in the outdoors. Too much heat (hyperthermia) can be as much of a problem as too little (hypothermia), and the shock from a lightning bolt, or burns from a bushfire can be potentially fatal. A snake bite or bee sting are obvious hazards, but more subtle problems such as the lack of oxygen in a closed-up tent where someone has been cooking can be equally calamitous. A little experience and care will help to avoid some of these problems.

Exposure

If you are exposed to cool conditions and no insulating clothing is worn, heat will be lost to the atmosphere by radiation, conduction and convection. Convection is the main source of heat loss, and the faster the air moves across unprotected skin the greater is the convectional heat loss. This is known as 'windchill'. The accompanying chart illustrates the relationship between temperature and wind speeds and its effect on unprotected skin. The body produces heat through muscular exercise and the burning of energy. If heat loss is not matched by heat gain then, after a while, the body will automatically start to generate heat through shivering. This is an early stage of exposure, which is also known as hypothermia. If cooling continues the body shuts down the flow of blood to the extremities and involuntary shivering begins.

Hypothermia is the chilling of the body to the point where the internal or

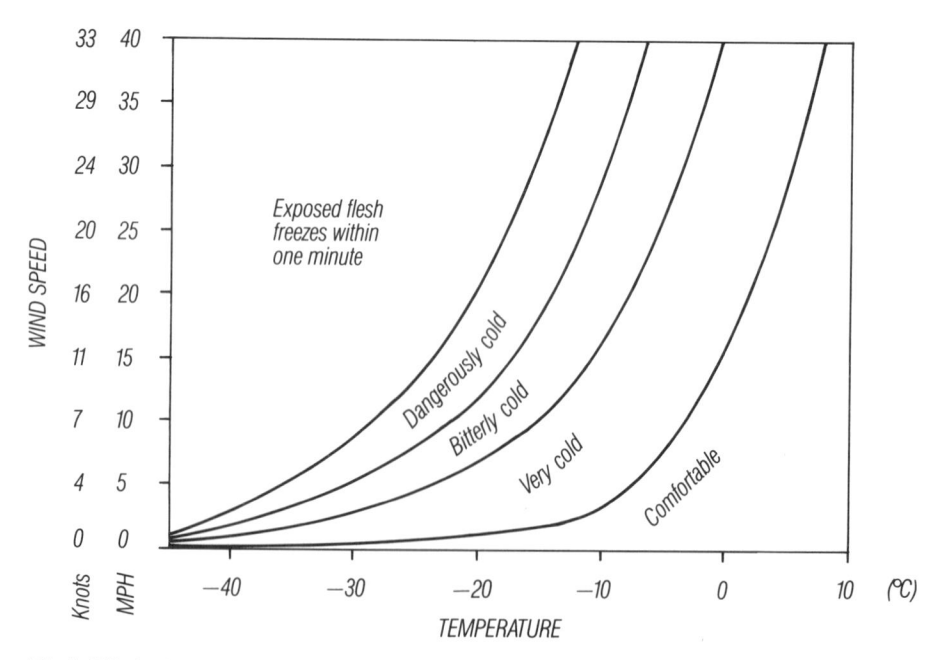

Wind chill chart

core temperature is seriously lowered. The normal oral temperature is 37°C (98.6°F), and a core temperature of below 35°C (95°F) is regarded as dangerous hypothermia. Exhaustion is often associated with hypothermia, and being aware of conditions that may lead to exposure is the first step to avoiding the problem. These are: insufficient clothing being worn, exposure to cold winds, fatigue, lack of fuel (digestible food), shock and imbibing alcohol. The onset of hypothermia is accompanied by stumbling, lack of response, slow reactions, lack of perception, slurred speech, shivering, swelling of the lips and hands. At an advanced stage the sufferer will fall down frequently and eventually collapse and become unconscious.

Warmth, food and rest will alleviate the early signs of exposure, but a serious case will require comprehensive and immediate treatment. Once the problem is recognised, the patient must be protected from the elements and further heat loss as rapidly as possible. Putting up a tent if available, getting out of the wind, and wrapping the victim in a survival sheet are the very first steps. Do not remove wet or damp clothing straight away as this may cause further cooling. Heat must be applied to the core rather than the extremities. If the patient is conscious give them warm sweet drinks and easily digestible food. Placing the patient in a sleeping bag with another person who puts their hands in the patient's crotch or under their armpits will help to apply heat to the core.

Medical help should be sought as rapidly as possible, and if evacuation is necessary the victim should be carried on a stretcher. Re-warming from serious hypothermia can be carried out in a warm bath where the legs and arms are left out, but this should be done under a doctor's supervision.

Heat exhaustion and dehydration

If exercising in the outdoors in high temperatures, especially over 30°C (86°F) it is necessary to drink copious quantities of water. In desert areas it is often better to try and minimise water loss rather than to carry enough to cope with high intake. Heat stroke can kill quickly and is usually first manifested by headaches, dizziness, rapid pulse, nausea, rapid temperature rise and collapse. The best treatment is to drink small quantities of water frequently. The victim should also be cooled externally by covering him or her with wet cloths, or totally immersing in water. An indication of the body's fluid needs is the colour of one's urine – if it is dark, more fluids should be drunk.

Lightning

At certain times of the year, in particular areas of the world and in certain types of terrain, electrical storms are very common. If you are in exposed positions in the outdoors at these times and in these places, the possibility of being hit by lightning becomes very real. The section on *Thunderstorms* in Chapter 3 covers what to look for and how to minimise any risks. Someone who has been struck by lightning, if still alive, may have no heartbeat, or not be breathing, and may also be in shock, and have serious burns. Immediate first aid must be administered.

Bushfires

Bushfires are a very serious proposition for people in the outdoors. Being caught out in the face of an oncoming blaze is one of the most horrific situations imaginable. Obviously the best defence is to avoid being in such circumstances in the first place when there is a high fire danger. Avoid scrubby country in hot, dry, windy weather, and seek out and heed the bushfire warnings that parks and local authorities give in summer months. If you do find yourself in situations of high fire risk make sure that you're not the person that starts the fire. If open fires are permitted, choose fireplaces very carefully and make sure there is plenty of cleared space around the fire. Never leave a burning fire unattended, and make sure it is completely extinguished before you depart from the campsite.

The main principles for survival in the face of a wild fire are: to remain calm and not to panic, to select an area where there is the least amount of burnable material, and to use every means possible to protect yourself from the radiation and the flames. Exposure to radiated heat which causes heat stroke is believed to be the main cause of death in those who are exposed to bushfires. As a bushfire passes, radiated heat is very intense but does not last for very long – less than four minutes is an average time. Do not try to outrun a fire unless the chances of escape are clearly very good. Fires can travel extremely quickly up hill, especially if fanned by a strong wind.

The best means of escape is to set up a barrier between yourself and the fire through the use of clothing, wood, earth, stones or metal. Woollen clothing and heavy boots will afford some protection (synthetics are often flammable). Wrapping yourself in a wet blanket or sleeping bag, or burying yourself in a trench, have proved effective means of surviving a bushfire. Where possible, take shelter in a car or building and make sure the doors and windows are sealed. Sizeable areas of bare ground or rock, a pond or running water are also possible refuges. In such situations lie face down and cover yourself as the fire approaches. Back burning (setting fire to bush or grass so that it will burn towards the oncoming fire) is a further effective way of creating a fuel-free area to take refuge in, but some previous experience of this procedure is advisable.

Floods and flooded rivers

Floods seem to be an increasingly regular result of today's weather patterns, especially in tropical and semi-tropical areas. The danger from flooding is potentially lethal in specialist activities such as rafting, canoeing, caving and canyoning. If bushwalking, the main thing to avoid in potentially threatening flood situations is camping in creek beds or low-lying areas. Crossing flooded rivers is a more likely problem to be faced with when travelling in the outdoors than being overwhelmed by a full-scale flood. Wading or swimming across flooded rivers is a potentially lethal situation, and if there is any doubt as to the condition of the river take precautions. More details of this aspect are covered in Chapter 8, in the section on River crossings.

FIRST AID AND SURVIVAL

TRAUMA AND INJURIES

After an accident the first thing to establish is whether the victim is conscious or unconscious. This can be done by shaking the victim gently by the shoulder and asking them for their name. If you can get them to respond to shouted commands such as "open your eyes", "squeeze my hand", "let my hand go", then they are conscious.

Whether they are conscious or not the victim should be checked for their ABCD: A - Airway – to see if it is clear; B – Breathing – if they are not breathing they should be given Expired Air Resuscitation (mouth-to-mouth); C – Circulation – if no circulation, cardiopulmonary resuscitation should be administered. In association with the question of circulation, you should also check to see if there is any

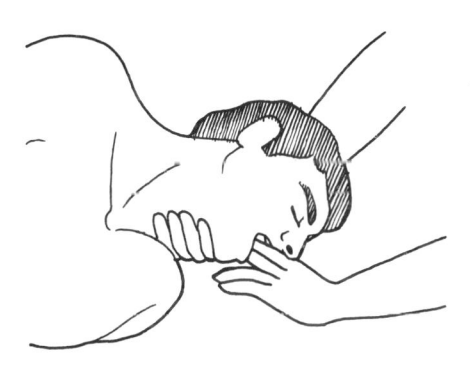

RESUSCITATION
1. Check airway is clear and that there are no obstructions

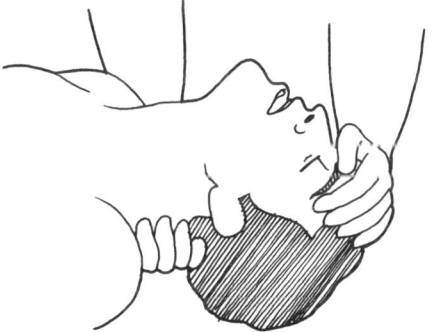

2. Tilt the head back, supporting it behind the neck, to allow air to enter the lungs

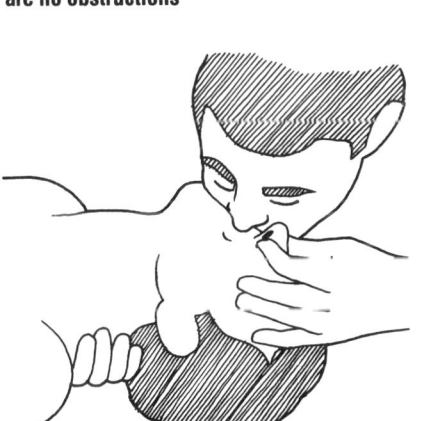

3. Pinch the nose and blow forcefully into the victim's mouth

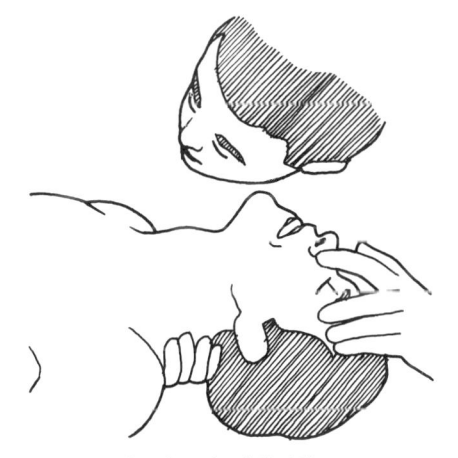

4. Turn your head to check that the victim's chest has risen, release grip on the nose and listen for exhalation. If the victim has not started to breathe, repeat

bleeding, which is then treated by applying direct pressure. Next, check for fractures or dislocations which must be immobilised if discovered. If a back injury is suspected then the patient's spine must not be bent or twisted. The D stands for degrees – check the patient's temperature to see if they are suffering from hypothermia.

Expired Air Resuscitation (mouth-to-mouth) and CPR (cardiopulmonary resuscitation) are detailed and important procedures that are best learnt from a first aid training course rather than a book. Good first aid manuals have detailed step-by-step procedures if you are not able to attend a course.

Shock is the result of injury or a fright, and should always be suspected when an accident has occurred. The onset of shock may not occur until some time after the accident. The signs are: the patient will feel cold and clammy, faint, have a weak pulse, and be breathless. Shock occurs when the body's circulation breaks down and there is insufficient oxygen supply to the organs through either internal or external bleeding, fluid loss from burns or other causes or from heart disorders. If conscious the shock sufferer should be kept lying down and warm, with their legs elevated. If unconscious they should be placed in the lateral or coma position (on their side with upper arm and leg drawn up to support them).

External bleeding is best treated by applying direct pressure with a pad pressed over the wound. This will stop most wounds from oozing or gushing. If there are no broken bones, the affected area should be elevated. The application of pressure to points may be used to slow the bleeding, but tourniquets should only be considered where a limb is partially or completely severed.

Fractures and dislocations in the outdoors are a considerable problem – especially if the victim is no longer mobile. Broken bones are usually the result of a fall and this often causes other complications, such as internal injuries. If there is any suggestion of a spinal injury, then the victim should not be moved – signs of this would be pain in the back or neck, or unconsciousness. Where there is an open wound, as in a complicated fracture, this should be covered. The broken area or limb must be immobilised as much as possible through the use of splints and bandages. Care should be taken to see that circulation is not restricted both by the fracture itself or the splinting. An inflatable air splint is

Place victim in the coma position and keep warm

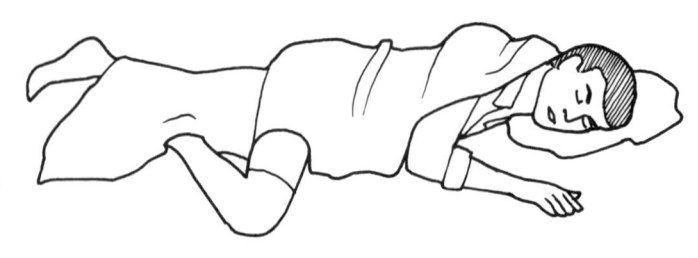

ideal, but temporary splints can be made from tree branches, the metal parts of internal frame packs, ski poles, and bandages, string or rope. Carrying a person with a broken leg over any distance is very difficult even with many people and a proper stretcher. Improvised stretchers can be made with whatever materials are at hand, for example, rucksack frames, climbing ropes and skis and ski poles.

If burns occur, where possible immerse the affected area in cold water immediately to minimise further tissue damage. The next best thing is to apply a clean, wet cloth to the area. The most important thing with this type of injury is to minimise the chance of infection, so lightly apply a sterile nonstick dressing or a clean bandage. Do not break any blisters or apply any ointments or lotions. Burn sufferers should be treated for shock, and the affected areas immobilised.

All snake bites should be treated seriously, although not all snakes are venomous. The victim must be kept lying down and, if feasible, you should apply a broad firm bandage over the bite. If the bite is on a limb, this area must be splinted and immobilised. The patient should be treated for shock and possible breathing failure. The victim must also receive medical attention as soon as possible, but with minimum exertion on their behalf – where feasible, helicopter rescue is preferable. If the snake can be safely killed and carried out without delaying the treatment of the victim, this will aid in subsequent treatment. At the very least, a written description of the snake will assist in identifying the species so that the appropriate antivenene can be applied.

MINOR AILMENTS

Any outdoor experience can be stressful, given the fatigue caused by unaccustomed sudden exercise, often severe climate changes, and the impact of unfamiliar food and drinks. The most common complaints you are likely to experience on the trail are blisters, stomach upsets, coughs, colds and sunburn.

Blisters

Properly worn in well-fitting boots, regular changes of clean socks, and the use of foot powder are the key to avoiding blisters. See Chapter 14, *Footwear* for more details. If you can feel a blister developing, stop immediately and apply some moleskin or a sticking plaster. This illustrates the value of carrying part, or all, of your personal first aid kit in your daypack where it is readily accessible. Once you have protected the hot spot, try to reduce the rubbing. This may be possible by simply adjusting your laces or changing your socks. With blisters that have burst remove the dead skin and apply Tincture of Benzine or some bland antiseptic and cover the affected area with a sterile non-adherent dressing.

Sore throats and colds

Sore throats and colds can quickly develop into serious complaints unless they are carefully monitored. They can sometimes be nipped in the bud by various preparations and treatments – the Sherpa people of Nepal, for example, swear by copious quantities of garlic and chillies, but these might not be to your taste. You are more susceptible to infections when you are run down and not eating properly, so get plenty of sleep and take it easy. Gargling aspirin or table salt dissolved in warm water, or sucking antiseptic lozenges and inhaling eucalyptus vapour will give some relief to a sore throat and cough.

Stomach upsets

The 'runs', or diarrhoea, is an all too common consequence of poor hygiene. Diarrhoea can occur in varying degrees of seriousness depending on the cause. Treatment ranges from doing nothing, except keeping your fluid intake up, to taking antibiotics.

Infectious diarrhoea in most cases is short-lived and requires no treatment. Taking antibiotics before it is necessary is inappropriate and may even prolong the illness. The best treatment is rehydration with treated or bottled water or carbonated soft drinks, and maintaining an adequate food intake is also important.

Where giardia, an intestinal parasite, is prevalent stomach illness often results from drinking contaminated water. The symptoms are rotten egg stomach gas, burps, vomiting and explosive runny stools, and you should consult your doctor regarding an appropriate medicine to deal with this.

Dry skin

Dry skin and painful cracks in fingertips and lips are common problems in the dry air in the bush, at altitude and above the snowline. Applying moisturising (sorbolene or lanolin) cream to your hands, and a lip-salve to the lips several times a day should help.

Sunburn

Prevention is the key to dealing with sunburn. In extreme sunny conditions carrying an umbrella and/or wearing a broad-brimmed hat and scarf, long trousers and a long-sleeved shirt will afford some protection. It is advisable to cover any exposed skin regularly with a 99 per cent protection (sun protection factor 15) sunscreen or sun barrier cream, and to take special care of your nose and lips.

These protective measures are particularly necessary if walking on snow. At high altitudes the earth's atmosphere is thinner, and so more harmful ultraviolet radiation is present in the sun's rays. The ultraviolet rays reflected from the snow can burn unusual places such as the insides of your nostrils, beneath your chin and underneath your nose. If you become sunburnt, calamine lotion will bring some relief.

Snow blindness

Snow blindness is caused by ultraviolet rays burning the cornea of the eye. When walking on snow always wear dark sunglasses or goggles as even in what might seem like cloudy or overcast conditions it is still possible for snow blindness to occur. Special glacier glasses are warranted if spending any length of time at high altitude or above the snowline. See Chapter 21, *Accessories* and the section on *Sunglasses* for more details on glasses and goggles. If glasses are not available, narrow horizontal slits cut in a strip of cardboard will help in an emergency. If you experience snow blindness, treat yourself with eye drops, cover the eyes with sterile pads, take pain-killers and rest for a day or so.

FIRST AID AND SURVIVAL

NATURE'S ANNOYANCES

Fleas, lice and ticks are not uncommon in the bush, but the effect of these pests can be minimised by washing yourself and your clothes regularly.

In tropical and wet temperate areas leeches lie in wait in low vegetation along paths and tracks for warm-blooded animals. They attach themselves to lower legs and ankles with amazing speed and usually without you being aware. They can work themselves through socks and the eyelets of boots, so regular inspections are advisable. If you feel any unusual skin sensations anywhere on your body, stop and check. Leeches can be removed by applying salt, alcohol, vinegar or a lighted match or cigarette. Avoid pulling them off by force as part of the head may be left in the wound, and this can lead to infection. Leeches secrete an anticoagulant, and even after they have been removed or fallen off, bleeding will continue. It is most important to clean these wounds with soap and water to prevent them from becoming infected. Applying certain insect repellents or Dibutyl Phthalate to clothes and skin, or rubbing feet and legs with tobacco juice, will also help to keep them at bay.

Prevention of mosquito bites is most important in a malaria-prone area. For details see the section on malaria prevention in Chapter 11, *Trekking*.

ACCIDENTS AND SURVIVAL SKILLS

Accidents are more likely to occur in the outdoors than in everyday life. Because of the often rugged nature of the terrain, and the likelihood that you are tired and feeling the effects of unaccustomed exercise, your balance and judgement are not as sharp. Slipping over on an icy trail could easily result in a bad sprain, or even a broken leg. Taking the wrong path, then trying to cut across country to regain the correct trail is also potentially disastrous. Crossing rivers and dealing with slippery paths in the rain are further problems that you could face.

Storms in the mountains can occur at any time of the year. In winter at altitude the temperatures will be much colder and you have to be prepared for bad snowstorms. If you are caught out alone in bad weather and do not have the protective clothing and experience to look after yourself, hypothermia and/or frostbite are a very real possibility. It is the simple mistakes, however, such as not watching where you put your feet, that are the most likely source of danger.

If seriously lost, the first thing to do is assess the situation carefully, and not panic. The main factors to consider are the adequacy of water, food and shelter. Water is the most important of the body's survival needs – it is possible to survive for weeks without food, but only a matter of days without water. Where the temperature is high and sweating is profuse, up to 5 L (9 pt) a day should be drunk – any less and dehydration can be a problem in a matter of hours. A minimum of 1 L (1¾ pt) of water a day is needed to survive.

Water can be found in the bush in a number of places. A solar still – or placing a sheet of plastic over a small bush at night – can yield a small but valuable supply of water. The presence of certain types of vegetation is a sure indicator of high levels of moisture below the surface, and by digging a hole in a soak or damp area water can often seep into the depression after a time.

Water, if present, is not always pure. Salt or salty water should never be drunk. Boiling water for long enough at a high temperature will kill most organisms that are likely to cause problems. At high altitudes water boils at a lower temperature, and so it takes longer and more fuel is used to make a given quantity safe. The best alternative is to add chemicals such as iodine. In the right dosage this procedure can be simpler and just as effective. Start with 5 g (0.2 oz) of iodine crystals in a 30 ml (1 fl oz) clear glass bottle with a leakproof Bakelite top. Do not use plastic containers as they are attacked by the iodine. Top up the bottle with water, then shake vigorously for sixty seconds and let it stand for a few seconds to allow the heavy crystals to settle. The water in the bottle is now a nearly saturated iodine solution that can be used to treat your water supply. To a 1 L (1¾ pt) water bottle, add between 10 and 20 cc of the iodine solution. This is equivalent to between five and ten drops per litre. After 20 minutes the water will be disinfected. The effectiveness of the solution varies with the temperature and clarity of the water. At body temperature, only 10 cc per litre is needed while if the water is near freezing or cloudy, 20 cc should be used per litre. The iodine crystals

To make a solar still, dig a hole approximately 60 cm (24 in) deep x 1 m (3¼ ft) wide and line with vegetation. At the centre of the hole, place a catchment container. Cover the hole with plastic and seal the edges with soil. Place a weight in the centre of the plastic ensuring that it is immediately above the container

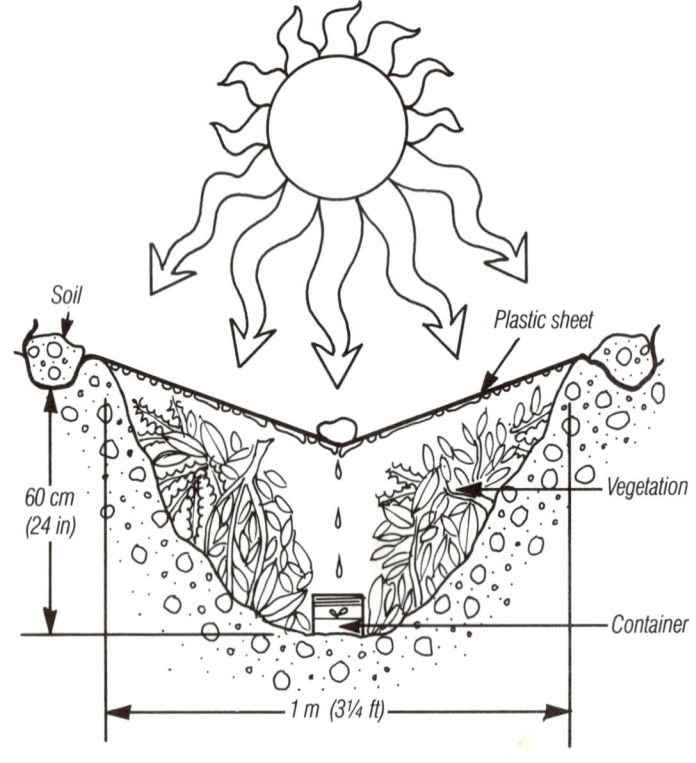

should not be used directly as iodine is highly poisonous in large quantities. These steps can be repeated hundreds of times without replenishing the crystals.

Portable water purification filters are now also available, but these are bulky and not effective against the hepatitis virus. Micro-filters however are very good at eliminating suspended particles and some organisms, but should be used in combination with iodine treatment for complete protection.

Search and rescue

Becoming lost is an all too common problem in virgin bush and rugged terrain, but for experienced people this situation should be only temporary. By careful use of a map and compass and studying the terrain (as discussed in Chapter 4, Navigation) it is usually possible to get one's bearings and then move on again in an orderly fashion. If you are seriously lost, there is often the possibility of getting out of trouble by heading to the nearest form of civilisation by following watercourses, or walking on a bearing to the nearest road.

Often, searches are commenced for parties in the outdoors who are not lost but just overdue. Before setting out it is important to notify appropriate people such as friends, parents, police, or park authorities of your plans. If you have left details of your route and destination, then if you have not turned up after a reasonable amount of time, the alarm will be raised and a search party sent out. If there has been an accident it is all the more important that you make it as easy as possible for people to find you or your party.

The remoteness of most true wilderness areas, and the minimal medical and rescue facilities available there, make even minor trauma potentially serious. If you cannot walk, yet are not too heavy, you may be able to be carried by a rescue team through rugged terrain. If you are a stretcher case it may be possible to obtain a helicopter, but this option cannot be relied upon. Helicopters require favourable flying conditions and have very limited payloads at altitude.

Helicopters are also very dangerous when operating and should only be approached from the front after having been signalled to do so by the pilot. Often the pilot will not be willing or able to shut the machine down, and so alighting is made more difficult by the noise and downdraught of the rotors.

Often it may be days before a search party will be called out and so, if lost or injured, it is best to carefully assess the situation and not waste undue effort or resources before the appropriate time. Searches are usually conducted on foot or from the air but if there are tracks or open ground vehicles may also be used. The best means of attracting attention varies, depending on the possible means of rescue. If foot parties are thought to be in the vicinity then calling out with cooee's may alert the rescuers, but this is difficult to sustain for any length of time. Better to use a whistle. Building signal fires that could be easily ignited if an aircraft is heard is a good example of how to spend waiting time positively. An extensive store of green leaves ready to throw on a fire to generate a big plume of smoke is another worthwhile diversionary activity. Avoiding panic

SURVIVAL KIT CHECKLIST

If a survival kit is to be of value it should be small and light enough to never be left behind. It should contain:
- Candle
- Compass
- Emergency shelter
- Energy bar
- Eye drops
- Fishing line
- Map
- Matches (in a waterproof container)
- Money
- Nylon cord (10 m / 30 ft)
- Pencil and waterproof paper
- Plastic bags (3 small for holding water, 1 large garbage bag)
- Pocket knife
- Signalling mirror
- Small torch
- Solar still (plastic sheet 1 x 1m (3 x 3 ft); plastic tube
- Sticking plaster
- Teabags
- Toilet paper
- Water purifying tablets
- Whistle

and keeping up a party's morale is the most important ongoing activity that can be undertaken.

Distress signals to attract the attention of a search party or aircraft are three long whistles, cooees, and mirror flashes repeated in groups of three every minute. SOS marked out on the ground in large letters, or one of a series of letters that is a code symbol for a short message: I stands for – require doctor serious injuries; II – require medical supplies; X – unable to proceed; F – require food and water; LL – all well; N – no; Y – yes; K – indicate direction to proceed, etc, can be used.

If you are lost or have to stay put because of an accident, but you have plenty of food and water, it is possible to survive for a considerable period of time. If you have run out of food but still have water, there are often edible native species to be found. Every biogeographic and climatic region, however, has a different selection of plants, so it is worth familiarising yourself with the main edible species before setting out. It is also worthwhile learning how to start a fire without matches, build snares and traps, and to fish. Like learning first aid, perfecting these skills can be interesting exercises in their own right. Once mastered such abilities will give you greater confidence to be able to head off into the outdoors with the knowledge that you can cope with almost anything.

PART 2
OUTDOOR ACTIVITIES

8
BUSHWALKING

A bushwalk is the easiest way to enjoy the outdoors. The skills are primal – everyone knows how to walk and of all the outdoor pastimes it requires the least equipment and specialist knowledge. This gives bushwalking a wonderful freedom and immediacy – to walk is to witness the world in the way nature intended: at eye level and a graceful pace.

There are, nonetheless, valuable lessons to be learnt. Walking may be instinctive, but the noble art of travel on foot has been in decline during this most sedentary of centuries. It takes practice to rediscover how to cover long distances and move with ease over difficult ground. If this sounds far-fetched then it is salutary to observe locals moving through countryside where there is no alternative but to walk. Watch a Nepalese porter carry a load over a steep pass, and you will see a study in poise, balance and control. Similarly, an experienced bushwalker learns nimble footwork, how to rest mid-stride when climbing, how to negotiate obstacles and maintain a steady pace. All this, at the same time as being involved with the unfolding landscape.

Just as there are many skills to refine, so it is possible to pursue bushwalking in many forms. It can be a relaxed day's outing along a marked track, for which you need only comfortable footwear, a map and daypack. Or you may enjoy overnight walks that take you further into the bush and embrace the delights of camping out under the stars. In its more extreme forms bushwalking can mean a week-long exploration of rugged, untracked wilderness; or tackling a long-distance walking trail that may traverse an entire range, cross state borders and take a month or more to complete.

So while bushwalking may be the most accessible of activities it need not be tame or low-key.

SETTING THE PACE

The key to good walking is finding a comfortable pace. Everyone has their natural stride and a pace at which they move fluently without undue exertion. Establishing this rhythm is not hard and to maintain it some people link their breathing with a pattern of strides, others do mental exercises, or fix their gaze on the feet of the person in front. Experiment to find a method that works for you.

All this would be fine if you only ever ventured onto a treadmill. However, bushwalking, by definition, takes you over fluctuating terrain and you need to keep on adjusting this pace according to changes underfoot, not to mention the constant flurry of signals from your body. The most common trap for new walkers is attempting long climbs at too fast a pace. With experience you will develop an impressive range of low gears to cope with heavy loads and steep gradients.

The other major complication is that there will be as many different walking paces as there are members in the group. This is a notorious source of disharmony on bushwalks. Slow walkers fall further and further behind, and arrive at a rest stop only to find the main bunch ready to set off again. Conversely, it can be equally frustrating for the fleet of foot to be held back by a mob of laggards.

There is no magic prescription for solving this dilemma. Traditional wisdom has it that a party's walking pace should be governed by that of the slowest member. This is certainly true at any time when navigation is problematic or when spirits flag, but on clearly defined trails a group may agree on a system that allows individuals to progress more or less at their own pace. Any such arrangement needs to be closely watched, as too much fragmentation can lead to a collapse of morale or one of the party becoming lost.

REST STOPS

One of the best ways to administer the walking pace of a group is to take short breaks during the course of the day. It doesn't really matter how often these rests are taken but there is a balance to be struck. Too many stops can disrupt a natural rhythm; too few can be taxing on energy reserves. It is better to have frequent short rests rather than one long break. The average stop should be for five minutes or so – dally much longer and you run the risk of getting chilled and muscles stiffening up.

When choosing a place to rest, use your imagination. No-one wants to squat in a muddy hollow. Look instead for spots with a pleasing aspect, somewhere comfortable to sit, and shelter if required. A rest stop is a time for drinks, snacks, photography or just lolling in the sun. It can also be an opportunity for energetic types to burn off their excess with side trips or reconnaissance.

UPS AND DOWNS

There is no escaping the fact that a lot of bushwalking involves climbing hills, and this can be hard work. Yet, in some cases, the climb is preferable to the descent.

There are a number of useful strategies for long climbs. If the idea of slogging to the top is too daunting to contemplate, then break the climb into manageable stages. Pick out natural features and head for them, moving at a comfortable, steady pace. As a distraction from the tedium, sing tunes, solve algebra problems or chant your mantra. Reward yourself with a brief rest as you arrive at each objective.

Prepared trails often zigzag up steep slopes in a series of rising traverses. This is a worthwhile tactic to adopt when you are making your way through untracked country. Generally speaking it takes longer than a direct assault on the fall-line, but is less punishing on limbs and lungs.

The key to enjoying the climb is to

maintain an even expenditure of effort. Take shorter steps rather than over-extending. Walk around obstacles like boulders and logs instead of clambering over them, and don't lean too far forward and risk losing your balance. One invaluable adaptation on sharp inclines is the rest step. This simply means that as you go through your stride you straighten each leg in turn so that your body weight is briefly supported by your bone structure, and the leg muscles get a momentary rest. This may seem a minor point but over a long climb you can feel the benefits.

During a long rest at the top of a hill it's tempting to think that the hard part is over, you've made it to the summit and it's all downhill from there. That may be true, but descending has its own demands. There's less heavy breathing but the strain on muscles and joints like ankles and knees can be intense. You need to concentrate on keeping your balance and careful foot placement to avoid twists and sprains. The combination of a heavy rucksack, gravity and a brain in neutral is one of the most common causes of bushwalking injuries. Blisters also often develop on long downhill stretches. Treat any potential blister areas before heading downhill, and adjust your laces to prevent your feet from rubbing and being cramped in the toe of your boot.

TREADING LIGHTLY

Even the most sensitive bushwalkers cannot avoid making some impression on the landscape. In spite of painstaking footwork small plants are crushed, stones become dislodged and a trail of boot prints is sometimes left behind. Unless bushwalkers evolve to grow wings this kind of disruption cannot be entirely avoided, but at least with a little care it can be kept to a minimum.

Walking lightly over the ground is largely a matter of attitude. In the past, bushwalking may have been regarded as a military-style forced march with hulking figures, wearing clunky boots and wielding machetes, swaggering through undergrowth. Thankfully, this is no longer the fashion. Apart from anything else, hacking a passage through the bush to conquer the wilderness is exhausting work.

If, on the other hand, the focus of the trip is an appreciation of the bush and how it works, the chances are that you will walk with some delicacy. It has to be admitted that some people are better at this than others. In most parties there will be people who by nature are clumsy and awkward on their feet. Others simply get carried away with being let loose in the wild. The ultimate aim is not to stifle enthusiam with dull reverence, but just curb wanton damage.

PACK CARRYING

All the skills of walking are complicated by the weight of a pack bearing down on you. While everyone has moments when their rucksack is a cursed enemy, it's important to make peace with your load.

Just lifting a laden pack off the ground is an art in itself. One way is to grab the pack by the haul loop or shoulder strap and raise it onto a knee; then swing the pack onto one shoulder and then your back as you put the other shoulder strap on. An alternative method with extremely heavy packs is to use both arms to raise the pack onto something like a rock or tree stump. Then put your back into the pack, slide the shoulder straps on and rock forward onto your feet.

Assuming you're still upright, it's time to fine tune the shoulder straps and hipbelt. If the pack fits your back and the load is evenly balanced only minor alterations should be necessary. No one adjustment will work in all conditions. Instead, as you walk it's a good idea to regularly loosen and tighten the shoulder straps to shift the load around. On trails and level ground use whatever position feels comfortable. On rugged descents it's important that the pack doesn't sway you off balance, so tighten all the straps, and if you have a sternum strap then use it.

Pack carrying will never exactly be a joy, but in time, like the tortoise, you learn to live with your home on your back.

ROUTE FINDING

How do you pick a line through a tangled stretch of scrub, stay on course for an objective several hours away, and avoid tripping over the fallen branch two paces in front – all at the same time? The answer is, with difficulty. Detailed route finding is the challenge that endures when all other bushwalking skills have been mastered.

There are no shortcuts to make you proficient at steering a course through wild country. Experience is the best teacher, and much can be learnt by following in the wake of a veteran pathfinder. What might appear to be a casual decision to choose a particular gully to climb, valley to cross, or bluff to avoid, may in fact be based on a host of factors all glued together by bush-sharpened instinct. When walking on a designated trail these decisions are almost invariably made for you, but that doesn't mean you shouldn't use the opportunity to establish your own route-finding skills. Even on marked trails the way forward can at times be puzzling and ambiguous.

The essence of route-finding is observation: the ability to assess the lie of the land and its relationship with the path you have planned and the ground you have covered. Use a topographic map to build up a big picture in your mind of the major landforms; the summits, river valleys, clifflines and ridges. From this picture features are chosen as objectives to aim for. Then plan what detailed line should be taken to each objective. It sounds straightforward enough, but what happens if your chosen landmark disappears out of sight as you enter dense forest, or when low cloud descends?

It's at such times that route finding skills are sorely tested. In cases where the ultimate goal is totally obscured you may need to follow a compass bearing. This involves walking in short stages between identifiable points along your route and using your compass to maintain the appointed bearing. In extreme circumstances such as whiteouts you need to create your own reference point by having a person advance as far as you can see, and then direct them into line with the bearing, before joining them and repeating the procedure.

There is considerable scope for error when trying to steer a straight line in the bush, but there are a number of tactics you can use when heading for a specific point like a campsite, road junction, or a landmark that may have become obscured. Establish a line to aim for along which your destination lies. This may already exist in the form of a river, ridge or track. If not, create your own line using a compass bearing from your destination to a prominent feature nearby. When heading for your line it pays to deliberately veer to one side of your destination. You then know which direction you have to go along the line to reach it.

As important as these skills are, most cross-country walking is made simpler by selecting a route that follows clear natural features, such as major watercourses and ridgelines. This allows you to concentrate more on the minutiae of walking over the terrain immediately ahead. At this level, route-finding is more a case of intuition than science — there are no rules to say what course to take through dense undergrowth, or which side of a creekbed will give the easiest passage. It takes a keen eye to interpret the grain of the land, the knit of different vegetation, and the pattern of rise and fall. Developing a talent for reading the signs and divining the way forward can take a lifetime, but these accumulated discoveries are the lifeblood of bushwalking.

CHALLENGING TERRAIN

Back-country travel can involve dealing with some unexpected obstacles and treacherous surfaces — there is a limit to the detail that maps can register. Escarpments, impenetrable scrub and scree slopes are often not shown. Nor can maps protect you from swollen streams, lingering snowdrifts, or slick, muddy slopes. It pays to be prepared.

Stone country

Sooner or later on bushwalks you will have to cross some rocky ground, follow a dry, stony creekbed, or descend a scree slope. The problem is that rocks can tip and give way, and of course they become slippery when wet. It takes agility, quick judgement and a lightness of touch to move efficiently over jumbled stones. A slow, deliberate approach often leads to problems as you strain to keep your balance. It is better to set a steady, fluid pace that allows you to compensate for shaky landings.

When travelling over rock on level terrain, give each other a little room in case of falls. On scree or steep boulder-strewn slopes take a diagonal traverse line, keep your weight over your feet and stay together so that nobody finds himself underneath falling debris. Walking on rocky ground is punishing on the feet, and presents a risk to ankles and knees. Your footwear needs to cushion you from the jarring, but not be so cumbersome as to inhibit your mobility or prevent your 'feel' of what's underfoot.

Thick scrub

While most vegetation is easy enough to thread a path through, some plant species seem to have evolved especially to defy bushwalkers. It's often worth making a considerable detour to avoid a bracken-choked gully, or dense, shoulder-height brush.

If you do have to force a passage through such undergrowth, take some precautions. In tall, clinging scrub make sure your pack has a trim profile; tuck away loose straps and remove anything dangling from the pack. Rainjackets and overpants, with their slick surfaces, help deflect branches and offer some protection from snagging and abrasion. Likewise, gaiters are an excellent defence against low, prickly bush.

Crashing through scrub is exhausting, so where possible seek a path of least resistance. Look for corridors established by native wildlife or depressions formed by water runoff. A strong stick can be handy to part and hold back bush at shoulder height. If in a group keep well back from the person in front to avoid branches whipping into your face. In the most extreme situations you may need to use your pack as a kind of battering ram by walking backwards or side-on to the scrub. As brutal as this may sound, in some areas a little bush-bashing is unavoidable.

Snow underfoot

Snow is a fickle medium for bushwalking. One moment you can be wading in knee-deep slush and then a few hours later you're skidding over slick ice. Most of the time, thankfully, it is somewhere in between. For traction on moderate snow slopes keep your weight over your feet and your boots flat on the snow so the tread pattern has maximum contact. This is more comfortable when you're following a diagonal traverse line. Depending on the steepness of the slope and the consistency of the snow you may need to kick steps using the toe of your boot to create a foothold. This can be tiring,

so move at a relaxed pace and take turns breaking the trail.

Boots for snow walking need to give support and insulation, and provide some kind of platform when kicking steps. A ski pole or long-shafted ice-axe is invaluable on long treks, not just for helping you make the ascent and keeping balance but also for controlling downhill manoeuvres. If the angle of the slope is too sharp to descend normally it is much safer to face the slope and kick steps. Should you slip on hard, packed snow your ski pole or ice-axe can be employed to brake your slide in a self-arrest. (See Chapter 11, *Climbing and Mountaineering*.)

Slippery surfaces

A slick, grassy hillside poses a challenge very similar to that of a snow slope. Once again, traversing is best and use large rocks and tussocks to help form a line of stable footing. A walking staff or improvised stick is handy, if only to lean on as you catch breath.

There's no magic answer when the ground underfoot turns to squishy mud or if you have to cross a swamp. Just grit your teeth and go for it. Ideally, wear a light pair of runners that can be washed and dried quickly. Gaiters offer protection and there are also some specialist gaiter/boot combinations that are worthwhile for regular trips into boggy country. (See Chapter 15, *Clothing*.)

Wading through shallow water is often necessary in gorges, when fording streams, and in country affected by tropical downpours. While going barefoot may seem preferable it is better to keep your footwear on (minus socks if you like) for support and protection against rocks and sharp objects. Leather boots are heavy and uncomfortable when wet, so here again runners are handy. Alternatively, some people use a pair of wetsuit booties or sandals when wading.

River crossings

Tiptoeing across a fallen log or leaping from stone to stone may be free-spirited ways to cross a river, but these methods have their perils. Nor are there such natural bridges always available when you want them.

The interplay of currents, submerged obstacles and deep holes can make even innocuous crossings hazardous. Doubly diabolical is a river in flood or a swollen mountain stream. There are many methods for dealing with these obstacles, but time should always be spent judging the strength of the current, the safest point to cross and where you might end up downstream. Whenever crossing water make sure that the hip belt of your pack is left undone in case you need to bail out.

If the stream is shallow enough to wade, then move slowly across with your body sideways to the current. Take short steps and test each foot placement. A long, sturdy stick is useful for keeping your balance and plumbing the depths ahead. There is also added safety travelling as a group. Line up, with the stronger members of the party upstream, link arms or get everyone to hold onto a solid pole, and walk together side-on to the current.

Deep, gentle rivers can be swum. Be prepared to be carried well downriver, and before jumping in choose a likely landing spot to aim for. A water-proofed rucksack offers excellent flotation. Lie with your chest on the pack, use your arms for steering, kick with your legs and go with the flow.

Using a stick approximately 2 m (6½ ft) long x 5 cm (2 in) thick as a prop can make a river crossing easier and safer

Stand in a line parallel to the current and link arms at the elbows to cross the river

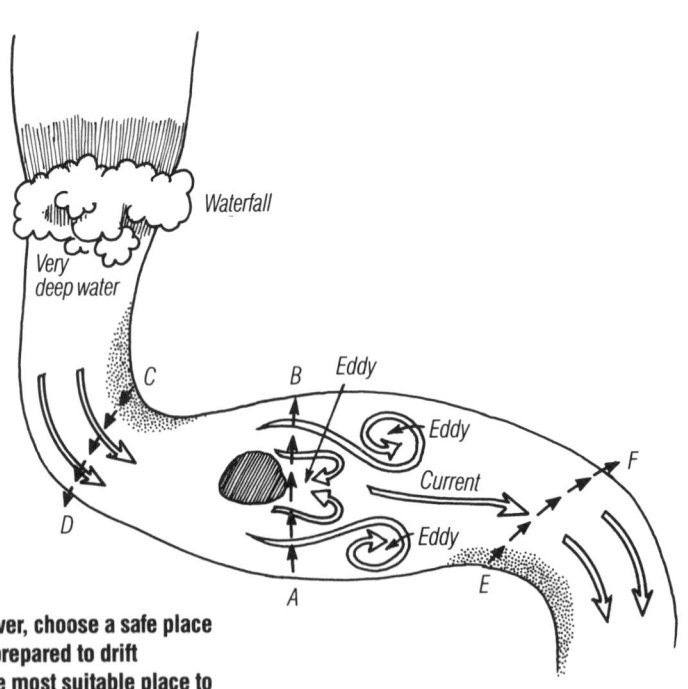

If swimming a river, choose a safe place to cross and be prepared to drift downstream. The most suitable place to cross is at A to B where the river is widest (as it is often shallower here). C to D, and E to F are river bend crossings

When confronted by a river in full flood the only sane decision may very well be to go back, find a way around the river, or simply wait a day or two for the level to drop. Once somebody is swept away by a crashing torrent, events happen at such a pace and with such violence that there is little that even a strong party can do to help, so play it safe.

Rock scrambles

By far the best tactic to adopt when a cliff blocks your path is to find a way around it. Scaling any kind of steep rock when wearing heavy boots and carrying a pack is a desperate situation, even for experienced climbers. At times, however, this is simply unavoidable when you are following a gorge, breaching a long escarpment, or crossing a rockband to the summit.

If heading into rugged country it's prudent to carry a length of rope to act as a safety line. Even more importantly, at least one member of the party needs to be a competent climber who can judge whether the climb is feasible and then lead the way. Some short rocksteps can be safely negotiated with only guiding words from above and below. In other cases a secure handline will give the security needed. For more difficult and risky ascents it can be necessary to haul the rucksacks up separately, and for individuals to be belayed on the climb.

When moving up steep rock fight the instinct to hug close to the wall. The key to efficient climbing is using deft footwork to support your body weight. If you're pressed hard against the rock you won't be able to see footholds and you increase the risk of losing control. Move smoothly up and try to anticipate what sequence of ledges and holds you will use. On loose or friable rock distribute your weight as evenly as possible by maintaining three points of contact, and be sure to test every hold. Going up is always easier than descending, so in case you reach an impasse, the cardinal rule is not to

---

DAY WALK CHECKLIST

Equipment
Camera
Daypack
First aid and survival kit
Map, compass, notebook
Matches or lighter
Pocket knife
Torch or headlamp
Water bottle

Clothing
Bandanna
Fibrepile jacket

Gaiters
Long johns
Shirt
Shorts
Socks
Sunglasses
Sunhat
Underwear top
Warm hat
Waterproof jacket
Waterproof overpants

Lunch and snacks

make any move upwards that you couldn't safely reverse.

Having covered the options of dealing with rock that you have to climb, what if you encounter a steep face in the course of a descent? The choices are similar, but more caution is advised given the added difficulty of down-climbing. If it seems risky, individuals can be belayed as they down-climb, or the alternative is to abseil. There are several classic techniques that require little or no technical equipment aside from a rope, but a crag in the middle of nowhere is hardly the place to learn this specialised and potentially dangerous art.

THE PATH AHEAD

There is a natural progression from daywalks to overnight trips to extended journeys. Discovering your physical capabilities and learning to feel at ease in the wilds is relatively straightforward. Combining this knowledge with everything involved in pack carrying and camping out is a much bigger step. To bridge the gap it is wise to start each phase on familiar, established trails. As your confidence grows, sharpen your planning, navigation and route-finding skills in untracked country.

Of course, events do not always conform to such logical steps. Your first walk may be a 30-day organised trek into Everest base camp, or after just a few day-trips your new-found bushwalking friends may invite you to join their two-week back-country traverse. With a little wit and commonsense most of us can adapt to suddenly being thrown into the deep end, and thankfully bushwalking is still one endeavour in which the most important qualifications have to be gained on one's own terms.

Bushwalking should never be seen merely as marching with blinkers on, from point A to point B. Some of the best walks are not lineal but form a loop and overlap in a collection of side trips or day walks from a base camp. There is endless scope for improvisation. Many skiers, climbers and canoeists also bushwalk and devise trips to combine a paddle with a walk, or an ascent with a range traverse or some other mix. A bushwalk can also be a springboard for any number of other engaging pastimes, from photography to botany and birdwatching, to stargazing. Of all outdoor activities bushwalking is the most infinitely varied and universally practised – it's the pursuit that takes us closest to our humbler origins.

9
CROSS-COUNTRY SKIING

Freedom is a word often uttered in the same breath as cross-country skiing. Indeed, of the many terms used to brand this winter activity, the most recently coined is *free-heel skiing*. This explains the essence of the activity: using boots that flex and lift at the heel, in unison with skis designed for swift travel uphill as well as down.

With this mobility comes the freedom to explore the back-country, seek out distant peaks to climb, and untracked slopes to ski. Implied too is a freedom from ski lifts, the cloying atmosphere of some resorts, and the cumbersome armoury of alpine boots and skis.

If cross-country hardware opens up new horizons, it also makes the high country accessible and affordable for a much wider slice of the population. No longer is skiing the province of the young and the affluent. The simplicity of the equipment and the flexible tempo of cross-country skiing makes it suited to all age groups. One of the most heartening sights is three generations of one family enjoying a day of skiing together.

All of this is not to suggest that cross-country skiing is merely a cushy option, or that the equipment by itself guarantees effortless freedom. While it's easier to make a start on free-heel gear, true mastery of the techniques can take several winters. Then there is the scope to apply these skills to steeper and more remote terrain. Bound up with this are the crafts needed to travel and live in a snowbound landscape, with its outrageous weather and strange sculptured spaces.

Cross-country skiing has many tributaries and an assortment of followers. The bushwalker who uses skis to cover distance and camp out amidst familiar territory, transformed by a mantle of white. The jaded downhill skier looking to spice up their steady diet of groomed slopes and lift queues. The competitive athlete, clad in lycra, pushing their limits in gruelling cross-country races. The telemarker whose passion for the sweeps and arcs of this graceful turn take them into ever-steeper gullies. The day skier who enjoys gliding over prepared trails and the bonhomie of a cross-country lodge. The expeditioner who uses cross-country skis for major overland traverses or for shuttling between camps on a high altitude climb.

Common to all of these branches is a set of basic skills. In recent years the adage 'if you can walk you can ski' has begun to tarnish. Certainly there are still people who are content to potter about on cross-country gear, but to treat skis as little more than elongated snowshoes is to greatly underestimate the power they hold. Refinements in equipment design and the growth of cross-country ski teaching have helped focus interest on the skills of the trade. These techniques can be employed, with minor modifications, even when touring with a pack. Once the threshold from walking to gliding has been crossed, snow travel becomes both easier and infinitely more satisfying.

THE BASIC SKILLS

Just as with learning to ride a bike, so it takes time with skiing to get your legs and arms to do new things, and then more time to assemble these movements into a co-ordinated whole. With abundant patience and perseverance you can chip away at these skills on your own. The trouble is that even if you know what you're meant to do, it's hard to see what you are doing wrong. A little professional instruction is highly recommended for correcting faults and easing the frustrations of your first hours on skis.

Diagonal stride

This is the cross-country skier's classic mode of locomotion. If you visit any area where free-heel equipment is in use, you will see lithe figures angled forward over their skis, waltzing along in rhythmic strides.

The diagonal stride is simply an extension of the natural walking action. You push off on one foot, transfer your weight forward onto the other leg and glide. You then push off on this ski, bring your trailing foot

The diagonal stride is an essential ski technique for cross-country skiing

forward, shift your weight across and glide again. Whereas walking is made up of short, clipped steps, skis allow you to extend your normal stride by holding your weight over the gliding ski mid-stride. Meanwhile, your arms follow their natural swing.

As you refine your stride you learn to generate more thrust from each push-off or 'kick'; you judge how far forward to slant your upper body; you smooth out your weight transfers and timing; you accentuate your arm swing to help your balance and through your poles provide a vital forward-driving force. Most importantly, you find yourself covering territory very rapidly. When you hit upon a natural rhythm your diagonal stride can be adjusted for subtle uphills and downs.

Skating

Until a few years ago skating on skis was a novelty act for downhillers crossing between lift queues, then it found its way into the repertoire of cross-country racers. Now it's been elevated up with the diagonal stride as a primary means of covering distance in open, undulating country.

The movements are not dissimilar to other styles of skating: you lift one ski, angle it outwards, then transfer your weight to this ski as it hits the snow. At the same time drive through with both poles and glide. You then bring the other ski forward, angle it out to the other side and transfer your weight across. It's best at first to drive through with your poles once every two steps.

Racers have devised numerous subtle variations of the skate. They also use specialised skis, boots and poles to generate the power and control they need. For the back-country skier looking to use the skate for some variety on the flats the most important innovation is a set of poles that can be adjusted up to nose height. This extra length is critical for the drive and balance that make a fluid skating stride.

Uphills

By shortening the length of your stride, leaning forward and moving fast it's possible to skate or diagonal-stride up long, gentle inclines and sharp rises. At some point, however, your forward momentum and the skis' ability to grip can no longer keep you from sliding backwards. To tackle steeper slopes you need uphill tactics.

The kick turn, the most comfortable approach on big hills, is to climb in a series of rising traverses. The angle at which you climb is ultimately governed by the grip of your skis. On moderate slopes you can change from traversing in one direction to the other simply by stepping around. In steeper situations it's safer to know how to kick turn.

With your poles planted for support, kick the downhill ski up until the tail is resting on the snow. Move your downhill pole out and around until it's planted behind you. Now swing your upturned ski around so that it's back flat on the snow, parallel to the uphill ski but pointing in the opposite direction. Transfer your weight onto this ski and swing the other ski around into line. This always sounds ridiculous on paper and it looks only slightly less absurd in real life, but the kick turn is an indispensable technique for back-country skiers.

The herringbone comfortably tackles

brief uphill stretches. From a parallel stride spread your skis into a V, angle the inside edge of each ski so that it 'bites' the snow, and walk up holding this stance. Your poles push from behind and help you balance. For even steeper sections, where holding a herringbone would be too strenuous, you can climb by sidestepping. This simply means edging up sideways, with your skis parallel across the slope, and moving one foot at a time.

Downhills

The fastest way down is a straight descent or *schuss*. This means skiing the fall-line; the shortest path to the bottom. Anything less direct is a downhill traverse. For schussing keep your skis comfortably apart, your legs slightly bent at the knees and your arms spread out in front. As you gather speed try to keep your upper body upright. To cushion the effects of bumps and dips in the snow, bend lower at the knees and slide one ski forward to distribute your weight over a longer axis.

Careering downhill is of course one of skiing's purest pleasures, and not to be spurned later on as you strive to execute perfect linked turns. Yet every schuss has to end. If you've picked the right slope gravity will slow you down gracefully, but sometimes the acceleration gets out of hand, or obstacles like rocks, trees or fallen skiers come into your path, and you need to bail out. Learning to fall is an essential skill. It's best simply to sit down and fall back into the slope. To get back up, arrange your skis across the slope and on the downhill side of your body, dig the edges in and ease up, looking nonchalantly at any passers-by!

Turns

There are many, more dignified ways of controlling your descent and changing direction. The simplest is the step turn. From a parallel stance lift up the ski on the side you want to turn to, step this ski around and as you shift your weight across bring the other ski into line. A full turn is best made up of many short, sharp steps. This turn is most useful for turning up hill and coming to a halt at the end of a traverse.

The snowplough, or wedge turn, is useful to add to your bag of tricks for added speed control and turning across the fall-line. This is the workhorse turn for all skiers; the one you use for sudden braking and emergency stops. From a relaxed downhill stance with your skis at hip width, push out with your heels so the tails of your skis spread to form a V, and the tips stay close together but just apart. As you push down harder with your heels and your feet widen, so the edges begin to bite the snow. The greater the pressure the more friction is generated and you come to a stop.

To convert the snowplough to a turn you keep up some momentum and apply extra pressure to one ski, say the right foot, and as you push out harder on the ski you will turn to the left. Conversely if you push out and weight the left ski you will turn to the right. Try to keep your upper body relaxed, and your ankles and knees flexed and responsive to the task of steering the skis. Practise turning uphill to a stop, then try linking short snowplough turns left and right across the fall-line.

CROSS-COUNTRY SKIING

The snowplough or wedge turn

Once adept at the snowplough you can safely venture into almost any terrain. It's also the first step to learning an assortment of snappy variations for carving corners, such as stem turns, stem christies and parallel turns. The chances are, however, that you will want to try your hand – or more accurately your knees – at the turn everyone else seems to be doing.

Telemarking has become the distinctive emblem of cross-country skiing: a sweeping, graceful turn that epitomises the freedom of the equipment and the back-country.

In a telemark position you sink down by bending at the knees, advance one ski forward and allow the other to stay back. Your weight is distributed evenly between both skis. The forward foot is planted firmly on the ski, the trailing foot is lifted at the heel with body weight transmitted to the ski at the ball of the foot. You create, in effect, one

The classic telemark turn

long ski. To make this ski carve and turn demands co-ordination. At the moment you commit the front ski forward you edge and steer this ski into the arc of the turn. The trailing ski edges to follow the same curve.

It takes time to fine tune the balance and timing for linked telemark turns, but when all the elements come together and you swoop down an open slope in a series of sumptuous telemarks it's like you're half-flying and half-skiing.

The same kind of breakthrough occurs when learning all the important cross-country techniques. You reach a stage when the exercise stops being a set of deliberate steps and becomes a fluent gesture; a reflex. Whether or not lights flash and bells ring at this moment, the significant point is that you never entirely lose the rhythm. After a long lay-off it will take only a day or two to recover the poise and polish you worked so hard to achieve.

TOURING

It's perfectly respectable for cross-country skills to be practised and enjoyed without leaving the comforts of civilisation. Indeed, getting the knack of downhill control with free-heel gear is demonstrably easier on groomed slopes and with a day ticket to ride the lifts. Similarly, most ski resorts have prepared trails for skating and diagonal striding. Yet to ignore the ability of free-heel skis to transport you to fresh slopes and wild peaks is to miss out on the cream of the cross-country experience.

Day tours

With a pair of skis on your feet you can cover a surprising amount of territory in a day. Indeed, this can be a trap for the unwary who may push deep into the back-country and may not be able to deal with bad weather or navigating a route home. Yet if you stick to marked trails, pole lines and snow-covered fire roads you are relieved of many of the uncertainties.

An outing can be planned like a bushwalker's day trip so you ski a long circuit, taking in scenic highlights, or you may prefer to ski to a summit, have a picnic lunch on top and spend the afternoon telemarking gullies on untracked snow. Whatever shape your day takes, the important thing is to get away and enjoy the liberty of open country, while saving enough energy for the journey home.

For any tour lasting more than a couple of hours you need to carry a well-prepared daypack, stocked with ample food, drink and spare clothing for the outing. (See *Day Tour Checklist*.) If you're attempting an ambitious day, then include additional items that you may need for an unscheduled night out. These include a down jacket, bivvy bag, snow shovel, torch and perhaps a stove. Such precautions may seem heavy handed but snow is an unforgiving medium in which to take risks.

Longer tours

When day trips no longer satisfy your appetite for the solitude and splendour of the back-country, it's time to consider venturing out overnight or longer.

The planning and preparation for extended touring is not radically different to what is needed for bushwalks

---

DAY TOUR CHECKLIST

Down or synthetic vest
First aid kit
Foam sit mat (ideally one that is removable from your pack)
Gaiters
Gloves and mittens
Lip balm
Lots of high energy snacks
Lunch
Map, compass and notebook
Peaked cap
Pile jacket
Pocket knife

Ski repair kit
Spare socks
Sun cream
Sunglasses and/or goggles
Survival kit (matches, whistle, cord, etc)
Thermal long johns
Thermal long-sleeved shirt
Warm hat
Warm stretch pants
Water bottle (plus, perhaps, a thermos)
Waterproof jacket
Waterproof overpants

of similar duration. There are maps to study, routes to be plotted and gear to be packed, but remember that in the mountains in winter the penalties for leaving behind something important, misjudging how much food to carry, or sloppy map reading can be severe.

Another point to remember is that while skiing is more efficient than walking as a mode of travel, your load will most likely be heavier: there is extra clothing, food and fuel to carry. Likewise, your tent and sleeping bag will be of the weightier variety, to cope with the exigencies of winter survival, and skiing with a load on board presents its very own challenge.

Skiing with a pack

Wearing any kind of pack can seem like a subtle conspiracy against the virtues of cross-country skiing – balance, speed and freedom. A monster rucksack, chock-a-block with all you need for a week of camping out, defies any finesse on skis.

Yet even if heavily laden it's still possible to cruise along much faster than you would if walking. The diagonal stride becomes the diagonal shuffle, with shorter steps and less exaggerated movements and weight transfers. Take downhill runs slow and easy. Make sure that heavy items are stowed low down in the pack, and tighten your hipbelt, shoulder and sternum straps. A big pack multiplies the forces generated in turns: your pack wants to keep on going downhill long after you have turned the corner. If you do take a tumble it's often easier to take your pack off before trying to get back on your feet. When downhills start getting out of hand, revert to the faithful snowplough for stability, or break up the descent into manageable traverses.

SNOWSENSE

On a bright, still day the high country can be deceptively benign. It seems as though you could ski all day without a care in the world. But, as any veteran tourer will testify, the mountains are prone to rapid and violent mood swings. In a matter of minutes a slicing wind can pick up, then a little later cloud pours in and you are snared by a blizzard.

After many seasons' experience of alpine weather there is still no way to predict with certainty how the dice will roll. Your only insurance is to go prepared for the worst. At the same time you need to accumulate all the wisdom you can about snow and its ever-changing textures and formations.

Even on fine days you need to be on your guard. Cold, dry air will quickly dehydrate you. Brilliant sunshine reflected off snow can cause severe sunburn, and in painful places, such as on the underside of your nose, chin and ears. The cool breeze you find so invigorating can burn the skin and crack your lips. Even short periods without sunglasses can make your eyes begin to feel like they are full of sand – the early signs of snowblindness. If a storm closes in you can be confronted with all manner of other winter nasties. Whiteouts that throw your navigation into chaos; the insidious onset of hypothermia at the end of a tough day; a troubling loss of feeling in fingers and toes.

The landscape around you demands constant scrutiny. Snow has an uncanny ability to alter its structure and stability. In the course of a day you can experience innumerable skiing surfaces, from deep fluffy powder and windblown crust, to wet sugary slop and rock hard ice. You need to adapt your techniques to each texture and consider taking evasive action to avoid more intractable surfaces. Be especially wary of ice. Take care skiing in the late afternoon and early morning when a sun-softened slope refreezes. Ski around icy patches, and if on an iced-up slope with a nasty drop below, contemplate removing your skis and kicking steps with your boots.

A snow-massed landscape also has larger formations that you need to deal with. Windswept cornices that overhang exposed ridges; small snowdrifts that lurk on the lee side of hummocks and boulders; steep slopes dangerously burdened with new snow that may avalanche. There may also be rocks, bushes and branches lying just beneath the surface of fresh cover, or suspect snowbridges across creeks. Some threats, such as avalanches, demand special study, but astute pathfinding is sufficient to help you skirt most of these obstacles.

Navigation and route finding in the snow are always challenging. The major problems are a lack of visibility and a loss of the detail and features that are so critical to precise map and compass work. Open, undulating terrain is often enigmatic in the extreme. The safest policy is to stay within range of clear natural landmarks like peaks and ridges. Avoid bewildering wooded slopes and meandering gullies. (For more on navigation in the snow see Chapter 4, *Navigation*.)

When things do go wrong, don't be driven by panic into any rash decisions. If you have lost your way, stop, conserve your energy, and quietly assess the situation. The right decision may be to backtrack to a known reference point, or to make camp and sit out bad weather. Charging ahead in the blind hope of finding your destination is sure to invite more problems.

SNOWCAMPING

With the right clothes and equipment, plus a little stoicism, it's quite feasible to live comfortably in the snow. The key is to stay as dry and warm as possible, but there will always be moments when cold insinuates its way into your bones. Particularly in the transition times: at the end of the day after the sun goes down, and before you have pitched the tent and taken in some warm food and drink; if you have to get up in the middle of the night to relieve yourself; and most of all in the mornings, when you ease out of your sleeping bag and struggle into every stitch of clothing and pull on frosty cold boots.

Shelter

It's imperative to have a safe haven from the elements. A sturdy mountain tent capable of withstanding high winds and snowloadings is ideal, although for overnight camps one can often make do with a good three-season tent that is carefully sited.

If there are huts in the area these can sometimes be used for cooking in and getting out of bad weather, but it is extremely foolhardy to rely on them as your sole means of shelter. They are invariably crowded and often difficult to locate. Should darkness descend before you can reach a hut you could face the serious problem of a night in the open.

Give yourself ample time to find a good tent site that catches the morning sun, yet offers protection from prevailing winds. Trees afford some shelter, but be wary of snow-laden branches that may dump on you in the night. Use your skis and then your boots to stamp down a firm platform. Pitching a tent in a gale can be a struggle, but make sure it is securely staked down with snow pegs. Building a snow wall around the tent base can keep out buffeting winds but it may also gather windblown spindrift. Once the tent is up make sure you keep snow and moisture out.

Snowcaves and igloos

A tent should always be carried, but in some circumstances it's worth considering a natural snow shelter such as a snowcave or igloo. Building these structures can take several hours so allow ample time for finding a site and doing the digging.

For snowcaves spy out a tall, deep snowdrift. Start by digging an entrance low down on the drift with a ramp back up into the slope (whoever is wielding the shovel needs to be rugged up in their waterproofs), and lay a groundsheet on the entrance tunnel to make it easier to remove snow excavated from inside. As a minimum you need enough height inside for sitting up, and sufficient width for everyone to stretch out in their sleeping bags. The ceiling should be arched for strength and smoothed over to prevent drips. You may also wish to create a vent hole using your ski pole.

A good snowcave is surprisingly cosy and gives complete protection from raging winds. With a little extra digging you can fashion your own five-star accommodation with spacious living, sleeping and eating areas. As candles flicker and the stove boils away there is no better place to be.

Igloos have their own appeal but they are more difficult to build. The trick is finding suitably firm snow that can be compacted and then cut into blocks. Start by stamping down a chosen site and leaving it to consoli-

A snowcave

date for an hour or so, then mark out the floor plan in the snow: a circle about 2 m (6½ ft) across with an entrance trench. Carve blocks roughly 500 mm (20 in) wide x 300 mm (12 in) high x 200 mm (8 in) thick from the entrance trench to begin with and work your way into the circle. The blocks are laid around the perimeter of the marked circle. After a foundation ring is established the blocks need to be laid in an upward spiral and angled at about 20⁰ inward. It takes considerable skill to complete the construction successfully but it can be fun giving it a go.

Sleeping

Sleep can be elusive if you are not adequately insulated from the snow. A thick, reliable, closed cell foam pad or self-inflating mat are essential. Without this even the finest sleeping bag will amount to nothing. You don't necessarily need an expedition-rated bag to sleep in the snow; a quality three- to four-season bag will suffice for some people if they are also warmly clad and well-fed. Wearing a hat to bed is a good idea. For added warmth try filling your water bottle with hot water, stuffing it in a sock and taking it to bed with you.

Cooking

While in dire emergencies it is sometimes necessary to cook inside your tent, this is not recommended practice. It's safer to create a kitchen area outside in the shelter of trees. Dig out a bench and seats, build a snow wall or rig a flysheet if you like.

If you have to melt snow for drinking and cooking, you'll need a powerful, efficient stove. Start melting snow as soon as you stop for the day. Make sure your stove is insulated from the snow (a small heat-resistant mat is handy) and sheltered by a windbreak.

Menus should be adaptable and include easy-to-prepare one-pot dishes. Hot soups and stews are perfect and the snow is an excellent environment to try out curry and chilli creations.

Snowcamping may not be everyone's idea of a good time, but there's something deeply satisfying about defying the privations of cold nights and waking to the sunrise with your skis waiting at the tent door.

10

CLIMBING AND MOUNTAINEERING

Climbing is the most misunderstood of all outdoor activities. Far from being the death-defying pursuit portrayed in the movies, climbing, at its purest, is graceful gymnastic movement on a steep ground. All the ironmongery, ropes and equipment serve only as a safety net. Unlike sports such as canoeing and skiing, where the hardware is essential for progress, rock-climbers rely on direct physical contact with their chosen medium – rock. Even in ice climbing the crampons and ice-axe function as natural extensions of the limbs rather than mechanical devices. While it's true that climbers enjoy working at the limits of their abilities, the risks taken are finely controlled. Few serious climbers could be described as reckless thrillseekers – they have a healthy respect for heights and their own human frailties. Climbing for such people is the noblest way to experience the exhilaration of high places, and the athletic challenge of the ascent. Climbers pay great – sometimes obsessive – attention to their gear, mostly in the quest for greater safety and security.

Climbing is an outdoor activity that many people take up as an extension of bushwalking or trekking. Others come to climbing from an interest in gymnastics or just a love of high places.

Easy climbing can be carried out with minimal equipment – some people even prefer to climb without any boots – but at its highest level climbing is a highly specialised and serious pastime. No climbing should ever be undertaken lightly, for there are many dangers for the inexperienced and unwary.

Climbing is an activity that comes naturally to young people. As most get older, become less athletic, and more reluctant to take risks, the thought of climbing often loses its appeal. Many people even develop a fear of heights; this fear is quite healthy but with experience it can be controlled. Climbing is also very much about overcoming mental barriers and learning to know one's limits: both psychologically and physically.

The term climbing is used in reference to both rock climbing and mountaineering but these activities today are almost completely different pursuits. Rock climbing is ascending small or large steep rock faces, while mountaineering is climbing up and down entire mountains. The level of difficulty at which a rope becomes desirable in both rock climbing and mountaineering varies greatly from individual to individual; it also depends very much on time of year. Experienced climbers may be confident ascending an exposed slope unroped (also called solo climbing), where a beginner or more cautious climber would require the security of a rope. Conditions can vary tremendously as well. What might be an easy scramble in summer may well turn into an icy 'slippery dip' in winter.

The myriad details of climbing are beyond the scope of this book, but instruction manuals such as *Climbing School* offer a comprehensive illustrated coverage of the theory and practice of all aspects of climbing. The following pages, however, outline some of the basics.

There are a number of specialisations in rock climbing such as bouldering, soloing, free climbing, and sport climbing. Some variations such as ice climbing and big wall climbing blur into the category of mountaineering. Mountaineering also has several specialisations – notably high altitude climbing and alpinism. If artificial means are used to ascend steep rock or a mountain face, the sport is called aid climbing. This is often a part of both alpine climbing and big wall climbing.

In days gone by there was often a sense of progression where individuals started out as rock climbers and passed through the various levels of the climbing game to expedition climbing. Today many individuals concentrate on just one aspect, be it rock climbing or bouldering, and are quite content never to set foot up a mountain. There are others such as the big wall climbers who will struggle up a mountain face and have no wish to proceed to the summit.

Climbing is a complex sport but there are few rules and regulations – that is unless you get into the area of competitive sport climbing. Overall, the pastime is governed from within through a code of ethics and informal debate rather than by imposed rules. Each style of climbing also has its own set of acceptable practices; these are not necessarily transferable. Using a ladder to cross a crevasse in the Himalaya, for example, is regarded as acceptable, but using this aid to get up the first part of a rock climb would not be sporting.

Climbing routes are given grades of difficulty, usually by the people who made the first ascent. These individuals are also entitled to give the route a name. Making a first ascent of a good high grade climb is the pinnacle of rock climbing. Such accomplishments are recorded in guidebooks which are periodically published by climbers for the more popular climbing areas or cliffs. The systems of ratings of the difficulty of climbs vary from country to country and there is a separate system of grades for mountain routes and rock climbs.

The Australian rock grading system is an open-ended numerical system with beginners' climbs starting around grade 5 or 6 and the hardest grades currently around 32. The United States, Great Britain and Europe each have their own unique systems. The American system is called a decimal grading – rock climbing with ropes being called the 5th class and the hardest grade currently being 5.14 c. In Great Britain, the home of rock climbing, climbers began by giving routes an adjectival grade. In the beginning the terms were meaningful with names such as Easy, Moderate, Difficult, Very Difficult, Severe. As standards have improved, the adjectival names have become a little more complex – namely: Very Severe, Hard Very Severe, Extremely Severe and Hard Extremely Severe. These grades give an impression of the overall difficulty and seriousness of the climb. As even harder routes began to be climbed the upper categories became very crowded and so a numerical system has been introduced; this refers to the technical difficulty of each pitch. European gradings are different again.

The grading of rock climbs serves to prevent individuals from getting into difficulty by tackling something that is way beyond their abilities. Grading also brings into the climbing arena a measure of competition – both between individuals and with one's self. Climbing is very much about personal challenge: pitting yourself against a route that is harder than you have previously climbed is one way of making progress in the sport.

Not everyone wants to climb at the highest level. Many just enjoy the delights of moving on rock without taking any risks, and without the encumbrances of ropes and technical equipment. The simplest form of climbing is scrambling; a more challenging form of scrambling is bouldering.

BOULDERING

Bouldering is climbing easy to very difficult moves, or 'problems' as they are also known, close to the ground where ropes are usually not needed or used. Bouldering is akin to outdoor gymnastics and often involves great feats of strength, balance, agility and stamina. Many climbers use bouldering as a way of training for rock climbing; to develop technique, fitness and strength. For some it is an end in itself – bouldering is the purist form of climbing. Boulder problems in some places also have their own system of grades: B1, B2, B3, etc.

SOLOING

Some extreme climbers like to ascend full free rock routes without ropes. This is known as free soloing and is the most serious form of climbing. If a hold breaks off or the climber runs out of strength on a steep crux it can mean a ground fall where broken bones and worse are often the result. Soloing is practised by the boldest climbers who usually have a policy of never climbing up anything that they are not prepared to downclimb.

Rope soloing is another variation – sometimes undertaken when a partner can't be found and a climber still wishes to climb protected. This is possible with the use of a rope and a specially made ascender such as the 'Soloist' that will hold a fall without damaging the rope. It is not recommended to use standard straight shaft ascenders such as Jumars, Gibbs or Petzel for this variation of soloing, and both a waist harness and chest harness are usually necessary.

ROCK CLIMBING

Free rock climbing is the most widely practised variation of the sport. Free climbing involves ascending steep cliffs, crags or rock faces in a series of stages called pitches up to 50 m (164 ft) in length, using just one's hands and feet to hang on to the rock. Often the 'routes', as the previously climbed ways are known, will be less than one rope length from top to bottom. Free climbing is relatively safe when proper climbing equipment (ropes, protection and belays) and procedures are employed by experienced people. Rock climbing is usually a team activity where two is the ideal number of people to have on a rope, although three is possible, if somewhat slower.

Ropework

To the uninitiated rock climbing can be a puzzling activity. The popular conception is often that the climber ascends a rope that somehow just dangles down a cliff. There is no such magic in climbing, however. In most instances the rope is not for climbing up, but just for safety in case of a slip or fall. In normal free climbing, the first person to move up, the leader, has the rope tied into a special harness around their waist. As he or she climbs, the person below, the second, pays the rope out through some friction device attached to an anchor on his or her body. This procedure is known as belaying. At regular intervals (more often on steeper, more difficult ground, or as often as the leader feels the need) he or she places some sort of protection device into a weakness in the rock if one can be found (a running belay), and then the rope is clipped into this with a karabiner. These running belays may be any one of a variety of metal devices such as expanding cams, wedges or stoppers or even natural features threaded with a tape sling or a pre-placed bolt or piton. If the leader happens to fall, then, providing there is not too much slack rope and the belayer is able to arrest the fall by locking off the rope, the leader will drop only twice the distance they have climbed above their highest point of protection. There is always some stretch in the rope, but this helps to absorb the shock of the fall and puts less strain on the falling leader, the belayer and the anchors. Most experienced lead climbers rarely fall – that is unless they are trying a route at the limit of their ability. In such circumstances, protection will usually be placed more frequently to minimise the seriousness of any plummet.

In the normal climbing situation the leader gets to the end of the pitch, which is often the top of a crag on short cliffs, or at some comfortable resting point, and there he or she attaches themselves to the rock and sets up a belay. Once the leader is safe, the second person then unclips themselves from their belay and commences the climb up the route – the rope being taken in by the belayer at the top as they move up. As they climb, the second also removes the intermediate protection equipment which they carry with them on a sling around their shoulder, or attached to their waist harness. Eventually the second arrives at the upper belay stance. At this point, if the climb continues for another section or pitch, the pair will often swap roles so that the second takes over the leading for the next pitch.

Top roping as it is called is practised on many crags and cliffs where individuals wish to experience the moves of a climb without the dangers of 'leading'. Here a rope is dropped down from the top and individuals climb up, either belayed from the top, or alternatively the rope can be fed through a screwgate karabiner attached to some bomb-proof anchors, and the belayer can stand at the bottom. Top roping is often popular for teaching and training on many small crags close to population centres.

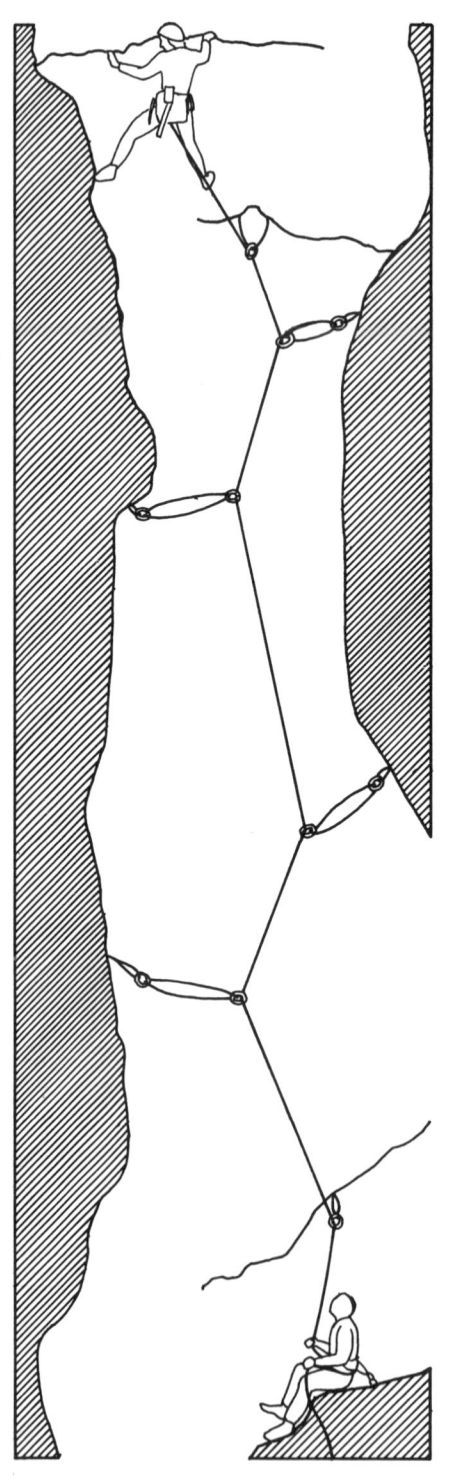

Leading is the most satisfying form of rock climbing because the elements of risk and judgement are added to the already considerable task of moving up the rock face. The judgement comes in the placing of protection as well as which hold to use. Questions of what type of protection, how often it should be placed and whether it is better to push on and conserve strength, or hang about on a crux, place a runner and risk falling off, face the lead climber constantly. Protecting a climb adequately is a cross between art and science. There is such a profusion of types of rock protection available today (see Chapter 20, *Climbing, Mountaineering and Cross-Country Ski Gear*) that it is possible to protect a wide variety of cracks, pockets and features. If the gear is not properly placed, however, it can move through the action of the rope running through the karabiner and 'walk', or even pop out.

With lead climbing the lead climber places protection in the rock at regular intervals and clips in the main climbing rope. Meanwhile, the belayer pays out the rope through a belay plate

Where there is little chance of protection from stoppers, hexes, wires or cams the trend today is to place bolts. These were first used by aid climbers and were drilled on a lead with a twist drill placed in a holder, and hit with a hammer, while being turned by hand. Today most bolts are placed by climbers hanging from an abseil rope. They are used extensively on the harder rock routes for protection, and for belay and abseil anchors. In some situations rock climbers are now even using cordless electric drills to place bolts on hard climbs.

The ethics of climbing are constantly evolving, and whether or not this sort of behaviour is acceptable depends on the region and the times. The main quest in the past has been to climb 'clean' – not to deface the rock in any way. Chalk, bolts, and in some places chipped holds, have all been criticised as being against this ethic, but many climbers argue that the routes could not be climbed safely without chalk and bolts. Chipping holds is nowhere yet viewed as acceptable.

Climbing technique

Good rock climbing is a combination or synthesis of balance, agility, strength and technique. The harder the climb, the smaller are the holds and the steeper the rock face. Strength does play an important role in the upper grades of climbing but, overall, good technique is the most important aspect of rock climbing.

Climbing technique is the way in which a climber uses their body, hands and feet to move upwards. There are a variety of basic moves which have to be learnt to be able to climb successfully. These range from jamming, bridging and mantle shelving, to laybacking, chimneying, offwidthing and smearing, to name a few. There is also a variety of different types of hand- and footholds with specific names such as pinch grips, fingerlocks, undercuts, sideholds, cracks, jugs, edges and pockets – all of which may be used in the course of a climb.

The secret of rock climbing is to conserve your strength wherever possible, and to move up in a series of waves, resting whenever the route allows. Most beginners tend to climb using mostly their arms to pull themselves up, then they look around for somewhere to place their feet. Good climbers use the strong muscles of their legs to push themselves upwards, and their hands mostly for balance. The steeper the climb the more you are forced to use your arms. When learning to climb it is worth following the principle of trying to have three points of contact on the rock at any one time. As the climbing becomes progressively harder, the opportunities to rest become less and less and so strength and stamina come increasingly into play. The harder routes often involve climbing through overhangs where maintaining even two points of contact is difficult. At the most extreme level of rock climbing specialised techniques such as heel hooks, one finger pull-ups and dynos (lunging for a handhold) all become part of a climber's repertoire. At all times the use of one's feet to take weight is critical to sustained climbing. Today's rock climbers are ascending routes of difficulty that were unimaginable ten years ago. Who knows what the future holds?

Abseiling

Abseiling (literally, 'rope down') or rappelling is descending a steep, sheer or overhanging drop rapidly by sliding down a rope. The person descending also has the control. The term abseil comes from the German, while rappel is a French word; both are used in the English-speaking world. In climbing jargon these terms are abbreviated to 'abb' off, or 'rap' off or down. Abseiling is used by mountaineers and sometimes by climbers as a fast, or indeed perhaps the only, means to get down a rock face or off a mountain. Cavers also use the technique extensively to descend into caves, and then climb back up these ropes using ascenders or jumars. The combination of these skills in caving parlance is called Single Rope Technique often abbreviated to SRT. Cavers have developed these techniques to a very high level as they often descend and ascend very large distances quickly in the course of exploring deep caves.

Abseiling or rappelling is to some an adventure sport in its own right and often abseilers may have no interest in climbing. To the uninitiated, abseiling is a thrilling and adventurous experience but to most climbers it is just a means to an end – getting down off a climb. When learning to abseil it is usual practice for the beginner to have a safety top rope as well, but this is rarely possible when abseiling as a means of getting down off a climb or mountain.

The source of friction, and hence control in abseiling varies acording to the nature of the activity. Initially, abseiling was accomplished by simply having a rope running from between one's legs across the back and over a shoulder. This is known as a classic abseil which is painful and potentially dangerous, but useful to know in an emergency. Other techniques involve the use of a piton across a karabiner or an arrangement of karabiners known as 'cross crabs'. Today, most climbers abseil with a figure of eight descender that is light and secure, providing it is attached to a proper harness with a locking gate karabiner. Climbers usually abseil on a double rope that is fed through a sling over a natural bollard, a chain, or around a tree or some other fail-safe anchor. In this situation both ends of the rope are at

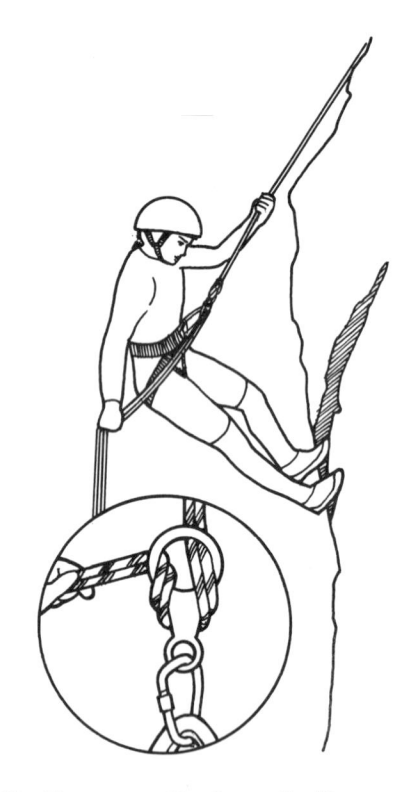

Abseiling or rappelling is a method for descending a steep drop. The inset shows the figure eight descender

the bottom of the abseil so that when all the climbers have descended, the party can pull the rope through and continue on another abseil if necessary, having left the minimum of equipment behind. Cavers abseil with more sophisticated descenders such as rappel racks and whaletales, where the amount of friction is variable. (See Chapter 20, *Mountaineering*.)

Abseiling is one of the most dangerous aspects of rock climbing and mountaineering, and one of the main sources of serious accidents and death. It should never be undertaken without careful inspection of the anchors, harness and abseiling devices. Always ensure that clothing, hair, etc. is not in a position to foul or be caught in the friction device, and that there is no chance of dislodging rocks on the way down or when the rope is pulled down. It is best to wear a climbing helmet in areas of questionable rock, and if possible always stand well away from beneath an abseil line once you have descended.

Sport climbing

Sport climbing is very hard rock climbing on short routes where the risks are minimised by the placement of abseil or bolt anchors. Rock climbing competitions have developed from sport climbing.

Competition climbing has been a feature of climbing in the Soviet Union for many years, and a version of competitive climbing on artificial walls is rapidly gaining in popularity around the world. Artificial holds are bolted onto panels attached to scaffolding towers that range from 10 m to 20 m (32-65 ft) in height. A circuit of competitions now exists under the auspices of the UIAA (International Union of Alpine Associations) in the United States, Europe and Great Britain, and such events are now also catching on in New Zealand and Australia. The competitions are usually judged on the basis of the maximum height achieved and the time taken. The climbers progress through a number of qualifications, heats and then a final. There are attempts afoot to have competition climbing declared an Olympic sport.

Artificial climbing walls are now also a feature of many sports centres in countries such as Great Britain, and increasingly in the United States and Europe. At first these walls were made with chipped and offset bricks, then natural rock was set into the walls and now specially made holds are available. These walls are seen as a way of developing strength and technique away from the cliff and are especially popular in places where the weather is less than ideal. Serious rock climbers are now into training with weights, inclined ladders, and specialised chin-up bars to improve their strength and stamina. Some even practise walking on a slack wire to hone their balance. Many of these people adopt Olympian training regimes and specialised diets and climb every day of the week.

Aid climbing

Aid climbing is ascending a rock face or mountain using artificial or mechanical means, rather than hanging on with hands and feet. Aid climbing mostly involves hanging off pitons or jam nuts but occasionally bolts are used. Aid climbers use several small portable steps called etriers, which are usually made of tubular webbing. Artificial climbing used to be widely practised on small cliffs with big overhangs, but today it is mostly restricted to big walls which may take many days to ascend. Aid climbing is very slow compared with free climbing and many of today's harder free routes were first climbed with aid.

Big wall climbing

This style of climbing was first developed in Yosemite Valley in California where there are giant walls of glacier-polished granite such as El Capitan, Half Dome and Washington Column — some of which are over 1500 m (5000 ft) high. The first ascents of these faces were accomplished mostly through continuous aid climbing. This is a very slow and tedious form of climbing and many hours can be spent ascending difficult aid pitches. The ropes of successive pitches are often left in place until sufficient progress has been made for the party to move off the ground or a ledge, and establish camp at the next convenient staging point. The great distances climbed mean that many days are spent on the routes, with bivouacs made on the ledges. Camping equipment, food and water are carried in a special haul bag that the leader pulls up with the aid of a pulley and Jumar system while the second ascends. As big wall climbing became perfected the technique developed to the extent that the second person climbed the rope with ascenders (see Chapter 20, *Climbing, Mountaineering and Cross-Country Ski Gear*) as they cleaned the pitch of pitons to speed the party's progress. Today, big wall climbing is practised on many of the world's most challenging rock faces such as Baffin Island in Canada and the Trango Towers in the Baltoro region of the Karakoram. The technique has also been refined to the degree that 'Porta Ledges', hanging bivouac platforms, remove the need for finding ledges to camp on.

Safety

Rock climbing varies greatly depending on the nature of the rock. Not all types of rock are worth climbing on — soft mudstone and chalk, for example, are usually unclimbable. The more solid the rock, obviously the safer the climbing. Different types of rock also weather in very different ways, which results in characteristic features and types of holds or friction properties. Granite, for example, often has a very rough surface and can result in giant slabs and boulders that are good for friction climbing. Limestone is often steep with cracks and pockets, while sandstone and quartz can be very compact and have complicated strata and a profusion of holds.

Much of the secret of safe climbing is being able to assess what is solid and climbable — most rock climbers will usually shy away from loose ground on a cliff. Despite routes being safe on the faces, however, it is often the tops of crags at the end of climbs that are unstable and the greatest source of danger.

Mountaineers do not usually have the same degree of choice in finding solid ground and are often required to move on rotten rock. This is just one of the reasons why mountaineering is more objectively dangerous than straight rock climbing.

MOUNTAINEERING

Mountaineering is about climbing with hands and feet up and down mountains. It usually also means carrying a pack, and being out for at least a full day, if not several days. The objective is usually the summit of the mountain. In the course of a mountaineering day it may be necessary to climb not only rock faces but also negotiate snow and ice – ice climbing. Glaciers also often have to be crossed, and if attempting the world's highest mountains there are also the problems of altitude, avalanches, rock falls, and storms.

Mountaineering can be categorised by the types of climbing that will be encountered: snow climbing; mixed climbing (snow, ice and rock), or just rock climbing. Alpine climbing is yet another term which is used to describe the sort of mountaineering which was first practised in the Alps of Europe. Here, routes are often climbed within a long day or with one or two bivouacs or overnight camps. The other criterion of alpine climbing is that the individual or party moves continuously up the mountain in one push. The alternative to this is 'siege-style' climbing where the group moves up and down the mountain via a series of semi-permanent camps that are established along the way. Ropes are often installed on difficult sections between such camps (fixed ropes) which make it safer and easier to move up and down the mountain quickly. This style of climbing was developed in the course of the first ascents of the high peaks of the Himalaya.

Mountaineering Techniques

It is vital for all mountaineers to become completely familiar with their ice-axe because on ice it is the only hope one has of being able to stop after a fall. The technique is known as making a self-arrest. After a fall, one has to try and roll into a position where you are facing into the slope and sliding down on your front, feet first. The adze or pick (depending on whether it is soft snow or ice) of the axe is held diagonally across the chest and gradually dug into the slope, which will hopefully slow one down to a gradual stop. Applying the brake too suddenly can cause the axe to be wrenched out of one's hands. It is also vital in such circumstances to keep one's feet up to avoid catching a crampon (spiked boot attachment) which could cause you to cartwheel or tumble out of control.

Many mountaineers need to wear crampons at some time in the course

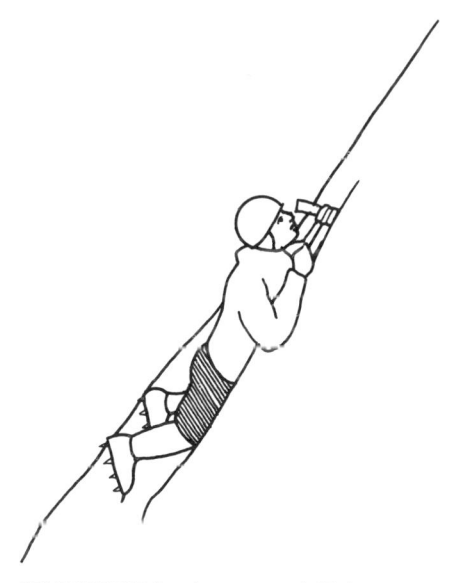

SELF-ARREST Bearing your weight down on the ice-axe will bring you to a halt

like across the slope with the sole of the crampons in full contact with the snow or ice. Here the ice-axe is used to keep balance, with the spike of the axe driven into the slope on the uphill side – this is called French Technique. On steeper slopes 'front pointing' technique is the most effective, but this is very strenuous and requires the use of an ice-axe and a second ice tool such

FEET FIRST FALL Turn over onto your stomach, gradually dig your ice-axe into the slope. Ensure that your feet are up so that you won't catch your crampons and lose control

of a mountain climb, whether it is to cross a glacier or traverse a snow slope. On such slopes the traditional means of crossing difficult sections was to cut steps with the adze of the ice-axe. This is a slow and tedious means of making progress, but if there are inexperienced members of the party it is often a worthwhile way of getting people across difficulties.

Today, the technique is to have an ice-axe and crampons, and walk crab-

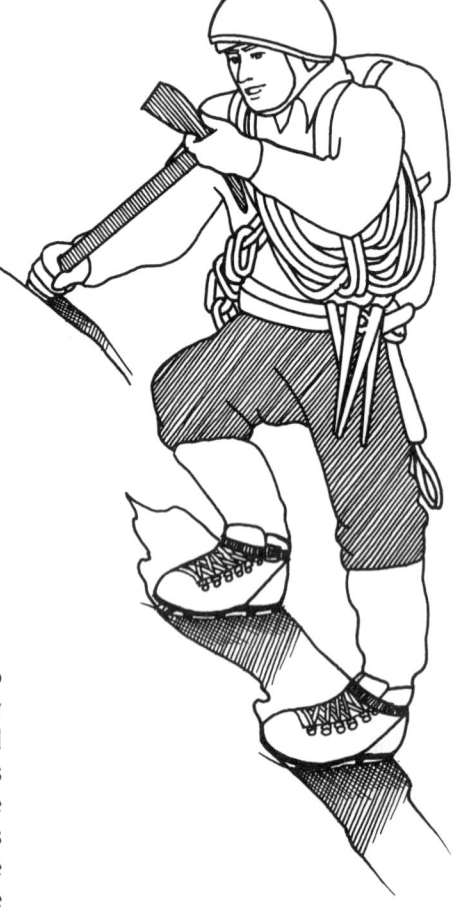

FRENCH TECHNIQUE Walking across the slope with the sole of your crampons in contact with the snow or ice, use your ice-axe for balance as an ice hammer or north wall hammer. In this case, the front points of the crampon – those that poke forward from the boot – are used; on each successive step they are imbedded into the ice with a firm kick. The picks on the ice tools are swung successively into the ice to give the equivalent of handholds.

To get protection or belay on ice and snow it is necessary to use specialised techniques and gear such as ice-screws, snow stakes, dead men and ice-bollards, and most importantly one's ice-axe. There will often be a mixture of ice and rock and in this instance it is possible to use pitons and nuts as well as or instead of ice-screws. A rock belay is always preferable to one on ice because ice is a fluid medium. When placing ice protection considerable fitness is required.

On snow, an ice-axe shaft driven in as far as it will go is the easiest and most common form of belay. This is the basis of what is known as a boot axe belay, where the rope is led around the shaft of the axe, which is braced with one's boot. A snow stake can be used in a similar fashion, or as a backup to an axe, and has the advantage of being able to be driven into the snow with a hammer without fear of being damaged. If necessary, a snow stake can also be left behind as an abseil anchor with minimal loss.

If it is at all icy, snow stakes and ice-axes are less useful than an ice-screw. There are two main types of ice-screws: drive-ins – those that are placed by being driven in with a hammer then screwed out, and regular ice-screws that are screwed in and out. All ice-screws and snow stakes must be inserted at an angle so that the force of

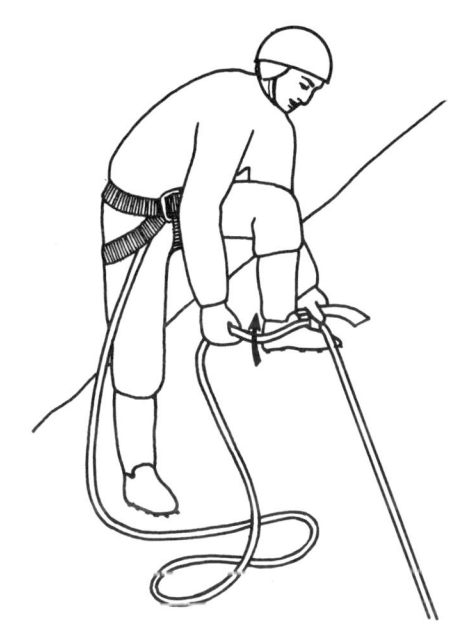

The boot ice-axe belay relies on the friction of the rope around the shaft of the ice-axe and boot

any load tends to pull them into a position at right angles to the face, rather than cause them to pop out. Similarly, dead men or dead boys must be placed carefully so that the wire traces are dug in and any load causes the device to be driven further into the snow. All anchors in snow and ice have a tendency to melt out under pressure; every placement left for some time, such as might be used on a fixed rope, should be checked regularly.

Glacier travel

The main objective danger on glaciers in the mountains is crevasses – clefts or fissures in the ice. The basic techniques for glacier travel involve being roped to one or more of the other climbers to minimise the likelihood of

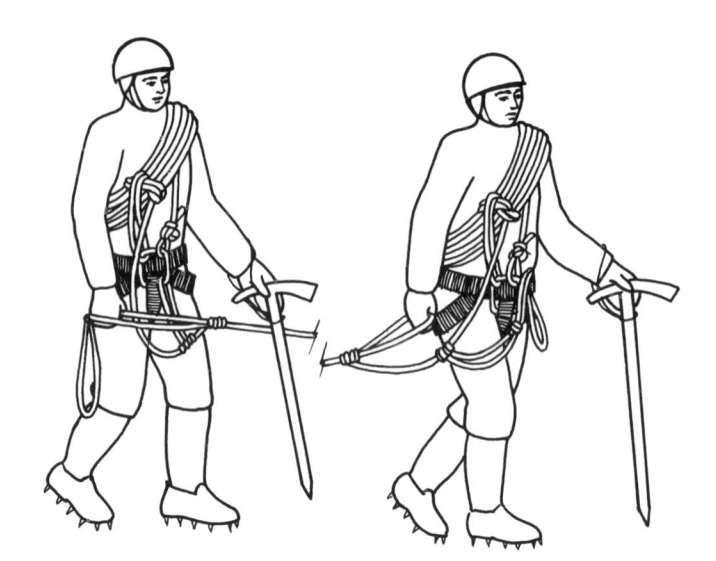

Safe glacier travel involves roping two or more climbers together to minimise the chance of falling into a crevasse

falling far if one breaks through into a hidden crevasse. Each individual on the rope has some form of device for climbing the rope – either jumars, CMIs or prusik knots. There are varying degrees of seriousness of falls. Often the fallen climber will be able to extricate themselves using front point climbing techniques. If the fallen climber is injured or unconscious, then a Z pulley system will have to be set up. This is time-consuming and technical, but often the only way of removing someone after a serious fall.

Objective dangers

Objective dangers in the mountains are those over which the climber has no control – avalanches, rockfalls, crevasses and storms. Whenever a climb proceeds to a high altitude all of these objective dangers are compounded.

Subjective dangers include falling off the mountain, and the problems of exhaustion and illness due to altitude.

There are many specialised books and videos which can provide the theory of how to avoid these problems but there is no substitute for good equipment, fitness, and most important of all, experience.

Mountaineering and rock climbing are both extremely enjoyable, and can be some of the most satisfying outdoor activities imaginable. If you have any interest in taking up these pursuits it is advisable to seek an introduction through experienced practitioners, but perhaps the best way is to take a course from a qualified instructor or guide.

11

TREKKING

Trekking at its best is found in areas, such as the Himalaya and the Andes, where there are no other practical forms of ground transport, either because the terrain is too rugged or too remote. Trekking in such regions involves going up and down hills, crossing passes, coping with high altitudes and extremely variable weather. It is not necessarily, however, a wilderness experience. Many popular Himalayan trekking trails are also ancient trading routes that carry a constant flow of local people and porters, mules, or yaks bearing supplies. These routes sometimes connect villages and pass through intensely cultivated valleys and hillsides.

Trekking anywhere in the world does not involve technical mountaineering, but it may mean going to higher altitudes than you would if ascending mountains. At times, it may also involve walking above the snowline.

Today the term trekking applies equally to individuals or groups and, more recently, to packaged commercial treks. Some trips cost little more than a few dollars a day if self-organised; commercial treks by contrast can cost you up to several hundred dollars per day.

Travel company brochures and documentaries often portray a very romantic impression of trekking. In reality, like many outdoor activities, it can also be frustrating, physically hard work, and at times potentially dangerous.

On commercial treks, with the support of professional leaders and staff, a lack of experience in outdoor living need not be a problem, but if you have never camped before, bedding down in a sleeping bag on a thin foam mat could be a shock to your system. Better to go on some weekend camping trips at home to see if you can cope with the day-to-day aspects of trekking before you take on the additional stresses of foreign lands, altitude and remoteness.

There are no real age barriers to trekking: all that really matters is your fitness, experience and motivation. Some children can manage easier treks and occasionally you will come across a fit seventy-year-old on a trail. Most trekkers, however, are aged between 20 and 55.

OPTIONS AND PLANNING

The style of trekking that you choose should be dictated by where you want to go, the time you have available, your level of experience in the outdoors, your knowledge of local cultures, how much adventure you seek, and what you can afford. Local regulations and weather conditions also have to be taken into account.

If you are fit and ready for an extended journey there are a number of choices. You can travel lightly 'living off the land', buying provisions en route and taking advantage of local hospitality; or you can be completely self-sufficient, carrying everything on your back or having someone else carry it.

Another set of possibilities is to travel alone or as part of a group, either organised by yourself or someone else. As a variation on backpacking, you can either trek by yourself, hire one or more porters to relieve you of your load, or hire a guide. When a guide is taken on they usually assume the responsibility for hiring porters, language translation and route finding. On each of these 'do-it-yourself' treks you have the option of staying in lodges or camping. If you camp you require more equipment, which means heavier loads or more porters, but you have more flexibility and added safety.

Organised and fully-catered group treks are the most self-contained form. If you are part of an organised group you will most probably have a team of local porters, a cook, a sirdar or head man, a leader, and in some instances, one or more sherpas or guides. The organisation of such a sizeable party is detailed and complex.

Preparation for trekking, like any big trip, should begin several weeks, perhaps months, before a proposed journey. The first step is to study reference books, guides or brochures (if taking a commercial trek) to see what the possibilities are. You also need to reflect on whether your experience and fitness match your aspirations, and the seasons you want to travel in.

How long can you be away for? Nowadays an average organised trek itinerary is of a week to twelve days in length, although more serious journeys can extend from three to five weeks. If you have no experience of walking and would normally never consider hiking for four or five hours at a time, then even a week may well be more than you would find enjoyable for a first-time trek.

People who have already trekked will be able to advise you on climate, conditions and customs. Be careful, however, not to take any one statement as gospel. Seasonal conditions, political factors and different perceptions can make one person's appraisal totally different to another's. As well as adventure travel company brochures, there are now many excellent trekking guidebooks.

You don't need to be a super-athlete to trek. No matter what you aim for, a gradual build up of fitness is recommended, especially if you are not used to regular exercise. The fitter you are, the more resistant you will be to infections and disease, and the more enjoyable your trip will be. Performing any aerobic activity such as squash, swimming, cycling or jogging two to three times a week for at least an hour is an excellent form of training. On a trek, however, you are likely to be going up and down hills much of the time. To strengthen the various muscles you will be using, perform part of your training on steep ascents and descents.

TREKKING

Pre-trek walks are an ideal opportunity to break in new boots which could help spare you the agony of blisters later on. If you plan to carry a heavy pack on trek, make backpacking part of your training routine. Rather than seeing the fitness build-up as drudgery, try to have some walks in interesting and scenic surroundings and to incorporate them as part of your relaxation at weekends.

CULTURAL CONSIDERATIONS

One of the great rewards of trekking is the exposure to and interaction with other cultures. This is particularly so in Asia, South America and Africa. The Himalayan countries are the most commonly visited by trekkers and so these are worth examining more closely. Each of these countries is based on a traditional society which is governed by varying ethical, spiritual and religious beliefs, customs and social mores. In the case of India the caste system, which dates back hundreds of years, is a further governing factor.

When you visit the Himalaya for the first time much of what you see and experience will not always make sense. As a traveller, however, you should try and be sensitive to native ways and to respect the local values. There are some aspects which are similar throughout Asia, and other considerations that are unique to a particular religion, be it Hindu, Buddhist or Muslim, or to a particular country.

A brief survey of some of these aspects will help you to avoid unintentionally offending local ways. People in Asia are, generally speaking, very modest. Nudity is not acceptable in many countries and you should always wear bathers or some clothing when swimming. Likewise, women should not wear shorts or have bare shoulders in temples and shrines.

Unless you want a picture of a saddhu or holyman who is traditionally paid for blessings, you should try to avoid paying for photographs. Be polite and ask for permission if you are taking close-ups. Likewise, always seek permission before photographing temples, stupas or monuments.

Tips, gratuities, bribes or baksheesh, no matter what you call them, are the same the world over. In the Himalaya it is no different. If you have had particularly good service from trekking staff, a guide or driver, some form of additional payment should be considered. Wages are usually very low in these countries and what is a small amount to you could well be a handsome tip to a local.

On organised group treks the tradition is to contribute whatever amount you wish to a kitty which is handed over to the sirdar at the end of the trek. He in turn divides the amount, pro-rata, among the staff according to their own system. Gifts of clothes and gear (no longer wanted) are also usually handled in this manner, but you may prefer to give an item directly to an individual who has helped you in a specific way. The sirdar should always be consulted if there is any doubt about the protocol. Porters are not usually tipped in cash but clean cast-off clothing is usually welcome.

Giving away pens, balloons, sweets or similar Western trinkets indiscriminately encourages begging and the 'something for nothing' mentality among children and some adults. If you have established a rapport with an individual over the course of some hours or days, then such a gift is more appropriate. There are other ways of 'breaking the ice' rather than giving away handouts. Becoming involved in a ball game, playing cards or trying your hand at shuffle board are possible conversation starters. Giving some pictures to a schoolmaster might be appropriate after a visit to a village school.

There is often no fixed price for goods or services in countries spanning the Himalaya. This is especially so when buying in a market from a souvenir stall, or paying for a taxi. Do not feel that everyone is trying to rip you off, it is just the way that business is transacted in much of the world. Ask around to try and determine what the going rate is for a similar item or service. If you can enter into the spirit of haggling, it can be quite enjoyable. Never accept the first price offered. Your counter bid could start somewhere around 20-30 per cent of what you were first quoted. The final deal is often struck at 40-50 per cent of the first offer. If you are not getting much response by starting at a very low bid, try walking away and see what result this brings.

If hiring a taxi, *shikara*, ponyman or porter, always establish the price before you take anyone on or step into the cab. With a porter or ponyman you should ascertain whether food and accommodation is included in the price, and the terms of payment.

Religion

There are a number of specific dos and don'ts that should be taken into account when travelling among Hindu people. Avoid wearing or carrying anything made of leather into a Hindu temple. Beef is prohibited among Hindus and no female animal is killed for food. Most Hindus cannot eat food that has been touched by a foreigner, and no food or offering should be touched on its way to a shrine. Both in India and Nepal always walk around a person and do not step over them. Do not offer anything with the left hand – this is traditionally reserved for cleaning oneself after going to the toilet. The right hand should be used if you receive or give anything and if using your fingers to eat with.

Buddhism also has its own codes and traditions that need to be respected. Always remove your shoes before entering a Buddhist *gompa* or shrine. Never touch a Buddhist child on the head and avoid pointing the soles of your feet at people. Always walk clockwise around a Buddhist temple, shrine, *chorten* or *mani wall*. If passing a mani on the trail, keep it on your right. Prayer wheels should always be spun in a clockwise direction. It is sacrilegious to remove any of the carved stones from mani walls. The inscriptions read 'om mani padme hum', the Buddhist mantra which translates to 'the jewel in the flower of the lotus'. Respect should also be shown to prayer flags no matter how tattered or torn they seem to be.

If trekking in parts of Pakistan or Northern India where Islam is the predominant belief, it is equally necessary to be aware of this religion's traditions. For example, it is necessary to remove your shoes when entering a mosque. In Islamic countries, women should dress modestly, wearing long-sleeved tops and long trousers or skirts. In mosques, women should also have their heads and shoulders covered. In some shrines women are not allowed inside the inner sanctum. Pakistani women seldom travel alone and it is offensive to Pakistani males to see European women travelling unaccompanied. There is virtually no open fraternisation between Pakistani men and women, but men will often hold hands out of friendship and nothing more. During the month of Ramadan, tea shops and food stalls – except railway station restaurants – are closed between dawn and dusk. Once the sun sets, however, it is business as usual.

National peculiarities

Indians have the opposite head movements to Europeans in response to questions. For example, the head being waved from side to side means yes. In Indian cities, shaking hands is accepted between males but Indian women do not shake hands. There is also much less open fraternisation between males and females. Shoes should always be removed before entering houses, and you must seek permission before taking photographs.

Because Pakistan is an Islamic state alcohol is not freely available. To buy a drink in Pakistan you need to have a liquor licence, which is obtained through having a tourist certificate. These are available from the Excise and Tax Office, or from some larger hotels authorised to sell alcohol to non-Muslim residents.

A Nepalese man dressed entirely in white should not be touched as he has had a death in his family and is considered contaminated. Most Nepalese remove their shoes before entering a house or a room. While this is not always practical when entering a village house wearing heavy boots, it should be observed in the cooking and eating areas. It is also not polite to enter these areas without being invited. Do not stand in front of a Nepalese who is squatting on the ground, eating. If you need to talk to him, squat by his side. Any food or utensil touched by a used knife, spoon or fingers is considered contaminated. It would humiliate a Nepalese if such food were offered to him. No used dish should be eaten from again without it being properly washed. It is not considered polite to open a gift in the presence of the donor. The most common greeting in Nepal is 'Namaste' or 'Namaskar' which is said with the palms of both your hands pressed together in front of your chest. The translation from Sanskrit is 'I bow to the God in you'. It is common to show respect to an older person by addressing them as 'daju' (elder brother) or 'didi' (elder sister).

HEALTH CONSIDERATIONS

Trekking can be more serious than walking at home because of the ease of getting to high altitudes, the remoteness of the regions visited in the event of illness or accident, and because of the poor general hygiene in such countries.

Preparations for trekking should begin a minimum of three months before you depart. These should entail a comprehensive physical examination, immunisations, the preparation of a first aid kit, and learning about the health problems you are likely to encounter. If you are signing up for an organised trek you are usually required by the travel company to have a thorough medical examination. If you are travelling on your own a medical check up is equally, if not more, important. It is necessary to inform the examining doctor of your full medical history, any medications that you are currently taking, and the exact nature of what you are about to undertake.

While you are away it is also prudent to carry a copy of your medical record with details of your blood group and allergies in case you should need emergency help. Leaving a copy of your itinerary and medical record with a close friend before you depart is also recommended. If you normally wear glasses or contact lenses, make sure that you take both a spare pair and your prescription with you. It is also wise to have a plentiful supply of any specific medications that you use regularly, or may need in the course of your time away.

Dental care is not up to Western standards in most countries where trekking is popular. It is therefore wise to have a dental checkup well before you depart. In cold weather and at high altitude, fillings have a tendency to work loose.

Researching the potential health problems of trekking is the next most useful preparation after your medical examination. In the Lonely Planet Guide *Trekking in the Nepal Himalaya*, there is an excellent section on health and safety. This covers diseases, treatments, a trekker's first aid kit and a list of medications and their use. Even if not trekking in Nepal, this section makes the book a worthwhile purchase. Comprehensive medical handbooks for travellers are *The Traveller's Health Guide* by Dr A. C. Turner, and *Travellers' Health* by Richard Dawood. The best specific book for altitude problems is *Mountain Sickness* by Dr Peter Hackett, a layperson's guide to the prevention, recognition and treatment of Acute Mountain Sickness.

Virtually all of the world's remote areas where trekking is practised have inadequate hygiene and sanitation. The third world cities and towns too have particularly poor public health. Before you go, make sure that all your immunisations are up to date, even though there are no official vaccination requirements for countries like Nepal. Certain vaccinations – cholera and yellow fever – are required by international health regulations, while preventative measures for other diseases such as typhoid, tetanus, polio, hepatitis, rabies and malaria are advisable. Your immunisation history must be recorded in a yellow passport-size booklet called International Certificates of Vaccination and should be carried with your passport when travelling between countries. These booklets are available from government health departments.

When travelling through most low-lying areas of the tropics on your way to a trek you are also potentially at risk of contracting the parasitic disease malaria from mosquito bites. There is very little risk of contracting malaria anywhere in the mountains as mosquitoes do not survive above 1000 m (3200 ft). Early symptoms of malaria are fever with shivering, feeling unwell, intense abdominal pain, vomiting and diarrhoea. If you suspect that you might have malaria, have a blood test and seek medical attention urgently – malaria can be a killer. Treatment should not be delayed if medical help is not available.

Precautions that can be taken to avoid being bitten include: wearing light-coloured clothing that covers your arms and legs after dusk; staying indoors and sleeping within insect-proof accommodation or under a mosquito net between dusk and dawn; using personal insect repellents on exposed areas of the skin twice daily; and using insecticide spray or coils to kill mosquitoes indoors. The recommended preventative tablets vary from doctor to doctor and country to country. Chloroquine and/or Maloprine (depending on the particular area to be visited) will help minimise the likelihood of contracting malaria.

Altitude and its effects

One of the delights of trekking, especially in the Himalaya, is walking in the shadows of the world's highest mountains. In such regions it is especially easy to get to high altitudes very quickly. This can result in a range of serious medical problems that most people would not experience in the course of walking elsewhere in the world.

The main problem, Acute Mountain Sickness (AMS), as it is correctly known, occurs if you ascend too rapidly to high altitudes. It is potentially very serious but can easily be prevented by understanding the causes, heeding any warning signs, and taking the necessary precautions.

Acute Mountain Sickness is caused by the body's lack of adaptation to the decreased amount of oxygen in the air. Although the proportion of oxygen in the air always stays the same, with an increase in altitude the overall air pressure decreases, and so there is less pressure to drive the oxygen from the atmosphere into your lungs. To compensate for this your breathing and heart rate increase. These and other factors lead to physiological problems where fluid accumulates in parts of the body where it should not be.

You can have problems with altitude as low as 2500 m (8000 ft) but it is more likely to occur when you ascend above 3000 m (10,000 ft). If you are trying to reach 5500 m (18,000 ft) you are considerably more at risk. The symptoms usually manifest themselves immediately, or within two to four days of reaching altitude. Anyone is potentially at risk regardless of age, sex or level of fitness. If you fly, ride or drive to a high altitude rather than walk you are more likely to have problems. Younger people tend to be more susceptible than older ones but only partly because they tend to climb faster. Overexertion and dehydration can contribute to Acute Mountain Sickness, which can occur in varying degrees of seriousness from mild to moderate to severe.

In its most benign, or mild, form the symptoms of AMS are loss of appetite, headache, lassitude (weariness), swelling of the extremities, nausea and sleeplessness, accompanied by irregular breathing. While these symptoms in themselves are not serious, they can quickly progress to a far more harmful condition. In the mild form the symptoms are annoying but can be coped with by taking aspirin – they are quite common and often people continue to ascend even with these problems. As soon as these symptoms progress to the point where you become quite uncomfortable, clear-cut measures must be taken to avoid potential tragedy.

With severe AMS there are signs and symptoms of high altitude pulmonary oedema and/or high altitude cerebral oedema. They can occur individually or together, and both can be fatal. The symptoms can either progress from mild AMS in a matter of hours, or begin with very little warning.

Sufferers of moderate and severe AMS are no longer able to make rational decisions for themselves. Where available, supplementary oxygen should be administered and they should begin to descend while they can still walk. If they cannot walk, victims should be carried by a yak, porter or mule.

The best way to avoid Acute Mountain Sickness is to make a graded ascent and acclimatise properly. A recommended rate is not more than 400-500 m (1300-1600 ft) per day. If you fly to high altitude airfields, it is advisable to spend time acclimatising at that altitude on arrival. The rule for ascent is to remain at the same altitude until the symptoms go away; if they worsen, you should descend immediately. The climber's maxim 'climb high, sleep low' is another expression of this rule.

Keeping your fluid intake up will help to reduce the likelihood of AMS. The decreased humidity of cold, dry, mountain air and sweating from the strenuous exercise that trekking and climbing usually entails, can result in extreme dehydration. There should be a conscious effort to drink more water – up to 5 L (9 pt) a day may be necessary.

Accidents

Trekking takes place mostly in remote areas, which makes even minor trauma or accidents potentially serious. If you can't walk after an accident and are not too heavy, you may be able to be carried by a porter. In certain areas it may be possible to ride on a yak or a mule. If you are a stretcher case, it may be feasible to obtain a helicopter but this option is very expensive and cannot be relied upon. The availability of aid and rescue facilities for trekkers and climbers varies greatly from country to country – generally it seems that wherever there is a strong military presence, the chances of rescue are greatly improved.

Hygiene

Commonsense and care is the key to dealing with most hygiene problems on trek. Treat all water supplies with suspicion. Do not take water into your mouth while under the shower, or clean your teeth with water from the tap. Better hotels will provide containers or thermoses of treated water for this purpose. In many towns and cities in the Himalayan region you can now purchase bottled mineral water. Bottled beer and soft drinks are usually safe to drink. Avoid eating suspect food and drinking tap or stream water; wash your hands thoroughly with disinfected water before eating or handling food; and treat any infections as soon as they appear.

GEAR FOR TREKKING

Given that trekking is little more than a style of walking – albeit in a foreign country where you may not have to carry your own equipment – the basic personal kit needed is much the same as you would require for an extended hike at home.

As is discussed in Chapter 15, *Clothing*, however, having proper clothing for a trek can make all the difference between an enjoyable trip and a disastrous one. On trek you could well experience a far greater range of conditions than you would ordinarily at home. Depending on the time of year and the destination, temperatures may range from 40°C (104°F) during the day to -10°C (14°F) on the same night, and if you are caught in a blizzard on a high altitude trek or mountain the temperature may not rise above 0°C (32°F) all day. Coping with everything from a heavy snowfall to a choking dust storm or monsoon rains can further tax both your humour and wardrobe.

Preparation for trekking involves spending time assembling a basic clothing kit in advance, or checking that all items are serviceable as many will often not be available overseas. If you buy at home you also have the advantage of being able to shop around at leisure and select each item carefully. As discussed in Chapter 15, *Clothing*, specialty outdoor equipment stores in home cities are the best place to purchase clothing as they usually have experienced staff who can advise you on what you will need for a particular region or season.

For those not already experienced and equipped for the outdoors, getting properly outfitted all at once can be a very expensive exercise. Much of the gear is so specialised that you may not have any further use for it once you return. Do not put your trip at risk, however, for the sake of a few dollars. Ask around friends and family to see what you can borrow before spending large sums of money. Some items may be able to be rented in the country of your destination, or possibly supplied by an outfitter if you are going on an organised trip. If you already have your own first class gear do not leave it behind on the promise that replace-

---

EQUIPMENT CHECKLIST

Camera gear/binoculars
Daypack
Inner sheet
Kit/duffle bag or large rucksack
Money belt
Personal first aid kit
Plastic mug
Pocket knife
Sewing and repair kit
Stuffsacks
Toiletries/toilet paper/towel

Torch/spare batteries
Umbrella
Water bottle

If Required:

Cooking gear
Eating utensils
Sleeping bag
Sleeping mat/Thermarest
Tent

ments will be supplied by the travel company.

As a rule, good equipment and clothing is not available in third world countries where trekking is popular. Nepal is the one place, however, where you could expect to be outfitted with quality gear. Secondhand clothing can be found in the trekking shops in the Thamel district of Kathmandu – expedition equipment often ends up here only hours after it has been issued to local staff. Bargains can be found at the end of the season when everyone is heading home, but when the demand is high, do not be surprised if shopkeepers quote you prices from the latest American mail order catalogue.

While it is better not to take the risk of relying on buying basic gear in Nepal or any other country, many of the more specialised items such as down jackets or sleeping bags can be hired from the trek outfitters, provided sufficient warning is given. In Kathmandu, trekking shops will also hire out gear.

Your equipment will need to be well-made, well-fitting and appropriate for the particular journey. The more serious the trek or climb the more vital the gear becomes. It is also important to have the right equipment for a trek; for example, plastic double boots are quite unnecessary for the Annapurna Sanctuary trek, but they could be a toe-saving investment for an ascent of Island Peak.

In addition to the clothing requirements which are outlined in Chapter 15, *Clothing*, the following equipment is essential for trekking.

If you are joining an organised group, tents cooking gear and eating utensils, sleeping bags and mats will usually be supplied. Most operators also prefer that your personal gear is carried in a kit/duffle bag, rather than a rucksack.

If participating in an organised trek, or going on your own but having porters carry most of your gear, it is advisable to have a larger than usual daypack. As well as water bottle, waterproofs and personal first aid kit you should be able to fit in an insulated jacket, gloves and warm hat, and perhaps a camera or binoculars.

If you are required to bring your own sleeping bag and mat, the choice will depend on personal preference, and where you are intending to trek. Some people are 'warm sleepers' and can be perfectly comfortable in a three-season bag (one that the manufacturers recommend for spring, summer and autumn) even in the snow. Others might need to wear long underwear or a tracksuit in an expedition sleeping bag (the warmest type usually made) under the same conditions.

If you are trekking to high altitude in the Himalaya and plan on camping you could experience temperatures as low as -10°C (14°F) or colder. This means that a four- or five-season bag should be considered. Just staying in the foothills, however, should mean that a three-season bag will be adequate. Even expedition-rated sleeping bags may be chilly if you are planning to climb in the Himalaya.

12
OTHER ACTIVITIES

No matter what the geography, or the season, there is an outdoor activity that you can pursue. Walking, climbing and skiing are essentially land-based, although airborne moments are not uncommon in the latter two pursuits. But what about the rivers and lakes; the deep ravines and the caverns underground; what about the skies above?

CANOEING

From its humble origins as a means of water transportation canoeing has evolved into a diverse and hugely popular outdoor pastime. Canoeing encompasses everything from shooting rapids to lazy drifting in the backwaters. It can take you to places that are impossible to reach by any other means. Although there is ample scope for drama and excitement, canoeing, as many people practise it, is the most leisurely activity of them all.

Canoe styles reflect both the waters that they are designed to travel on and the personality of the user. Kayaks give the best combination of speed and control for the independent paddler on fast or exposed water – they are powered by a double-bladed paddle and you sit in a cockpit. In rapids and white water the manoeuvrability of a

The style of canoe varies according to the water activities you wish to pursue. Canadian canoes are ideal for covering distances in comfort and style

The kayak combines speed and control on white water

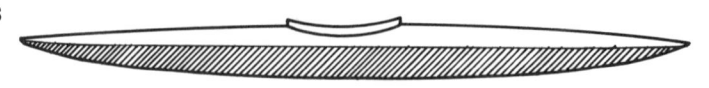

slalom canoe is unsurpassed, although these are not often seen except in competitive events. For covering distances in comfort and style, the ideal craft are two-person Canadian canoes. These can be open or decked and you use a single-bladed paddle from either a sitting or kneeling position. If you have a yearning for open water and the challenge of expedition-style trips, sea kayaks offer virtually unlimited potential.

There's much more to handling a canoe than dangling a paddle in the water — even getting into a canoe takes a little practice at first. Once underway, a repertoire of paddling techniques — bow strokes, sweeps, J strokes, draw strokes, etc — are needed to control a canoe efficiently in all waters. Perhaps the most important skills are being able to recover from a capsize or a swamping, and to rescue a paddler separated from their craft. The eskimo roll is the canoeist's means of escaping, Houdini-style, from difficulty, although it is a consummate skill to perfect. Needless to say, anyone contemplating canoeing needs to be a strong swimmer.

Specialised equipment for canoeing, apart from paddles and boats, includes a quality buoyancy vest, and items such as spray decks and helmets if travelling along rough water and rocky river beds are planned. Canoeists benefit from the kind of lightweight, fast-drying clothing discussed in Chapter 15, *Clothing*. A wetsuit is an alternative in winter.

Canoe touring is rather like bushwalking afloat, with the important difference that weight is less critical so one can be more liberal with food luxuries. Space, however, is not unlimited so lightweight, compact camping equipment is still very appropriate. Ideally, gear should be stored in watertight plastic barrels, or specialised canoeing dry bags, and securely stowed in the canoe.

RAFTING

For running wild rivers rafts are often the only solution. They offer a comfortable ride and can carry a mountain of gear. Although rafts can provide an extra margin of safety in tumbling rapids, they are by no means as precise in their movements as a skilfully paddled canoe. For this reason any river descent needs to be carefully planned, taking into account water levels, river hazards and the experience of party members.

Large rafts that take four or more adults are too bulky and expensive for most individuals to contemplate, but these are commonly used on the bigger rivers by commercial operators. For wilderness rafting one-person rafts are effective in narrow gorges and on rivers where a lot of portaging is likely.

Such craft are, however, notoriously difficult to steer and easily tipped.

The same strategies for packing and waterproofing gear apply for rafting as for canoeing. Rafting has the potential to be one of the most exhilarating things you can do in the outdoors with the least number of technical skills required. A raft is also a wonderful floating platform from which you can watch the world go by.

CANYONING

There are wet, exciting places where even the smallest raft can't go. Canyoning is a hybrid outdoor activity which combines the skills of caving, abseiling, bushwalking, swimming and paddling a 'Li-Lo' to descend narrow gorges. As a sport it has been perfected in the Blue Mountains of New South Wales where streams have carved deep chasms through the soft sandstone.

Typically, a canyon trip involves a bushwalk to an access point, then a series of steep, often wet, abseils punctuated by stretches of walking or rock scrambling and long swims through icy-cold pools. It requires solid ropework skills and a stout constitution but the rewards are great.

Given the potential hazards and the difficulty of rescue, a canyoning party has no alternative but to be thoroughly prepared and well-equipped. Canyons are only really comfortable in midsummer, and by their very nature they are susceptible to flooding so choose your days carefully.

A rugged daypack with a waterproof liner to take spare clothing, food and other equipment is essential. A thin wetsuit is useful for most canyons, but many people get by with thermal underwear and fibrepile clothing. Light sandshoes are the best footwear. Specialist equipment includes a proper climbing harness, descender, prussick cords, slings and karabiners. If a long swim is likely, a Li-Lo makes life easier.

Canyoning is best attempted only in the company of an experienced person who knows the descent, and, in particular, the right point to enter and exit the canyon.

CAVING

The joys of the subterranean world can seem obscure to most people – caving, like rock climbing, confronts some instinctive fears, but unless you are a confirmed claustrophobic it can be 'deeply' satisfying in more ways than one. As a pastime caving does not enjoy the popularity of many other activities; a large part of this has to do with the cavers themselves who usually prefer not to advertise their activities. Some cavers indeed are as introverted and darkly mysterious as the habitats they enjoy.

In essence caving means travelling through natural underground formations. This may involve only walking through large caverns, but caving at its most physical includes a range of manoeuvres – from scrambling and crawling, to tight squeezes, abseil descents and other complicated ropework.

If the idea of grovelling around in dark, muddy passages sounds off-putting, bear in mind that the experience of caving is like no other. Only in caves do you appreciate the meaning of pitch black, the feeling of total silence, and the wonder of natural limestone formations. After a while you begin to realise why cavers are so protective of their underworld.

The equipment needed for caving has to endure some brutal treatment. This is not the environment for flimsy, lightweight gear or prissy clothing. At least two reliable light sources are the core of a caver's kit. The main light is usually a professional miner's light that is mounted on the helmet with a battery pack at the waist. Additional lights are usually compact torches. A construction site hard hat gives necessary protection, mainly from knocks in tight chambers but also from the risk of rockfall. Climbers' helmets have the added advantage of being lighter and more comfortable. High-cut leather boots are preferred over sandshoes for muddy caves and when grovelling over rough ground. The caver's uniform is a pair of heavy-duty overalls which keep out the worst of the mud, dirt and gravel. More technical clothing layers are essential if traversing cold, wet caves.

Caving has many sub-branches. Far from being a case of aimlessly wandering underground, most serious cavers pursue their sport in a methodical, even scientific way. Exploration has obvious appeal and new cave extensions are being mapped constantly. Cave archaeology attracts the more painstaking and meticulous type. Sport caving can include serious scuba diving and mind-boggling vertical logistics normally grouped under the heading of single-rope techniques.

Caving skills are not widely promoted. The only sure way to get into caves and back out again is to join a caving club or speleological society.

PARAGLIDING

At the other end of the scale from caving is a sport which has all the hallmarks of being the latest fad, but is in fact a highly practical solution to the climber's dilemma of descending from high summits.

Paragliding, or parapenting as it is known in Europe, is flying using a wing-style parachute that is capable of gliding and soaring much like a hang-glider. The difference is that a para-glider weighs only 5 or 6 kg (11-13 lb) and can be easily stowed in a rucksack. This makes it highly portable and instantly appealing to alpinists looking for a fast way down.

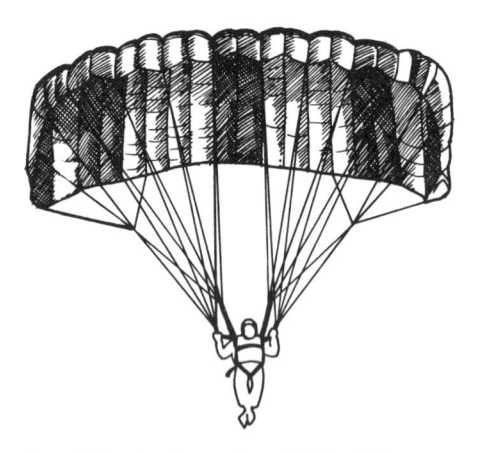

Paragliding involves using a lightweight parachute style canopy for airborne descent, catching the thermal air current and short cross-country flights

Unlike a hang-glider, however, a para-glider has only a glide ratio of 3:1. This means that it travels forward 3 m (10 ft) for every 1 m (3.3 ft) it drops (a hang-glider by contrast can have a glide ratio of 14:1), so in calm air paragliders descend at approximately 200 m (650 ft) per minute. In 1988 the Frenchman

Jean Marc Bovin descended 2100 m (7000 ft) from the summit of Mt Everest to the Western Cwm in 11 minutes.

Paragliding is a relatively recent phenomenon, having originated in Europe just over a decade ago. Now there are some 100,000 paraglider pilots worldwide, and the sport is popular in ski resorts, mountain sites and anywhere with good take-off conditions. In Australia paragliding is conducted under the auspices of the Hang-gliding Federation of Australia. It is necessary to take a course with a qualified instructor, and a recreational licence can be obtained after a seven-day course.

The reliability of the equipment and its correct application are the first essentials of paraglider safety.

Landings and take-offs are usually practised on small hills or sand dunes. The chute is laid out on the ground behind the flyer and if the right combination of wind and updraft prevails the chute will inflate after a few steps forward and become airborne. The flyer is suspended in a full body harness. Turns and climb and descent rates are controlled by left and right steering toggles. Tandem paragliders are used by many instructors to give training flyers a taste of the experience.

It is possible to soar to several hundred metres in a paraglider, so reserve chutes are worn by serious flyers. Two-way radios, helmets, altimeters and air speed indicators can also be used, but at their simplest paragliders offer both a radical way of descending, and a new way to enjoy the skies, even in back-country areas.

MOUNTAIN BIKING

Cycle touring on conventional 10 speed 'racing' bikes has always been

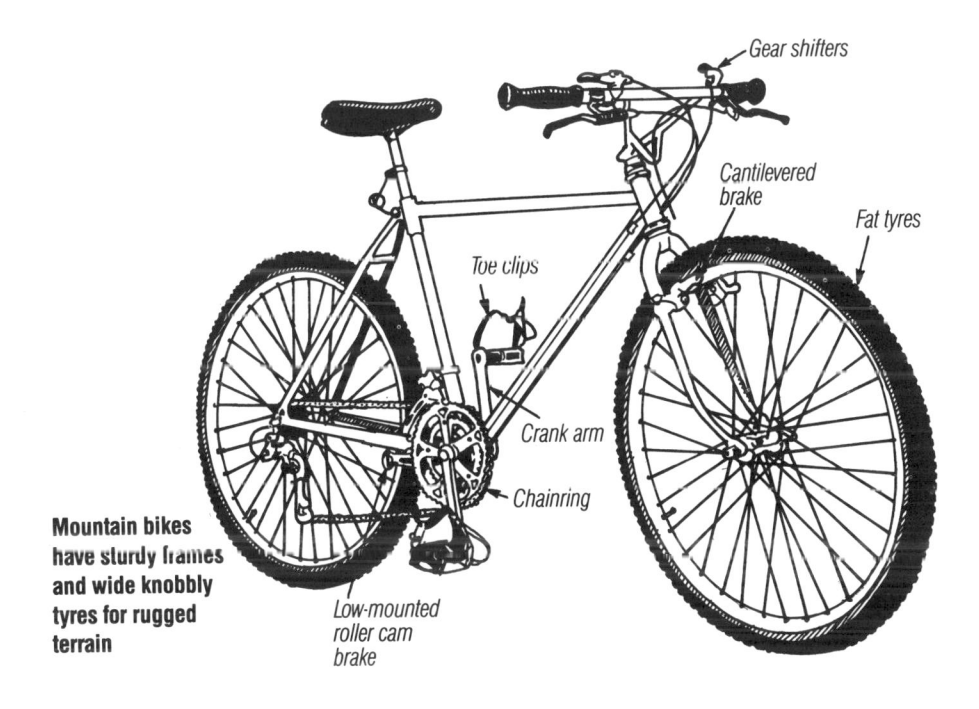

Mountain bikes have sturdy frames and wide knobbly tyres for rugged terrain

Gear shifters
Cantilevered brake
Fat tyres
Toe clips
Crank arm
Chainring
Low-mounted roller cam brake

popular, but these machines are relatively fragile. Tours meant staying on smooth road surfaces and coping with high-speed traffic as well as tedious town-to-town itineraries. Then around ten years ago another type of cycle appeared on the scene – with a sturdy frame, fat knobbly tyres and straight handlebars. The mountain bike was born and with it came the freedom to tackle dirt backroads, fire trails and all manner of fearsome terrain, including boggy hollows, creekbeds, rocky ground and sandy flats.

Mountain biking is mostly enjoyed on day trips, but with panniers and lightweight camping gear multi-day trips are quite feasible. Like any 'off-road' vehicle mountain bikes can cause a lot of damage so when planning trips take care to avoid sensitive surfaces, such as alpine meadows or fragile hillsides. Existing roads and appropriate trails should be followed wherever possible.

There are many styles of mountain bikes, each catering to different uses. For touring and speed on gently undulating terrain it's better to have a longer wheelbase and chain stays. Thinner tyres mean less friction on good surfaces and gearing needs to be efficient at higher speeds. On steeper and bumpier terrain a shorter wheelbase, chunkier tyres and more angled front forks help make a bike more nimble. A comfortable seat is essential. Higher handlebars suit fast pedalling on the flat, while lower handlebars keep your weight over the front wheel on the rough stuff. Most bike frames are made from chrome-molybdenum steel tubing that is butted at the joints, although aluminium frames are also common. Given the brute force required on slippery inclines, most bikes have triple cranksets for extra low gears. As well as strength, mountain bikes need to cope with a lot of wear and tear from dust, mud and water. Sealed bearings, and quality alloy wheel rims and stainless steel spokes are essential.

Clothing for mountain biking needs to be light and snug fitting. Lycra cycling shorts and tights are popular but layers of mainstream outdoor clothing including long underwear and fibrepile work just as well in the backcountry. Good wind and rain garments are essential. Tailored cycling shells fit the best but a more general purpose anorak and overpants combination are fine as long as the pants are not too baggy. Specialised mountain bike shoes and boots have grooves in the soles and top straps to mould with the pedals for added comfort and power.

Though hardly an activity suited to fragile wilderness areas, mountain biking is nevertheless an exciting way to explore the back-country areas. There is also scope to have fun on hair-raising descents and dicey trails.

ORIENTEERING

Orienteering combines the skills of navigating by map and compass with route finding through the bush under the umbrella of an organised event. At one extreme it can be fiercely competitive, demanding a high level of fitness and cross-country running skills, at the other it can be a leisurely day's outing for all the family. Among bushwalkers and skiers it is regarded as one of the best ways to hone land navigation techniques in a controlled setting.

An orienteering course is a series of

OTHER ACTIVITIES

checkpoints scattered around an area of bush. The idea is to find as many checkpoints in the shortest possible time. Details of their whereabouts are given at the start, and you transfer this information onto your map. The key is to plan which checkpoints to go for and in what order, depending on the lie of the land. Checkpoints are identified by a marker and you carry a card which is punched at the appropriate checkpoint as proof that you have visited it.

Most orienteering events have several courses of increasing length and difficulty to cater for various age groups and abilities. Individual checkpoints are given a score according to how hard they are to reach. The winner will have accumulated the most checkpoints, or the highest point score in the fastest time.

The orienteer needs little specialised equipment. A good quality map case, compass and watch are obviously essential. Light but sturdy running shoes are best teamed with clothing appropriate to the weather. On longer events a waist pack or bum bag is handy for carrying a water bottle and windshell.

Competitive orienteering events, including national championships, are held regularly and most clubs welcome new members. Rogaining is another branch of the sport which involves much longer courses lasting several hours and sometimes all night. Here the emphasis is just as much on effective route finding in rugged terrain as on map reading. Endurance rather than speed is tested and the competitors need to be well prepared with adequate clothing, drinks and light foods.

MORE OPTIONS

There is no shortage of other avenues to outdoor pleasure. Ingenious new sports are being dreamt up and old pastimes revived. At some point, however, usually when technology takes over, an activity ceases to be part of the tradition of lightweight, low-impact travel. The following are worthy options to consider.

As an alternative to cross-country skiing some people prefer to travel across the snow on snowshoes. Although it seems ponderous compared with the speed and grace of moving on skis, there are many densely wooded and broken slopes that can be ascended only with snowshoes. Lightweight alloys, neoprene lacing and snug bindings make the latest snowshoes more manoeuvrable than the original model featuring wooden frames and leather lacing.

Snowboarding is the closest thing, yet, to surfing on snow. A snowboard is like a very wide and squat ski with fixed bindings. Best suited to very steep slopes and soft snow, snowboards allow for spectacular descents using techniques remarkably similar to those used on a surfboard or skateboard. Not surprisingly it attracts the same sort of crowd: those who revel in the speed and stunts.

Mountains are the breeding ground for many other fringe activities, for example, talus running, which involves descending rocky slopes on foot at breakneck speed. In Great Britain there is a long tradition of fell running, a branch of cross-country running in punishing mountain terrain. Mountain marathons are the nearest equivalent in Australia. Another variation is the Three Peaks Race, a competitive event combining sailing and mountain running that has been held in Tasmania in recent years following on from the success of similar races held in Great Britain.

Though ocean sailing may seem far removed from the realm of rucksack sports, there are some strong parallels. Expeditionary voyages to remote areas for climbing and exploration are a venerable part of the outdoor tradition. Also popular are shorter journeys in coastal waters using lightweight camping gear and travelling by assorted small craft including sailing dinghies, catamarans and sail boards.

The scope for integrating different activities is virtually unlimited. The challenges offered by the outdoors, far from being exhausted, are only just being realised. So, as well as striving for excellence in a single pursuit, or seeking out more extreme wilderness areas, there is also the option of combining pastimes and plotting ingenious lightweight expeditions.

13

OUTINGS WITH CHILDREN

Sharing the outdoors with children can be the most rewarding and challenging thing you can do in the wild. The secret is to allow children to introduce you to the bush as seen through their eyes. The usual measures of a day's success – the distance covered, summits climbed, destinations reached – have to be set aside in the presence of young imaginations expanding to meet the natural world.

Travelling through the bush with children of any age is slow, to the point of being best regarded as a long rest stop broken by short bursts of forward progress. It's also physically demanding. Small infants can be carried, but even with a good papoose carrier the load is rarely stationary. There is additional clothing, food and equipment to be borne by whoever gets to shoulder the main pack. Older children may be capable of carrying part of their kit but not for great distances. The logistics even for gentle overnight trips can be formidable.

It's virtually impossible to maintain the same tempo with children as that which you may be accustomed to on adult trips. In any case an outing with youngsters is not simply a scaled-down adult adventure. Children see the world differently and at the same time adults shoulder new responsibilities.

So travelling with children means quality not quantity, and the activity provides the opportunity to experience the wilds and each other with an intensity that is rare in a group of grown-ups. Families have the freedom to interact as a tight-knit group. The divisions between child and adult activity that are necessary for day-to-day survival at home can be temporarily suspended in the bush – out there you work together, solve problems as a group and share in the high times.

The type of trip you choose is largely governed by the age and personality of the child. Many people walk successfully with young babies who are often quite content on their parent's back. There they have a passing parade of things to observe and the motion of the carrier helps them to doze. The routines of feeding and nappy changing help break the journey.

A baby in a carrier is, however, vulnerable to the elements and other intrusions like low branches and insects, so protection from wind, sun and rain is essential. Perhaps the biggest dilemma is what to do with dirty nappies. Even the most ecologically-minded people find the idea of washing nappies in the bush too much. Disposable nappies can

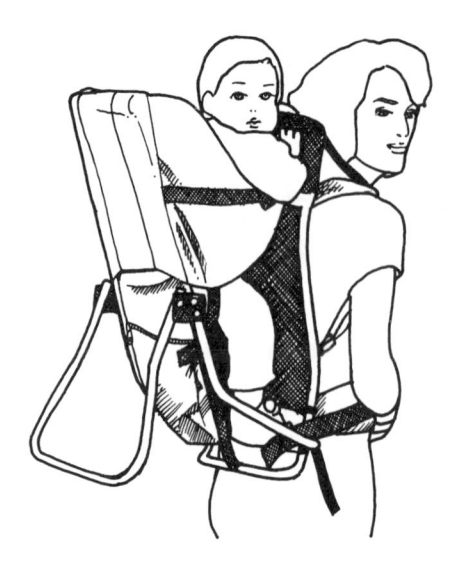

A child carrier is an ideal way to transport young children about on family outings

make life easier but they must be carried out, so a garbage bag is essential.

Older babies are still quite portable but those at the crawling stage can quickly become restless in the confines of a carrier. Once on the ground they need to be closely watched. Aside from the problem of a crawler disappearing into the undergrowth there is an array of stones, sticks and plants that they will want to put in their mouths. Other hazards like stoves and campfires are just as irresistible to the explorer on all fours, and somehow the toys you take along never have the same attraction as they do at home.

Toddlers who are too heavy to carry, but not able to propel themselves for any distance, pose a special problem. Many parents find the age between two and four the most testing time for serious outdoor pursuits. Some families give up altogether on the idea of going bush in this period, yet at an age when a child's learning is such a delight to observe there are benefits for both parent and child if some contact with the natural world can be maintained. This experience also provides a foundation for more ambitious outings later on. Short day trips with plenty of variety and frequent rest stops are the answer.

Even when a child is capable of walking several kilometres and wearing a small daypack it can be hard work to keep them motivated. For a four-year-old the notion of walking for pleasure is not necessarily a natural one. The pace should be gentle and the timetable very flexible. Journeys will need to be punctuated not just by rests but by entertaining games and diversions. The best incentives are the natural ones – the promise of a swim in a creek or a cave to explore – but when a child is tired or irritable the lure of a snack bar may be the only thing that registers.

Young people like to feel that they are part of the decisions made on the trail. As well as taking responsibility for carrying some of their own gear children need to be actively involved in the tasks of navigating, cooking meals and setting up camp, no matter how much extra time it takes initially.

Clearly some children are better suited temperamentally than others for the experience of the outdoors. Most children are more adaptable and tougher than their parents realise, but a teething baby is unlikely to fare any better in the wild, and sleeping or eating difficulties at any age may be compounded in strange surroundings. Every child needs to be introduced to the bush in gradual stages. It might be simply a question of waiting until a child reaches a certain point in their development, but even then some individuals never make the transition and prefer the routines of home life.

PREPARATION

Preparation for any trip with children begins well before you leave home. A child born and raised in the city often finds the outdoors not so much new and exciting as almost alien. If not carefully managed, a child's first experiences of being in the wild and camping out can be troubling and even off-putting for all concerned.

A lot of these anxieties can be avoided if you introduce a child to the bush at an early age and in measured doses. The young baby learns to appreciate the sights and sounds of nature in the raw — they accept that being in the bush is part of their relationship with their parents.

Older children are best treated to a series of short day outings in nearby parks, where they can learn to respond to the outdoors in a relaxed setting. Gradually, you can increase the adventure with more arduous terrain and staying out in rough weather. Much can be done at home to prepare children for camping out in the wilds. A night spent in a tent pitched in the backyard helps ease any fears, and using camping stoves and campfires at home is worthwhile.

These preliminary experiences are the time to foster a healthy respect for the environment; good habits come mostly from the example parents give. Young children are happy to touch and observe and it's simple enough to reinforce this gentle awareness with nature games. Children also usually understand basic rules about what to do with rubbish, going to the toilet and so on, but there will come a time when youngsters want to play by themselves and use whatever comes to hand, so branches are broken, rocks trundled and dams built. As every parent knows, an active four-year-old can be highly destructive, without meaning to be so.

There is a fine line between giving children latitude to learn through play and enforcing a stifling code of conduct. Just as adults value the freedom of the bush, so children should be encouraged to see the outdoors as a place of uninhibited fun. Nevertheless, it's important to explain certain ground rules before going bush. Once a trip is underway parents need to be alert to a child's needs; boredom is often the cause of unacceptable behaviour so there is a need to keep children entertained in ways which cause the least impact on the environment.

There is no doubt that the outdoors can be a potent learning experience for children and it's understandable for parents to hope to pass on their knowledge and skills, but children have a way of seeing through situations contrived to teach them 'lessons'. They are happiest when they feel part of what their parents are doing and sharing the parents' discoveries as well as making their own.

ACTIVITIES

Day walks on prepared trails are the easiest and safest starting point for any youngster's outdoor career. Many parks have excellent nature paths that help introduce children to environmental themes. Whether you are carrying a young baby or shepherding five-year-olds, don't expect to walk too far or fast. It can take at least twice as long to cover the same distance with children in tow.

When the time comes for more extended trips and overnight camping it's very common to ferry provisions, equipment and young charges into a base camp from which daily excursions can be made. Carrying heavy packs and motivating children to keep walking on multi-day treks is only really possible when you're dealing with energetic eight- or nine-year-olds.

Around this age many children are also ready to take on more adventurous pastimes. Cycle touring is a great way of combining skills that almost every child is eager to practise with the outdoor experience. With a little planning to avoid strenuous ascents and long hauls on dirt roads it's possible to devise itineraries that are interesting for everyone.

Skiing with a young baby may appear out of the question, but many people do it. The secret is to have a means of transporting the baby that is safe and comfortably warm. A sled or pulk does the job admirably. Older children of course revel in the snow and can easily outski their parents by the time they are five. Extended ski touring is safest left until the child has the stamina and skills to endure buffeting winds and severe cold. In any winter activity proper clothing and footwear is particularly critical as small bodies do not tolerate cold as well as adults.

Children have a natural affinity with water, and river-based trips have a decided appeal as long as parents are prepared to closely supervise water play. It is also essential for youngsters to understand the importance of not polluting creeks and waterholes that provide the main water supply for other bush travellers. Canoeing and rafting trips should be undertaken only when children are proficient swimmers and have strong paddling skills of their own. Even then, the trip needs to be well-planned to avoid dangerous rapids or exposed open water.

The right child at the right age can attempt almost any outdoor activity if it's well managed. Many a ten-year-old has proven adept at scaling rock faces that have defeated much older climbers. Similarly, some kids think nothing of scrabbling through a dark cave or descending a long abseil, but there are just as many children who have been coaxed into such positions only to find themselves freeze with fear. With high-risk activities adults have to finely judge each individual child's progress and be competent to retrieve the situation if problems develop. What is an adventure for an adult can quickly become a frightening ordeal for a young child.

CAMPING OUT

A night spent in the bush, camping out under the stars, can be a marvellous family experience. The first priority is to find a safe location – avoid sites near steep drops or treacherous streams. Choose areas with resilient surfaces that are located well back from water supplies. It's wise to spend time with toddlers and older children surveying the camp, pointing out hazards and clearly identifying the boundaries that they must stay within.

Remember, too, that even well-mannered children can cause havoc to fragile environments.

Most children want to help out with pitching tents, collecting firewood and unpacking gear. It makes sense to encourage this participation, no matter how long the job takes. Involving small children in the preparation of the evening meal is trickier – stoves and campfires are difficult to cook on at the best of times. When it's dark and everyone is hungry the last thing you need is a small helper to knock a pot of noodles into the coals. Often it's safest if one adult is delegated to keep little ones amused.

In the evenings a campfire is good entertainment for both children and adults alike, but be sure you choose the right area and the time of year when fires are acceptable. Even then children should be educated to regard campfires as a special privilege. When the time comes for sleep, smaller children are best bunked down with their parents. At some point, though, most youngsters will want the adventure of their very own tent.

Either way, once a child is toilet-trained parents have to be prepared to accompany a young one to the toilet in the middle of the night. In the bush the same rules apply for children as for adults: choose a place well away from camp and any permanent water. If defecating dig a small 'cat' hole, and if possible burn toilet paper. Needless to say, parents have to take time to educate children in this procedure.

GEAR FOR KIDS

Good quality clothing and equipment for children is notoriously difficult to source. Most parents are unwilling to part with much money for items that may be outgrown within a year or two, but children as much as adults need dependable gear. The solution for many families is to make their own.

Clothing and footwear are most important, not just to protect the child from the weather but to make them feel comfortable. The same principles for clothing outlined in Chapter 15 apply to children. Like their parents they need a flexible set of clothing layers. Waterproof rainwear is essential and warm clothing should be light, cosy and fast-drying. Fibrepile is possibly the perfect children's wear fabric. Good hats, mitts, gloves and socks are a must for winter trips. It may take some legwork to track down high quality fabrics, but that's the key to making children's outfits durable and functional. Proper walking boots are virtually impossible to obtain for children until they are near their teens, so often it's a question of making do with well-fitting training shoes or joggers.

A simple, child's sleeping bag is easy to make using lightweight fabrics and a good synthetic fill. Different styles will suit different ages, but most children don't like the feel of a hood and are better off wearing a hat to keep that area warm. Rucksacks are not as simple to stitch together on the family sewing machine, but fortunately they are more widely available in styles that can be adapted to suit small children. Daypacks of various sizes work well, and when the young pack-carrier begins to carry more substantial loads there are many rucksacks with adjustable back lengths so that the right distance between shoulder straps and the hip belt can be maintained.

Parents carrying babies and infants have a range of options. When a baby is only a few months old they can be quite comfortably transported in a sling that holds the baby against the parent's chest. Then there is a choice of papoose-style carriers which usually have rigid alloy frames and padded shoulder straps and hip belts. It pays to test drive these carriers in the store with your live cargo. Some versions can be stood on the ground, which makes them useful for feeding and rest stops, although children should not be left unattended in carriers.

PART 3
OUTDOOR EQUIPMENT

BUYING OUTDOOR GEAR

In the bush one's needs are relatively few, also there is a limit to what can be carried in a rucksack. The gear you take has to be strong and functional. Even though it is only a means to an end, there is much satisfaction in using well-made equipment. In the wild you work with your gear day after day and you learn to value the tools that perform well, and last.

Initially the task of buying the equipment you need can seem daunting – a gear list can include up to a hundred separate items. Given the increasing specialisation and technical nature of outdoor gear, it is rare these days for those starting out to buy all that is needed in a single visit to an equipment store. Making informed choices takes time, and good quality gear is expensive.

For most people the solution is to spread major equipment purchases over at least a year or two. During this time it makes sense to rent or borrow some of the more costly items. This gives the opportunity to assess your needs. Equipment is a favourite topic of conversation in the bush and fellow travellers are usually the most reliable source of advice about gear. Many stores hire out packs, tents, stoves and sleeping bags, as well as more technical hardware like skis and canoes. Few go to the extent of offering footwear or clothing for rental and, in any case, these are generally considered the best items to buy first.

WHERE TO BUY?

Shops that specialise in equipment for the rucksack sports offer not only the best choice of quality brands but are also often owned and staffed by people involved in outdoor activities. The advice they give is usually based on first-hand experience in the field and they are only too willing to share their ideas. Naturally each store will have particular brands they promote, but if you shop around then comparisons can be easily made.

Other traditional suppliers of outdoor gear include army surplus and disposal stores. There are bargains to be found in these stores and a few may carry more reputable equipment brands – along with some pretty unsavoury 'military' paraphernalia. They are probably best known as a source of heavy duty outdoor clothing, like woollen pants and cotton shirts. These stores are somewhat disorganised and the staff have little appreciation of what is needed in the bush, so finding what you want is not easy. More mainstream department stores and discount chains usually have a camping section but it's rare to find any quality lines, and even harder to get good advice.

Mail order is a worthwhile alternative if there is no specialist backpacking store in your area. Most of the larger retailers offer a mail order service and have detailed catalogues that can be sent upon request. Buying by mail order works best if you have a good general knowledge of the gear and a store you like dealing with. Many stores are happy to exchange items that don't prove to be the right size, colour or style, but the postage costs can soon mount up. Obviously there is nothing quite like making direct comparisons 'in the flesh'.

Second-hand gear is widely available through the club network. Often there is nothing wrong with what is sold second-hand – many people just want to update or upgrade their gear. Some groups also arrange special days when used gear can be swapped or purchased. It is also worth keeping an eye on shop or club noticeboards for gear bargains.

WHAT TO SPEND?

Outdoor gear is one of the last refuges of solid, hard-wearing products. In this disposable age, it is refreshing to find items that are designed and built to last a lifetime, for example, a good sleeping bag can keep for twenty years or more, while most packs and tents should give a decade of reliable service.

When shopping for outdoor gear look for brands that have proven themselves over the years, and are recommended by specialist backpacking retailers. Cheap imitations are often a false economy in the long run. The better brands will cost more, but in return you will usually have a product that has been constructed with pride and is backed by a guarantee.

While it is worth seeking out quality brands, that doesn't mean the most expensive items are the best. In every equipment category there is a range of models, including flagships, loaded with features to justify a high price tag. These are the jackets with multiple pockets, flaps and zips, and the rucksacks with countless compartments and straps. In most instances the 'bells and whistles' are unnecessary and simply mean more moving parts or things to go wrong.

Canny buyers of outdoor gear know that even the best stores have end of season sales. Likewise most shops regularly have discontinued lines at reduced prices. All manufacturers have seconds – items with minor cosmetic flaws – which are sold through factory outlets and some stores. Substantial savings can be made if you shop around.

Ultimately, what you outlay on gear should reflect the kind of activities you plan on pursuing. Expedition-style equipment is overkill for occasional weekend outings. Likewise, there is no point in forking out for costly hardware if you are unsure whether the outdoors will be a lifetime passion, or a one-year fling. Wherever possible wait until your future directions are clear.

There are alternatives that help to keep the total expenditure to a minimum. For many activities an economical synthetic sleeping bag is more than adequate, as is rainwear that's waterproof but with no pretensions of being able to breathe. You should never compromise on some items like footwear, but with judicious buying there's no reason why you can't kit yourself out for less than many people spend on a resort holiday.

One final option is to make your own gear. If you enjoy tinkering and are handy with a sewing machine, this can be an inexpensive solution for many equipment needs. The key is finding quality fabrics and components. Larger outdoor stores generally carry suitable fabrics, including ripstop nylons, Cordura and canvas, as well as an assortment of buckles, velcro and webbing. Sailmakers and workshops that make canvas awnings are other good sources of materials. Start out with simple items like flysheets, stuffsacks and inner sheets before attempting anything more elaborate. If you have access to an industrial sewing machine, then making packs and gaiters are further possibilities. Some companies also sell kits for gear which you can sew yourself. Check magazines for details.

CRITERIA

Anything you carry on your back has to justify its weight. Every gram saved makes wearing a pack less of a chore. So when purchasing equipment, weight is a major consideration. This may seem obvious with big items like tents and sleeping bags, but it applies to all gear from accessories through to the rucksack itself, many of which are heavy even without a load.

Look for equipment whose design has the strength of simplicity. Added features must be of real practical benefit for your chosen activity, otherwise they just add weight and increase the chance of equipment failure in the field. Durability is perhaps the most important aspect of gear selection. Pay special attention to construction details, like evenness of stitching and reinforcement at stress points.

Finally, personal factors come into play. Some people are by temperament more adept at making lightweight gear survive the trials of the bush while others need sturdier gear. The best equipment allows you to enjoy the outdoors with a minimum of fuss.

14

FOOTWEAR

Long gone are the days when it was deemed necessary to wear most of a cow hide on each foot, in the form of heavy leather walking boots with wide stitched welts and stiff mid-soles. There are still grizzled veterans who swear by their 3.5 kg (8 lb) stompers, on the grounds that nothing else stands up to the rough and tumble of bush-bashing, but in an age of more discerning attitudes, people are voting with their feet for boots that are kinder to their toes and the trails they walk on. The big beefy boots have returned from whence they came – out to pasture.

This shift in interest coincided with marked improvements in boot construction and the adaptation of running shoe design to more rugged outdoor needs. A decade ago lightweight boots emerged with combination fabric and leather uppers and at the same time a rash of chunky joggers started to appear in the windows of equipment shops. For a while it seemed that the classic, handcrafted European walking footwear was lost to posterity, but recently the pendulum has swung back in favour of light boots with all-leather uppers for serious back-country use.

As a result there is now a much wider range of outdoor footwear to choose from. This is just as well, for few items of gear exert as much influence on a trip as what's on your feet. Heavy boots make long walks a drudgery. The old chestnut 'a pound on your feet is worth five on your back' still holds true. Ill-fitting boots are even worse, making every kilometre a misery and causing blisters, the bane of bushwalkers. In the city, dud footwear is an irritation; in the bush it can render you immobile and jeopardise everything.

COMFORT

The three most important attributes of footwear are comfort, fit and more comfort. While the new profusion of walking boots, with their brash colours and features, may offend purists who would have us all wearing standard issue, army-style clodhoppers, the simple increase in styles means that there is a better chance of finding something to suit your feet. If there is one consistent point about feet, it's that most people believe theirs are somehow different.

Yet comfort goes beyond locating shoes that conform, by happy coincidence, to your foot shape. A good boot needs to offer protection from sharp stones, sticks and spiky undergrowth. It should cushion you on hard, jarring surfaces and for sudden landings. It also has to grip on steep and slippery ground. When carrying a pack in jumbled terrain you require stability and ankle support. A good boot helps keep out rain, mud and snow; it will insulate when necessary, yet still breathe and be fast-drying. A good boot will go the distance.

You might think that footwear with all these credentials is an impossible dream, but such boots do exist, albeit at a price. Some people are not prepared to fork out for premium boots, and so look for a compromise. Others are content to wander about in a pair of tennis shoes and make up for their deficiencies by developing tough ankles, living with wet feet, and, most of all, walking with special care and precision.

At some stage choosing footwear comes down to the purely personal and subjective: what 'feels' right for you. But before jumping to conclusions it's wise to assess your needs, evaluate what styles are available, and try on as many as you can. To make sense of the comparisons it's important to have an understanding of how footwear is put together.

DESIGN AND CONSTRUCTION

In general terms footwear has three parts: the sole, the mid-sole and the upper. The materials used and the way in which the components are assembled largely determines the life and performance of a boot or shoe.

Sole

This is the most obvious feature and perhaps the easiest to judge. The traditional deep-lugged Vibram sole is still found on some hefty mountain boots. Though sturdy and hardwearing, this pattern chews up trails and retains mud and stones between its lugs, which means more weight to carry around. This sole has been replaced by a host of new designs that have more open and shallower tread patterns which are lighter and shed mud. Likewise, shoes from the makers of running footwear come in an array of sole configurations, each supposedly conferring special properties to the shoe in question.

It's not worth fretting over these claims. Just look for a sole pattern that gives good grip and is comfortable underfoot. The harder the sole rubber the more durable it will most likely be. Conversely, softer rubber generally means better grip. If this is high on your list of priorities, some manufacturers now also offer walking footwear which uses the same 'sticky' rubber employed in rock-climbing shoes.

Mid-sole

This is the structural heart of the boot: the platform responsible for support, cushioning and flex. In older style boots with stitched welts, the mid-sole included one or more layers of leather. The great majority of lightweight walking shoes and boots now use mid-soles made from EVA (ethylene vinyl acetate) or a form of micro-porous foam rubber. Stiffer, more robust boots with leather uppers commonly have a nylon mid-sole, graded to the size of the boot.

Within the mid-sole there's normally a steel shank to ensure that the boot flexes at the ball of the foot and not under the arch. On top of the mid-sole there may be a leather or fibre board deck. Over that sits a removable insole or footbed made from a light foam and shaped to the foot.

Upper

The prime function of the upper is to comfortably cradle the foot. Classic walking boots have single piece leather uppers that have been carefully lasted to the foot shape. The absence of seams, except for a backstay at the heel, makes the boot durable and minimises the opportunity for water to enter through stitching. This is still the favoured type of boot for rugged off-trail walking, but they are expensive.

Uppers that combine panels of Cordura-style nylon with leather patches at critical points have their own merits, including a lower price tag. They are usually lighter and more able to breathe. Being more flexible, these uppers are also easier to break in. Careful design of the panels also allows the upper to be shaped to the foot. The main drawbacks are the extra seams that are exposed to abrasion and vulnerable in the wet, unless the boot has a waterproof liner that breathes.

The upper has to protect the foot with a reinforced toe section and a firm heel counter to prevent the upper from distorting. Most boots have some form of lining to provide a smooth, soft contact surface with the foot and help the boot keep its shape. This is traditionally a supple calf leather or a fabric like Cambrelle which has the advantage of being more able to breathe and faster drying. The collar at the top of the boot should be padded out of kindness to your tendons, and should fit snugly around the ankle to keep out stones. Likewise, the better tongues are padded and attached to the boot with gussets that prevent snow, sticks and gravel from entering. Lacing systems vary, though it's popular to have a set of eyelets or D-rings lower down, with hooks for the top of the boot.

Construction

The way the sole, mid-sole and upper are joined together greatly affects the performance of a boot. A few years ago the orthodox view was that for a boot to last it had to be stitched together in a heavy welted construction. A glued or cemented boot was a bit of a gamble, especially in wet environments. Now, thanks to dramatic advances in the way that differing materials can be permanently bonded, stitched welts are becoming the exception.

For the record, there are two main methods of constructing a stitched welt. The sturdiest is probably the Norwegian welt, where one row of stitching angles inward to sew the insole to the upper, and an outer row of stitching joins the upper and the mid-sole. With the Littleway welt the upper is folded under, between the insole and the mid-sole, and stitched on the inside. A similar technique is still quite common on the better European walking boots where the upper is sewn as well as glued to the nylon mid-sole.

Now, however, most outdoor footwear is simply bonded together. This saves weight and cost. Doing away with welts eliminates the vulnerability of

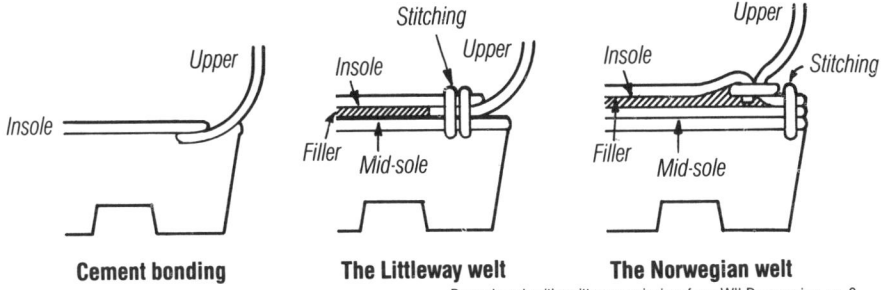

FOOTWEAR

Cement bonding   **The Littleway welt**   **The Norwegian welt**

Reproduced, with written permission, from WILD magazine, no. 8

external stitching to wear and water penetration. Most beneficial of all, it produces a neater boot with a trim profile for nimble footwork.

SHOES

Within the walking and climbing fraternity there have always been those who are happier with a pair of shoes on their feet. Even before the influx of high-tech running footwear the humble sandshoe was often worn in preference to boots. The sandshoe was light, cheap and kept you in touch with the earth. All the same they were often worn more as a badge of defiance; a snub to the exotic, imported boots.

This debate has been long since overtaken by the fashion for wearing sports shoes almost everywhere. Basic tennis shoes are still popular for the outdoors, as are many mainstream running shoes, but some models are just too light and flimsy for walking with a pack. Others cost so much you wouldn't dare get them scuffed or dirty.

More practical are the purpose-built shoes for walkers. These borrow heavily from athletic shoe technology but they are much sturdier. Instead of light mesh fabrics they use tough Cordura nylons, with leather reinforcing at the toe and heel. The soles are thicker with lugs for traction, and have high toe rands to protect against

A lightweight shoe suitable for trail walking

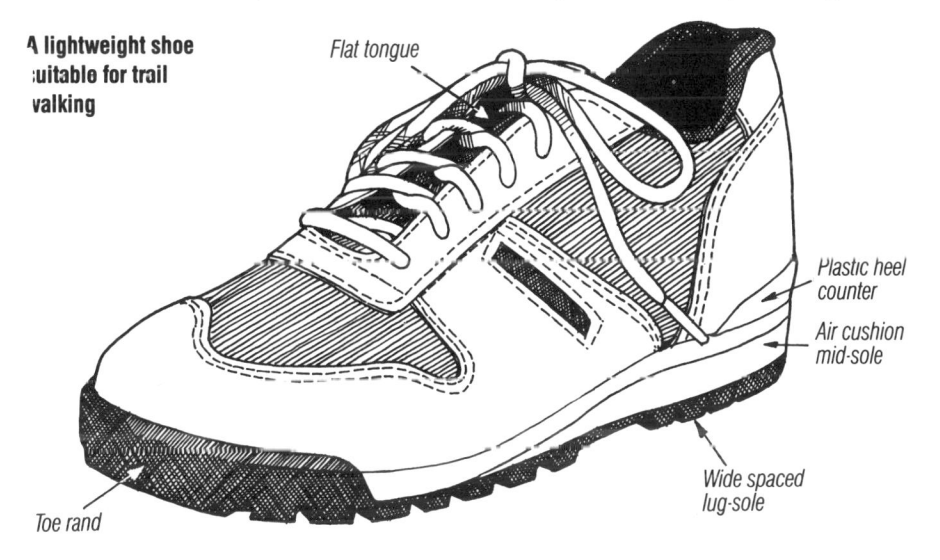

knocks. Uppers are firmer and better padded. These lightweight shoes are ideal for daywalking on trails, and are also popular for use on mountaineering approach marches.

Another category of shoes has emerged with the advent of 'power walking' as a form of aerobic exercise. These have light leather uppers and all the looks of a casual shoe, but boast more supportive insoles and improved flex and cushioning. Though undoubtedly comfortable, they are too dainty for anything more than padding around town or strolling with the dog.

Many legendary makers of bushwalking and mountaineering boots now also offer a line of shoes. These too have the familiar fabric/leather upper, but the craftskill and rugged build reflects a quite different pedigree. In most cases they are cut-down versions of a boot design, with the same heavy-duty sole and stiffer midsole. Such shoes are chosen for their durability and quality feel. They perform well on treks and in more punishing terrain.

On the right feet a good pair of shoes can venture almost anywhere that boots dare go. They are lighter and more responsive – your foot enjoys greater freedom and flexibility. Shoes are versatile, too. A pair of heavy boots can languish in the cupboard for most of the year, while shoes tend to be used in between trips.

LIGHTWEIGHT FABRIC BOOTS

For some people shoes simply don't offer enough support and protection – they hanker after the security of footwear that extends above the ankle. If you have accident-prone joints or are shouldering a big pack in difficult country, boots are more than justified, but it's fair to say that the need for boots is sometimes more perceived than real.

The lightest boots also exploit

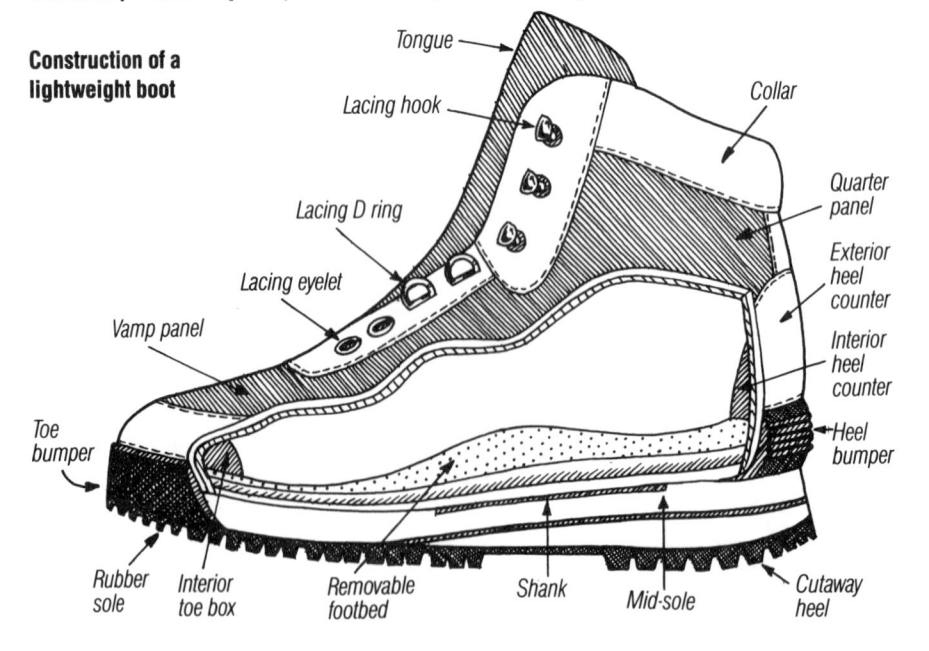

Construction of a lightweight boot

Labels: Tongue, Lacing hook, Collar, Lacing D ring, Quarter panel, Exterior heel counter, Lacing eyelet, Interior heel counter, Vamp panel, Toe bumper, Heel bumper, Rubber sole, Interior toe box, Removable footbed, Shank, Mid-sole, Cutaway heel

Leather boots are hard-wearing, waterproof and offer protection to the foot

running shoe technology with foam mid-soles and fabric panels, but are cut higher to cover the ankle. In the better models the foot is well-supported by a heel counter, with an additional plastic stabiliser mounted at the base to prevent the boot from rolling and losing its shape. The ankle area is normally reinforced with a leather wrap which can be snugly laced.

These boots, like the shoes of the same format, are supple and easy to wear. They are fine for established paths and general bushwalking. Indeed, they are often better engineered and more durable than a cheap pair of leather boots, but in the eyes of some people they are not stout enough for prolonged back-country wear.

LEATHER BOOTS

The latest generation of leather walking boots are not much heavier than the running shoe inspired lightweights. The major difference is in the increased stiffness of the upper and sole, and the protection that this affords.

In a quality boot the leather used for the upper is 2-3 mm (approximately $1/10$ in) thick and has been kept on the last long enough for the boot to retain its shape for many years. Unlike combination fabric/leather boots which flex freely all around the foot, a leather boot tends to encase the foot and bends only where it needs to. The sole is typically a single-piece moulded rubber format which is bonded to a nylon mid-sole.

All of this translates into a firmer, more stable ride. This is invaluable when carrying heavy loads up steep and rocky slopes. Leather boots are also harder-wearing and more weatherproof in snow and the wet. For mountain walking many people would not use anything else.

Leather walking boots with stitched welts, though less common, are far from extinct. In Europe and elsewhere they are still *de rigueur* for alpine treks where crampons may be needed.

A word about leather

There's leather and there's leather. After tanning, cow's hide is split into layers – the outer layer, the side the cow wore exposed to the elements, is called top-grain leather. This is naturally strong, resilient and waterproof. As such, it is the best leather for walking boots. The other layers are known as split-grain leathers and have a suede look on both sides. The better split-grains are still quite serviceable and are often employed in lightweight fabric/leather walking footwear.

ACCESSORIES

Socks

Good socks keep your feet warm, padded and comfortable. While there are no rules about which socks to wear, or how many, there is some empirical evidence.

By far the most popular socks are knitted in a plush pile with at least 50 per cent wool content. Some synthetic fibre (normally nylon or rayon) improves the durability of the sock, but it's the wool that provides the warmth and the essential wicking ability.

One pair of good socks is usually adequate when wearing light boots or shoes. For stiff leather boots a second thinner pair is often worn underneath to help minimise rubbing and blisters. Many other permutations are possible, including none at all. Trial and error will reveal what your feet enjoy the most.

Several specialist socks are now available. These include thick winter socks made from wool blends incorporating Hollofil, Thinsulate and other such insulations. Other styles are available in warm, wicking materials like polypropylene and Hydrofil, as well as tape-sealed Gore-Tex socks for the wet.

Whatever socks you choose, it's important to keep them clean and to carry some spare pairs.

Gaiters

If you only ever intend travelling along manicured paths gaiters are not necessary, but for walking through snow, mud and any type of scrub, gaiters are one of the best things invented.

In their simplest form gaiters are short tubes of fabric, with elastic top

Gaiters provide protection to the legs when walking through snow, mud and the bush

BUYING FOOTWEAR

- Try on as many different pairs of boots and shoes as possible. (Wear the socks you plan to use.) Getting the right fit can take time. Be aware that many top brands offer boots in differing widths and in models specifically lasted for the female foot. Look for the lightest footwear you think will do the job.

- Check for length. Before lacing up, shift your foot to the front of the boot. If one finger fits snugly behind the heel, the length is normally good; any more, and the boot is too big. With the boots laced, your toes should be a thumb's width back from the front of the boot.

- Check for width. A good fit will have ample toe room and hold the ball of your foot firm. Any undue sideways movement means that the boot is too wide. All boots will 'give' a little in width after use.

- Check for depth. Can you wiggle your toes up and down? Watch out for excessive pressure on the instep.

- Check for heel lift by climbing up and down stairs or doing a few knee bends. Some slight heel movement is to be expected, but nothing more than about 3 mm ($1/10$ in).

- Feel the shape. Are there any points that might rub and cause blisters later?

- Spend time walking around the store: take as long as you like. (Some stores may even allow you to take the boots for a test drive on the carpet at home.)

- Buy what feels most comfortable. All other factors — durability, weatherproofness, looks, etc — are secondary. If in doubt, don't buy.

and bottom, that slip over the top of your boot. Such puttees keep out the small stones and grass seeds that intrude into boots at inopportune moments.

More substantial and more common are the calf length gaiters made from canvas, nylon or Gore-Tex. These seal lower on the boot and are held in place by a strap under the boot. They normally have a full-length zip or snap and velcro closure for ease of use. This style of gaiter deflects rain and debris, as well as helping defend against snake bite.

The ultimate in gaiter protection encloses the boot completely and has a snug fitting rubber rand that seals around the sole. These 'Yeti' gaiters were designed by Berghaus to protect boots and their wearers from damp boggy ground and deep snow. The vulnerability of the rand to abrasion limits their use, but the Yetis are unsurpassed in the wet and the lined versions are standard equipment on mountaineering expeditions.

Other footwear

There's a lot to be said for carrying something light to wear at the end of a long day in boots. A pair of thongs, sandals, slippers or featherweight runners will give your feet a break, allow them to air and at the same time do a favour for heavily tramped campsites. In winter a pair of down or synthetic-filled hut booties can seem like heaven, especially if your digits have been cramped and cold all day in ski boots.

TAKING CARE OF YOUR FOOTWEAR

Any walking boot or shoe needs some breaking in. With lightweight fabric/leather footwear it may only take an hour or so. Solid leather boots can take several days to break in; do this in gradual stages by taking short walks or wearing the boots around the home. One solution for very stiff boots is to saturate them with water and walk around for a few hours until they dry and take the shape of your foot.

At the end of a day's walking give your boots a quick clean and leave them to air. Never dry boots by a campfire or expose them to any severe heat. This cracks and shrinks leather, and may cause the sole, mid-sole and upper to separate.

After a trip, make sure that boots are cleaned, dried and stored in a dry place. Leather boots should be treated with a silicone-based waterproofing compound which conditions the leather. Avoid oily preparations that cause the leather to stretch and the boot to lose its shape. Combination fabric/leather footwear should be scrubbed clean and a silicone spray can be applied to enhance the boot's water repellency, though this is a temporary measure at best.

With even little amount of maintenance good boots will last many years and take care of your feet in all terrains and weather. Of all outdoor equipment they become entwined with the memories of miles covered and hard ground won.

TAKING CARE OF YOUR FEET

- The best way to take care of your feet is to give them time to adjust to the demands of walking and the shape of your boots. Even the toughest feet will become sore in unfamiliar footwear. Work up to long trips with a series of shorter walks.

- On the trail, respond quickly to any sign of soreness or rubbing by covering the affected area with a strip of adhesive plaster or moleskin. (For more on blisters see Chapter 7, *First Aid and Survival*.)

- Keep your feet as dry and clean as possible. Change your socks regularly. Take time to bathe and massage feet at the end of the day.

15

CLOTHING

Evolution has not helped us weather the outdoors. Our bodies perform best in a narrow temperature range and even slight fluctuations can throw us out of kilter. We cannot endure extremes of wind, cold, rain and heat for any length of time. Nor does the human hide afford much defence against nature's harsher facets. Unlike other creatures, we require a collection of garments to counter the elements and maintain a comfortable personal climate.

In fine, mild conditions one's clothing needs are minimal. For many outdoor pastimes a light shirt and pair of shorts are ideal, with a jumper and rainjacket just in case. Mostly, you can get by with hard-wearing, everyday clothes, but there will come times when more specialised attire is called for. If wild weather sets in, clothing is relied on for protection as much as comfort. On extended trips into remote wilderness or mountain areas what you wear can be a matter of survival.

FUNCTIONAL LAYERING

In these circumstances each garment has to be highly functional and perform in unison with other garments as a complete outfit. The familiar practice of wearing a number of clothing layers is thus refined to a fine art. The underlying principle is that several thin layers are more versatile than a single thick one. Outdoor clothing is usually seen in terms of three layers: underwear to keep the skin surface dry and comfortable; insulation to provide increasing degrees of warmth; and shellwear to keep out wind, rain and snow. To this triad should also be added a fourth more general purpose layer of shirts, pants and shorts or skirts.

Recent advances in fabrics and garment design have greatly improved the utility of these layers. Just a few years ago the only sources of bush clobber were 'op shops' and army surplus stores. Now it's possible to buy garments that fulfil the layering roles but are more durable, lighter in weight, faster drying and much easier to care for than ordinary clothing. Whole ensembles are designed around specific activities to ensure freedom of movement and the right mix of insulation, moisture transfer and ventilation.

Outdoor clothing has come of age and entered the orbit of mainstream fashion. While arch traditionalists look upon the tutti-frutti colours and bewildering price tags with a jaundiced eye, the practical benefits of the new generation apparel are undeniable.

FIBRES AND FABRICS

The impetus for this change has come from the ingenious application of synthetic fibres. The vast sportswear industry has spawned a host of new fabrics with excellent characteristics for use in the wilds. While conventional materials have been pushed to the sidelines, many loyal followers still prefer the feel of natural fibres and are more at ease in clothing that doesn't have a petro-chemical heritage.

Natural fibres

Wool is the classic material for outdoor wear. It's durable, warm and retains much of its insulation value when damp, but a wet woollen garment is heavy and slow to dry. Wool also tends to be scratchy and irritating against the skin. In contrast *cotton* has a soft, natural feel. It's ability to soak up moisture and cool by evaporation makes cotton the preferred cloth for summer shirts and shorts, yet this feature is a serious liability in cold weather.

Silk has long been used in underwear. It's light, supple and surprisingly strong. Silk also traps warmth and stays warm when wet, but the fabric is expensive and needs to to be washed with care. For the same reasons that *down* is still the favoured insulation in sleeping bags, it has retained its popularity in clothing for extreme cold. Though bulky to wear, down garments are extremely light and pack away into a tiny bundle. Down however is virtually useless when wet.

Synthetics

Of the synthetics, *polypropylene* has been widely accepted as a material for underwear. Its fibres are hydrophobic – which means that they refuse to absorb water. A polypropylene garment thus wicks moisture away from the skin with great efficiency, and dry skin is warm skin. *Chlorofibre* shares many of the virtues and drawbacks of polypropylene but being constructed with a thicker, brushed inner surface it offers greater insulation.

A more versatile fibre is *polyester*. It's strong, hard-wearing, easy to clean and will not shrink. In its latest incarnations polyester makes excellent underwear. There are intricate polyester knits which transport moisture away from the skin by capillary action. In other formats it is chemically treated so that moisture rapidly disperses and evaporates from the fabric.

Polyester is also constructed into thicker insulating materials. Conventional *fibrepile* has a dense inner layer of fluffy fibres attached to a knitted backing. Recent variations include *fleece* which uses finer fibres to create a plusher feel, and *Polarplus* which is a double-sided pile, that doesn't pill like its predecessors. *Polarlite* is simply a lightweight version of Polarplus.

When more insulation is required synthetic fills like *Hollofil* and *Quallofil* (see Chapter 16, *Sleeping Bags*) are often employed as a substitute for down. Both offer superior warmth when wet but are heavier and bulkier than down. There are also a number of micro-fibre insulations, the best known being *Thinsulate*. These rely on a bonded mass of fine fibres to create a vast surface area and trap more warm air for a given thickness of insulation. In simple terms, this means more warmth for less bulk.

Nylon is used extensively for outdoor wear. Even the lighter weight nylon fabrics are tough, hard-wearing and quick to dry. Traditionally, nylon has been used for shell garments and was a noisy cloth with a cool, clammy feel, but with refinements in yarns and weaves it has become much better natured and now performs a multitude of roles.

Taffeta is a plain weave nylon which is soft and supple with a slick, shiny surface. *Ripstop* has thicker reinforcing threads woven lengthwise and crosswise into the cloth at regular intervals. This helps prevent tears from spreading and gives ripstop its unmistakable chequerboard appearance. *Taslan* is a strong, abrasion-resistant nylon with a rougher, more natural feel – the result of the yarns being treated by a blast of air. *Tactel* is similarly treated, but uses very fine yarns in a dense weave to produce a soft, supple cloth which has the feel and look of cotton.

There is also a legion of fabrics using blends of different fibres and yarns. As well as the ubiquitous polyester/cottons for general purpose garments, there are cotton/nylons for wind shells, wool/nylons for socks, and innumerable fabrics that use either Lycra or Spandex for active sportswear.

UNDERWEAR

On warm days you probably need only the kind of underclothes you would normally wear at home, but in cold, fickle weather more specialised garments are invaluable. For outdoor use the term underwear takes on a broad meaning. It encompasses a range of light shirts and pants that can be worn on their own or under other layers.

Moisture is ever-present in the outdoors, in the form of perspiration caused by exercise, condensation from outer garments, and damp, humid air. The prime function of underwear is to deal with this moisture and prevent the chilling effects of wearing clammy clothing, especially at rest stops. The best underwear both absorbs sweat and transports it rapidly out through the garment, where it can evaporate or be taken further by other layers.

Underwear's secondary role is to provide insulation. Most modern underwear fabrics are made from fibres with low thermal conductivity. In other words the garments feel warm while being worn, and by keeping the body dry they also minimise heat loss caused by evaporation. For additional insulation, some versions have a dense brushed surface which traps warm air.

Comfort, however, is more than dry skin. For underwear to make the grade the fabric has to have a soft, pleasant feel against the body. Garments need to stretch or be shaped for freedom of movement, and they should be hard-wearing enough to be worn for days at a time and used alone as a light layer for active wear.

Most underwear is available as long and short sleeved crew neck tops, long john pants and assorted polo neck skivvies. The style you choose will depend on the activities and climates you enter into, although most people usually end up buying a couple of sets. Crew necks are good for moderate conditions. Higher necks keep out the winter cold, but when you're working hard it's important to have a collar that opens for ventilation. A popular combination when on the move is one or more shirts on top and long johns under a pair of shorts. This works in all but extreme conditions, and when you stop you can pull on light shell garments to block out the wind.

Stretchy, body-hugging fabrics are better for strenuous activities like skiing and cycling, where a garment's wicking ability is paramount. Light, fast-drying polypropylene underwear has been dominant in this category, but the garments do not wear well and the hydrophobic properties makes rinsing out body salts and oils difficult. Polypropylene also shrinks alarmingly when washed or dried at high temperatures. Increasingly popular is underwear made from lightweight Polartek and Drytech which is much easier to care for, and has an impressive wicking performance.

For more severe cold, and less energetic activities, Chlorofibre and the thicker weights of Polartek are probably the most popular fabrics. These styles have a looser cut to allow the fabric to loft. A roomy fit also makes a garment easier to ventilate and more versatile when worn on its own.

INSULATION

Maintaining a balance between the body's heat production and heat loss can seem a complicated business. You start the day rugged up, then peel off layers as you warm up, only to fling them back on when you stop for lunch or a rest break. Instead of one heavy coat that gives you only two options – on or off – it's important to have several light insulating garments that can be manipulated to keep you comfortably warm.

Taken to extremes, this could mean stopping every few strides to fidget with your clothes. More likely, you will find individual garments with a tolerance for varying conditions. Some materials have the ability to breathe and release surplus heat, or the garment design may allow for ventilation to regulate warmth. It's important to distinguish between pure cold and windchill. To keep warm you may need only to slip on a windbreaker rather than adding thicker layers.

The most versatile insulating garments used in the outdoors are made from fibrepile. They are lightweight, soft to wear, and offer the same warmth as wool for around half the weight. Best of all, they are warm when wet and retain very little moisture. A saturated pile garment can be wrung out and worn straight away, and fibrepile jackets stay comfortable in a wide temperature range. As the tempo of

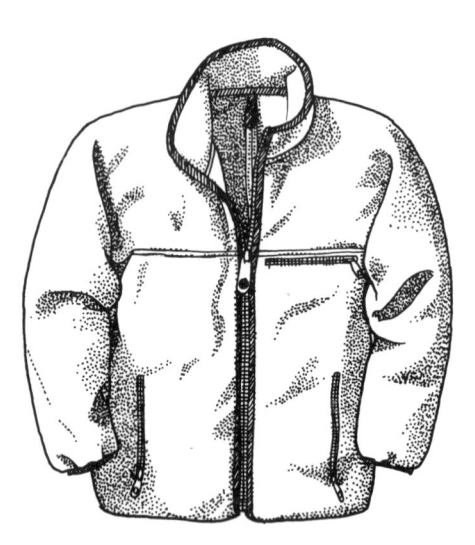

A fibrepile jacket is lightweight, warm and retains very little moisture

activity changes, a full-length zip allows you to adjust airflow through the garment. Though fibrepile's insulation value is affected even by light breezes, by adding a basic windproof outer you have a potent combination. Fibrepile is also fashioned into pullovers, vests and pants, the latter being excellent for snowcamping but usually too hot for active wear.

The nearest equivalent for general purpose warmth is a woollen shirt or pullover. A wool garment can be more windproof and pack down smaller than fibrepile, but wool needs careful handling and is heavier, particularly when wet. Yet many stalwart outdoor people would not be separated from their checked wool shirts. Aside from sentiment if you're on a tight budget it's better to use existing woollen pullovers and spend any spare money on good underwear and shellwear.

When the temperature and your exercise rate drop you need clothing that keeps a dense layer of warm air snug against the body. Padded jackets are the popular answer to winter cold but they are cumbersome to wear. A vest is often a better layering garment — it insulates the critical torso area but leaves your arms free to be active, an important consideration for skiing and climbing. Unlike heavy jackets vests are more easily worn with underwear and fibrepile, or under a shell garment.

Micro-fibre insulations perform well in a niche between the flexible warmth of fibrepile and the full-on heat of a down jacket. Their low bulk suits light, close-fitting garments like vests and pullovers which are also easily ventilated if required. The fill is normally enclosed in a windproof outer shell that sheds snow and drizzle.

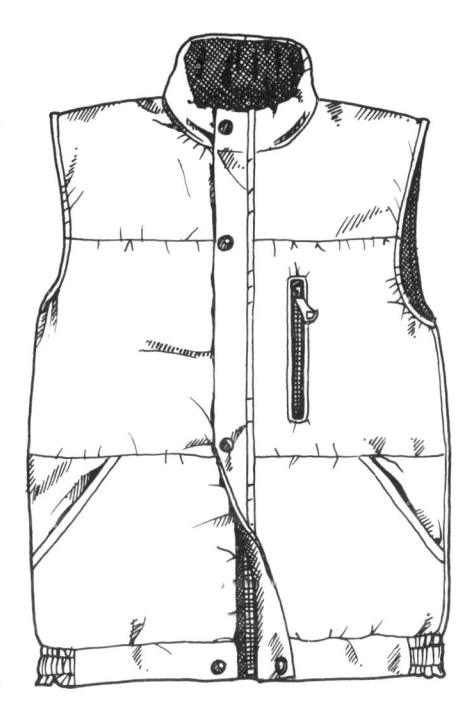

A padded vest is an ideal layering garment as it insulates the torso but keeps your arms free for movement

For the extreme dry cold of high altitude and low latitudes the ultimate defence is a thick down-filled expedition duvet with hood. The most advanced down garments have the same features to restrict heat loss as are used in technical sleeping bags. To protect the down against moisture the outer shell is usually a waterproof/breathable fabric like Gore-Tex.

RAINWEAR

A rainjacket is the most important outdoor wear item of clothing. When conditions are at their worst your comfort and safety can depend on having a barrier against lashing wind, rain and snow.

Waterproof fabrics

The first duty of shellwear is to be waterproof. For this you need garments made from a durable, proofed fabric. The traditional cloth was an oiled japara. Then came garments in dry japara – a polyester/cotton fabric with a thin coating of polyurethane. These were lighter and did away with the unpleasant oily smell and feel of the old japaras, but neither version is particularly waterproof, and both cloths are easily torn and abraded.

A tougher, more impervious option is a proofed nylon. This is usually coated with several layers of polyurethane or a thin skin of neoprene rubber. Both of these proofings deteriorate with wear and will eventually peel off. Hypalon is much more durable and waterproof; this rugged elastomer coating is waterproof to 1170 kPa (170 lb per sq in) – nearly 10 times that of other proofings.

The main handicap of these compounds is that they are just as efficient at keeping water in as keeping it out. Condensation is trapped within the garment, and the inner layers and the wearer are destined to become increasingly damp. The answer is a fabric which is both waterproof and breathable, by virtue of a micro-porous membrane or coating.

Gore-Tex is the most celebrated of these materials. It consists of a thin membrane derived from Teflon which has 3½ billion pores per sq cm (9 billion pores per sq in). These holes are large enough to allow water vapour to pass out, but too small to prevent liquid water droplets from entering in. This membrane is normally laminated between a tough outer fabric and a tricot knit liner. Gore-Tex performs well in most conditions, but if you're using it in humid climates or during vigorous exercise the membrane may not be able to cope with the rate of vapour transmission needed.

While Gore-Tex remains the material with the best combination of waterproofness and the ability to breathe, a range of alternatives are now available. Some, like Sympatex, use a similar membrane, while Entrant and many others use coatings impregnated into the fabric. These coatings are heat treated to form a honeycomb of holes less than 2 microns in diameter that

A waterproof rainjacket is an essential article of clothing when outdoor conditions are at their worst

prevent the passage of water but allow vapour to escape.

A key feature of the latest rainwear fabrics is an outer finish to repel moisture. The latest compounds are normally tagged Durable Water Repellency (DWR). As the name implies, these treatments have a much longer life than silicone-based sprays. DWR treatments encourage water to bead up and run off the fabric.

Shellwear design

Waterproof fabrics and finishes are only half the equation. Shellwear needs to be carefully designed and constructed – every needle hole is a potential leakage point, so the better jackets have minimal seams and avoid seams in shoulder areas which are highly exposed to rain and the pressure of pack straps. These days the seams on every serious rainwear garment are heat-sealed with tape to prevent water entry.

It's not as easy to prevent moisture from penetrating the more obvious openings on garments. Zips on jackets and overpants are most vulnerable. To deter wind-driven rain, flaps should overlap the zip inside and out. Even so, in downpours moisture will often wick in across the garment's linings. Cuffs normally have adjustable velcro closures that can be cinched tight. Likewise, the hood on a jacket has to close around the face and have a peaked visor to shield the opening from driving rain. While external pockets should be protected by a broad flap of fabric, it's also useful for pockets to have small drain holes.

Beyond keeping you dry, shellwear has to be sturdily built. A tough,

A windshell anorak is lightweight, breathable and windproof

abrasion-resistant fabric is essential to survive the wear and tear from scrub, rocks and rucksacks. Ease of ventilation is also a concern in steamy weather and during strenuous exercise. Garments should have a loose cut to allow for airflow, and zips with two-way sliders for easy opening. More sophisticated jackets also have zips under the arms or mesh in the pockets to prevent overheating.

Some shell garments are so stiff and ill-fitting that any activity is a struggle. Comfortable outer clothing starts with a soft, supple fabric that is tailored for movement and shifts easily over other clothing. If you have to wear a rainjacket all day small details make life bearable: things like pull tabs for working zip sliders with cold or gloved hands; cord grips to hold drawcords in place; and snug hoods that move with you and don't restrict vision.

Selecting shellwear

When trekking and bushwalking a thigh or knee-length jacket gives the best coverage. With such jackets you can happily sit where you please and there is no need to wear overpants in mild weather. For activities like skiing, canoeing and climbing that involve a lot of bending and dynamic movement shorter jackets and anorak styles are preferred. Cyclists need specialist jackets with long tails and well-cut sleeves that don't bind. In habitually cold, windy environments drawcord waists and hems help seal in warmth and stop jackets from flapping in the breeze. Mountaineering shells are worn for days on end. As well as being stormproof and easy to ventilate they have to accommodate both climbing harnesses and rucksack waist belts. Climbers and skiers also need jackets with several roomy pockets to hold mitts, goggles and a host of other items.

Overpants are essential for protection in wintry conditions and when wearing shorter style tops on rainy days. The simplest pants have a baggy cut with short calf-length zips so that they can be pulled over boots. More elaborate designs have a slimmer, more anatomical shape and full-length side zips so the pants can be put on while wearing skis or mountaineering boots. This arrangement is also used in bib-and-brace style salopettes which stop cold air and snow from getting into gaps between pants and upper garments.

Ultimately the style of rainwear you choose and the material it is made from is a matter of personal assessment. As you weigh up the merits of different garments remember that the aim is clothing that will keep you dry. If you plan on spending long periods in storms and wet weather it's worth investing in specialised garments that employ the latest waterproof fabrics that breathe. But there's no point in being seduced by this expensive technology if your rainwear is destined to spend its days buried at the bottom of your pack, only to emerge for the occasional shower. You'd be better off buying a reliable knockabout jacket and spending what you save on, perhaps, a better pair of boots.

EXTREMITIES

Protection from the elements is particularly critical for your head, feet and hands. A light, floppy hat with a broad brim is imperative in summer. Ideally the same hat will give some shelter from rain as well. The traditional Akubra style bushman's hat is favoured by many walkers but is not as well ventilated as a panama or straw hat. The combination of a scarf and snug peaked cap is better for climbing, cycling and paddling where a wide hat might obscure your vision.

Given the potential for heat loss from the neck and head area a warm hat is an indispensable part of a winter wardrobe. The traditional woollen ski hats and beanies are still seen but Polarplus is a softer, friendlier material for hats. Balaclavas either made of wool, or one of the technical underwear fabrics, are preferred in sub-zero cold. Other variations include peaked skiing caps lined with fibrepile, Thinsulate or an equivalent. Warm scarves don't make much of an appearance in the outdoors. Instead the gap

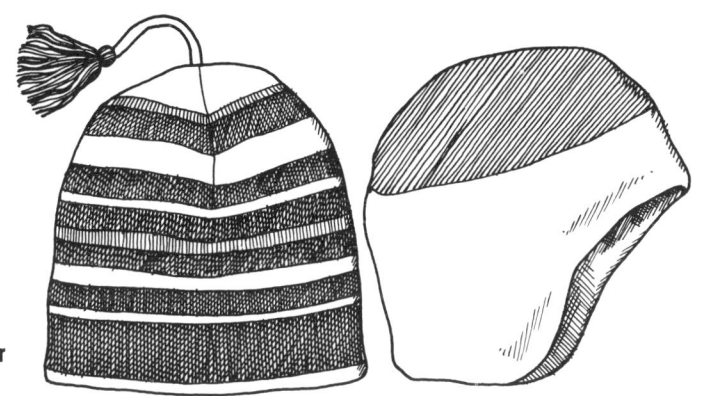

Warm hats are essential for winter activities

between hats and collars can be sealed with a neck gaiter – usually a simple tube of Polarplus fabric.

Gloves are usually needed only in the depths of winter, and even then a medium-weight pair of woollen gloves is usually adequate for bushwalking. Fingerless gloves are quite handy for climbing, camera work and cooking over a stove, but for any activity that takes you above the snowline something more substantial is required. Mittens are more thermally efficient than gloves and the ultimate in woollen mittens are Dachsteins. Even when coated with ice these legendary mitts can still keep your hands warm. They are commonly used in conjunction with a thin liner glove made from a light underwear fabric, and perhaps a waterproof overmitt.

A closer fitting alternative is a

BUYING CLOTHING

- Few people buy a complete outdoor wardrobe in one hit. To begin with you probably need buy only key items like rainwear and underwear. Make do with existing clothes until you have the cash and experience to buy the rest.

- Think in terms of clothing layers, the likely conditions you will encounter, and the degree of protection needed.

- Some manufacturers offer complete clothing ranges with garments that can be zipped together and which have compatible features such as pocket openings and vents.

- Keep in mind how each item will layer with others. There must be ample room under shell garments for insulating layers. Make sure that different fabrics don't grab and bind when layered.

- Take time to try garments on and assess their shape and fit for your chosen activity. Canoeists and climbers need clothes with maximum arm movement. Skiers want flexibility in the legs.

- Look for clothes that you feel comfortable in and which have the versatility to be worn around town as well.

gauntlet style fibrepile mitt with a waterproof outer shell. When dexterity is required for pursuits like skiing and ice climbing a Gore-Tex glove insulated with fibrepile or Thinsulate is usually chosen. The best gloves are anatomically cut with straps that adjust across the back of the hand and wrist for a snug fit.

There is a range of warm, comfortable socks for outdoor activities. Once again a layering approach with a thin lining sock and a thicker insulating sock is best for cold climates. (See Chapter 14, *Footwear*.)

GENERAL CLOTHING

In addition to technical layers a range of multi-purpose garments is used for outdoor wear. On all but the most frigid days shorts are the ideal legwear. Almost any style will do as long as they are roomy and not too long. Cotton or canvas shorts with double seats and big pockets are very popular.

Although not as hard-wearing nylon and polyester/cotton shorts have the advantage of being lighter and faster drying.

Wool breeches or knickerbockers were once the classic pants for cross-country skiing and alpine wear. Unlike full-length trousers they don't bind at the knee and the velcro cuffs can be undone for ventilation, but the current fashion is for light lycra tights or ski pants made from a stretchy, fast-drying fabric.

Long pants are usually worn only for warmth and as protection from mosquitoes or cool breezes. Jeans are usually too tight for comfort, and when wet they have all the appeal of chain mail. Light nylon track pants are easier

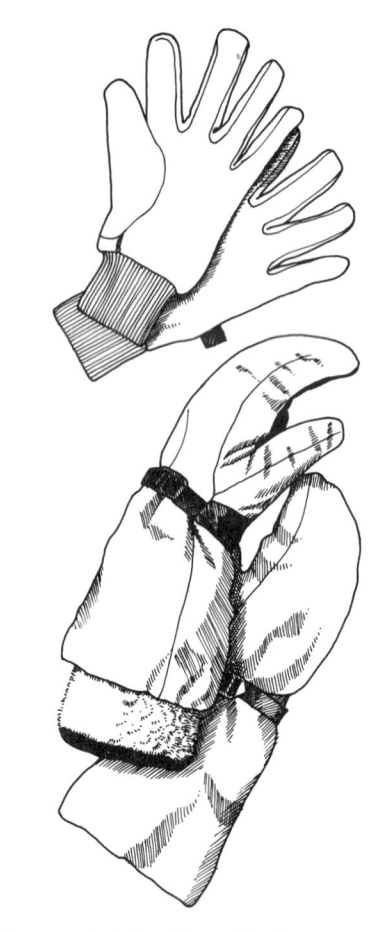

Gloves and shell mittens will allow you to carry on with your activities while keeping your hands warm

to wear, while ex-army woollen trousers are robust, cheap and warm. For layering over long johns, and protection from windchill, a pair of light polyester/cotton or nylon trousers is more flexible. Whatever pants you opt for they need to have a baggy fit and ample pockets for carrying odds and ends that are accessible even when wearing a rucksack hip belt.

The traditional bush shirt is made from sturdy cotton or canvas with two button-down chest pockets. This style works well in hot weather but lightweight shirts made from technical underwear fabrics are lighter and more versatile options. Long-sleeved shirts and high collars are important for sun protection.

One of the most underrated clothing items is a pullover or simple jacket designed to take the edge off bleak winds. These are usually made from a tightly woven nylon or polyester/cotton that is breathable but showerproof. They can be used as a shell over underwear and insulating layers, or worn for extra warmth under rainwear.

Although no substitute for fully-fledged wet weather gear these windshells are light and compact to carry. In many situations they offer a better mix of comfort and weather protection.

CLOTHING FOR TREKKING

Trek clothing requirements are virtually identical to those of bushwalking at home, with the exception of cultural considerations and the fact that you will often be walking at higher, and therefore colder, altitudes.

From the cultural viewpoint, modesty is far more important than it is at home. No-one should wear brief shorts and singlets, and it is highly recommended that women wear skirts or long culottes, rather than shorts, to avoid offending local people.

Warm waterproof clothing is of paramount importance, as is protection from the sun which is much stronger at high altitudes. The checklists on page 145 and below cover clothing needs for anything from a short bushwalk to a four-week Himalayan trek.

CLOTHING CHECKLIST

Bandanna
Fibrepile jacket (or warm sweater)
Footwear
Gaiters
Light gloves
Light long pants
Long johns
Long-sleeved shirt
Long-sleeved underwear top
Shorts
Short sleeved underwear top
Skirts/culottes for women
Socks (4 pairs)
Sunglasses
Swimming costume
Underwear (3-4 changes)
Warm hat
Waterproof jacket
Waterproof overpants

Wide-brimmed sunhat
Windshell top

Additional items for winter wear/trekking
Extra long-sleeved underwear top
Extra thick socks (2 pairs)
Extra warm hat or balaclava
Gloves
Insulated mitts
Insulated vest
Tent booties
Warm pants or extra long johns

Additional items for snow wear/high altitude trekking
Fibrepile pants
Goggles/glacier glasses
Insulated jacket
Waterproof overmitts

16

SLEEPING BAGS

Of all the major categories of outdoor gear, sleeping bags have changed the least. While modern tents and packs bear little resemblance to their ancestors, sleeping bags have retained the same fundamental shape, construction and fill.

The key to this history of enduring design has been the pre-eminence of down as the preferred sleeping bag insulation. Despite worthy efforts by manufacturers to devise a man-made alternative, down is still unrivalled for warmth, compressibility, lightness and longevity. Down bags also have a sumptuous feel and softness: a characteristic that makes them treasured articles, redolent of great times in the bush.

This quality comes at a high price – a good down bag has always cost roughly the average weekly wage. Yet when a sound night's sleep is sometimes the key to comfort, and perhaps survival, in the outdoors, and given the ability of a well-made bag to last a lifetime, it's hardly an extravagant investment.

A sleeping bag cannot create warmth; its job is to conserve the heat that your body generates. This is done by stabilising warm air in the small pockets created by the insulation. True down, as opposed to feathers, consists of light, fluffy clusters which trap still air between their countless tiny filaments. In synthetic fillings fine polyester fibres perform a similar role. In theory it is the thickness and evenness of insulation which determines a bag's ability to retain heat.

In reality, a host of other factors come into play. Cold ground, for example, will lead to substantial heat loss by conduction, so an effective insulating mat between the bag and the ground is essential. If sleeping out in the open, any breeze will cause warmth to be dissipated through convection. At a practical level a sleeping bag can also only be efficient if features designed to minimise heat loss, like adjustable hoods, draft flaps over zips and down collars, are used to effect.

THE HUMAN ELEMENT

In addition to all of these external factors, the most crucial element of making a sleeping bag work is its occupant. If your body is not producing enough heat to keep you and the bag comfortably warm then no amount of insulation will help. The only solution is to get your metabolism out of the doldrums by exercising, munching on energy-giving food, or having a hot drink. You may need to do this before retiring or during the night, after your heart rate slows and the air cools. Such measures usually become necessary when sleeping out in low temperatures, but just as everyone has their own metabolic rate, so there are wide variations in our ability to tolerate and adapt to chilly conditions. If you are a cold sleeper – or the sort of person who needs two pullovers when everybody else is happily wandering around in shirt sleeves – you will most likely need a warmer bag.

Other individual quirks also influence a sleeping bag's performance. If you are especially tall or bulky a standard sized bag may not be thermally efficient, either because you poke out of the end, or your shape stretches and compresses the filling. You may be a notoriously restless sleeper who spends your nights tossing and turning – a bag with a slender profile will be restrictive and keep you awake. Or perhaps you find the very idea of a sleeping bag confining and claustrophobic. If so, it's worth tracking down a bag with a roomy, accommodating shape.

INTENDED USES

Even if the principles of sleeping bag design have altered little, this doesn't mean that one bag will suit everyone, in every circumstance and all weather. Thankfully there is a great variety of bags available to cater for specific needs. To decide what style bag will serve you best, you need to arrive at a working definition of what you want the bag to do.

Where and when will you use the bag?

You may start your outdoor career with a conviction that you will only ever venture out for coastal trips in summer, but it rarely stays that way. Nevertheless, if your passion is for warm weather excursions, a light, easily ventilated bag will suffice.

The overwhelming majority of people head into the wilds over the spring, summer and autumn period. It's no surprise therefore to find a galaxy of bags catering to the conditions expected during these months. For example the classic three-season down bag has about 700 g (25 oz) of fill distributed in a semi-rectangular shell. This will keep most people cosy when the temperature nudges just below freezing, yet still be comfortable on balmy summer evenings.

It's a much harder decision if you want a bag to span from summer to the occasional midwinter foray. If you're naturally warm-blooded, the insulating properties of a three-season bag can be enhanced by using a bag liner, and wearing thermally efficient clothing. But confirmed cold weather addicts, and anybody who gets the shivers at the mere thought of snow, usually end up with two bags: a lightweight utility model, and a plump, cosy one for bleak winter nights.

What do you want to use it for?

The criteria that make a successful bag can be assigned differently according to your chosen activity.

For canoeing and rafting, weight and bulk are less critical than a bag's ability to withstand the moisture that is ever-present in a watery environment.

On the other hand, if you're into long-haul bushwalking or cycle touring, lightness and compactness are paramount. Travellers, likewise, need a bag that will take up the least space in their luggage, yet be versatile enough for nights in hostels and campgrounds.

When snowcamping, dependable warmth means everything. The favoured snow bag is generously filled and has features that keep heat in. Meanwhile, mountaineers need portable, highly efficient bags that integrate with their clothing and bivouac gear for lightweight ascents.

Finally, for general camping and only occasional overnight walks, the priorities become more commonplace: a bag that is durable, economical, and easy to use and care for.

FILLING

To a large extent the nature and arrangement of the filling dictates the ability of a sleeping bag to meet the needs outlined in the previous section. Ironically, this most critical ingredient is concealed within the bag's shell. This is hardly a problem with proprietary brand synthetic insulations, where the quality is assured. While down is subject to certain standards, bag manufacturers often blur the picture with hyperbole and claims that the geese or ducks that provide their down are somehow superior. Be ready with a pinch of salt!

Down

For a given weight of fill, down harbours more warmth than anything else, and when required it can be compressed into a miraculously small volume. These two facts alone account for its popularity in sleeping bags for serious lightweight trips. Down has other fine attributes as well. It's extremely resilient and will spring back into shape repeatedly during years of use. Down also breathes and keeps you comfortable in a wide range of temperatures.

As a filling it does have its drawbacks. Most damning is down's vulnerability to moisture. There is no more miserable an experience than a saturated down bag: all the insulating power is lost and it will take an age to dry. Even if you take care to protect a down bag from getting wet it will still retain moisture from your body and humidity in the atmosphere. Other negatives include the high cost, the difficulty of cleaning a down bag, and the fact that some people are allergic to the stuff.

To assess the down quality in a bag start by looking at the contents label. This will be described as something like, 90 per cent down, 10 per cent small feathers, indicating the ratio of true down clusters or plumules to the more familiar feather structures. The higher the down content, the more efficient the bag.

You can verify this labelling simply by feeling the down in the bag: the softer the better. If you come across a lot of bits of quill and feather be wary. Finally, lie the bag on the floor to assess its loft, or the thickness of the bag, once the down has had a chance to expand. Look at equivalent bags from brand to brand to make a comparison.

Synthetics

In its rudimentary generic form polyester is a solid core fibre of uneven quality. This is the filling used in the cheapest bags, the ones with lurid checked inners sold by discount stores.

For serious outdoor use there are several specialist synthetic insulations. The most common is *Hollofil* in which the fibres have a hollow core that saves weight and traps more air than a solid fibre. *Quallofil* is similar except that the core is hollowed by four channels, yielding more surface area, and in theory more warmth for weight. Both of these fills are crimped and silicon treated to help them loft and for easier stuffing. They are, however, short-staple fibres that need to be stabilised by a scrim. *Polarguard*, by contrast, is a solid, continuous filament fibre that comes in batts, making the bag simpler and more durable in construction.

The principal advantages of all these fills is their resistance to moisture. A sodden bag will never be comfortable but in a dire emergency a damp synthetic bag still promises a measure of insulation. Equally important, it will dry quickly. For wet environments and any water-based activity, synthetic bags are ideal.

They have other virtues as well. Unlike down, the fill doesn't immediately flatten under body weight, which means some extra padding and insulation from the ground. Synthetic bags are also more robust, easier to care for, non-allergenic and, most persuasive of all, cheaper to buy.

Against this a synthetic bag is 30–40 per cent heavier and, when packed, around twice the bulk of a down equivalent. Another telling factor is that with regular use synthetic fills will gradually clump and lose their lofting power. A well cared for down bag has the potential for three to five times the effective life of a synthetic bag.

Clearly both down and synthetic fills have their advantages. People initially often choose a synthetic bag on the basis of price alone. If your budget is tight there is more value in buying a good synthetic bag than a cheap down model, and later, if the need arises for a warmer winter bag, you can always opt for down the second time around.

There are, however, no hard and fast rules. A lot of canoeists happily use down bags and take precautions to keep them from getting damp. Conversely, many bushwalkers minimise the shortcomings of synthetic bags by using a special compression stuffsack, and selecting an efficient mummy-shaped design. This point raises another important aspect of sleeping bag performance.

SHAPE

The simplest form of sleeping bag is a rectangle with a zip down one side and across the bottom. Roomy, easy to ventilate and simple to use, rectangular bags are nevertheless bulky and heavy for the warmth they offer. This, and the fact that they often don't have a hood, relegates the rectangular bag to low-key camping and use as a quilt.

Much more common are semi-rectangular shapes which taper slightly towards the foot of the bag. This brings more of the filling closer to the body, where it counts. Some designs have only side zips, while more prevalent is a dual zip arrangement with a second zip along the foot of the bag. Semi-rectangular bags offer a practical compromise between efficiency and roominess.

The semi-rectangular sleeping bag is tapered in slightly at the foot of the bag for added warmth

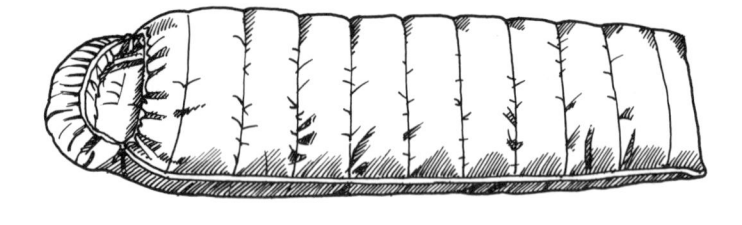

The mummy-shaped sleeping bag is the most efficient bag as it is contoured to the body and is less weighty and bulky for the warmth it provides

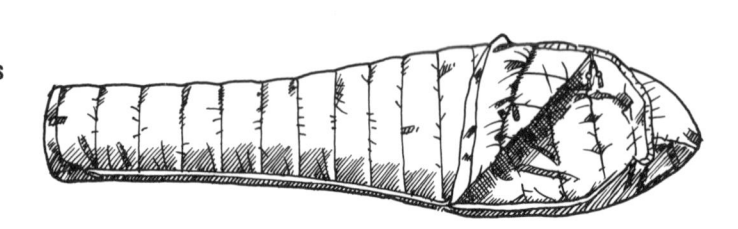

The most effective use of materials is achieved by a mummy-shaped design which contours close to the body. This means less weight and bulk for a given warmth of bag. There are no corners or wasted spaces in the bag to be warmed. The foot section of any decent mummy bag will be carefully designed for ample toe room and added insulation. At first a body-hugging mummy bag can feel confining, and when you roll over the bag moves with you. Depending on the zip configuration this type of bag can be harder to ventilate.

No one shape suits everybody. Ultimately it comes down to personal preference, although the mummy-shaped bags are likely to be warmer.

CONSTRUCTION

Beyond fill and shape lies the question of how a sleeping bag is put together. Just as the filling is hidden from view, so too are the intricacies of construction.

In the case of down bags this becomes critical, given down's tendency to shift around. To help ensure good distribution the down is contained in compartments. The crudest method is to stitch the inner and outer shells together at regular intervals. This is a simple and inexpensive solution but it leaves cold spots along each stitch line. Such sewn-through bags are only really suited for indoor use and summer camping.

To create an even layer of insulation the better down bags have fine mesh internal walls, or baffles, sewn between the shells. The result is a series of box-like chambers running laterally around the bag, which allow the down to loft freely and to a consistent thickness. Many literally baffling variations on the box-wall have been devised, including slant wall, v-tube, trapezoid and vertical cross baffles. Whether one has any merit over another is much less important in the field than most ardent designers like us to believe.

In more sophisticated four-season

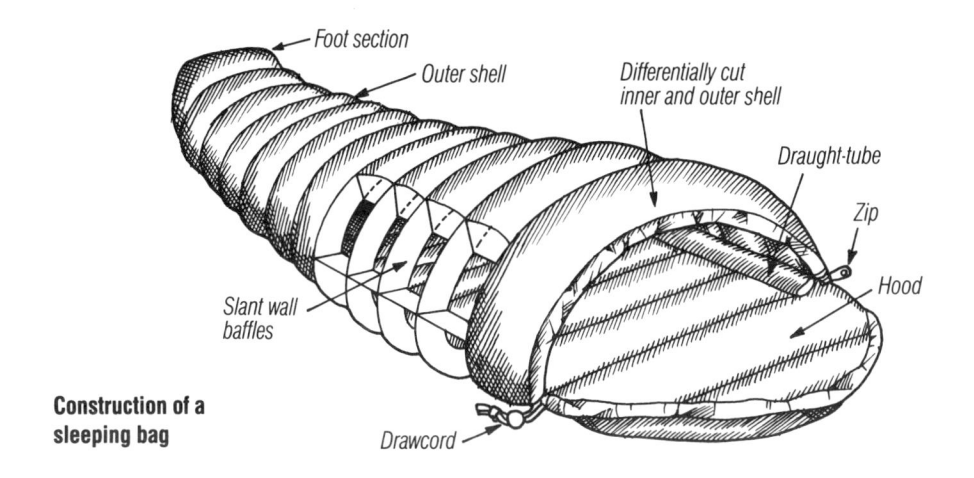

Construction of a sleeping bag

Labels: Foot section; Outer shell; Differentially cut inner and outer shell; Draught-tube; Zip; Hood; Drawcord; Slant wall baffles

bags there is also a side-block baffle, which prevents cold spots caused by down migrating within these chambers from the top to the underside of the bag. These baffles are not included in most three-season bags, which allows you to push the down to the top or base of the bag according to the need for more or less warmth.

The construction options are similar for synthetic bags. The basic models are sewn-through in a variety of quilting patterns. To combat cold spots warmer bags align two sewn-through layers so that stitch lines are off-set and potential cold spots in one layer correspond to the thickest part of the insulation in another. In advanced Polarguard constructions the batts are sewn in an overlapping sequence to create a shingle or multi-layered construction.

Most good down and synthetic bags are cut differentially so that the inner shell is smaller than the outer.' This allows the fill to loft fully and not be flattened by the inner pressing against the outer. Another common feature is differential fill – this allocates more filling to the top compartments of the bag, which tend to be more exposed to the cold than those underneath the body.

DESIGN DETAILS

In the battle to retain warmth within the bag as the mercury falls, even the smallest features become critical.

Given that up to a third of your body heat can be lost through your head it's imperative to have a snug hood. The more elaborate designs are closely contoured to the head shape, generously filled and have a two-way adjustable drawcord for closing the hood around your face.

A zip along the edge of a sleeping bag is a prime source of heat loss. A draught-tube is the answer. In its crudest form this is an insulation-filled flap of fabric that drapes over the zip, but is sewn through where the zip is attached to the bag. Better versions are constructed so that there is a uniform layer of fill across the zip area. Expedition-rated bags sometimes have two overlapping draught-tubes.

As you move inside the bag, so you tend to pump warm air in a bellows action out through the hood opening. To keep out cold draughts and seal in the warmth, winter bags commonly have an insulated collar or muff which can be drawn in around your shoulders. This also helps prevent condensation from your breath from circulating down into the bag.

MATERIALS

Shell fabrics

Noble japara was once *the* sleeping bag fabric. As comfortable and familiar as cotton feels, it's heavy, not especially tough, and it has an unfortunate affinity for moisture. It has all but disappeared from use as a sleeping bag fabric.

Taking its place is a new breed of high thread count taffeta and ripstop nylon fabrics. In the most advanced weaves these lightweight nylons have up to 3500 multi-filaments per sq cm (9000 multi-filaments per sq in), making them strong and highly wind and moisture resistant. Best of all, they are silky soft and supple with little of the cold, sticky feel of the original nylons. Still, if you have an aversion to synthetics against your skin use a cotton inner sheet.

In specialist sleeping bags for expeditions and high altitude mountaineering Gore-Tex or a similar waterproof/breathable fabric is used for the outer shell and hood of the bag. This protects the loft in the bag by defending against moisture found in snowcaves, tents and open bivouacs, as well as accumulated vapours from breathing. Such shells do, however, nearly double the price of a sleeping bag.

Zips

Most bags have continuous coil nylon zips. These are strong, self-repairing and easy to use. The biggest hassle with any zip is its uncanny ability to become snagged with the shell fabric. To alleviate this, bag makers place tape behind the zip, or stiffen the draught-tube. Almost all sleeping bags these days have two-way zips, with a slider at either end for easy ventilation.

To join two bags together the zips need to be compatible and if you want both hoods on the ground, you should have one bag with a left-handed zip and the other with a right-handed zip. As pleasant as sleeping with a partner might seem, sleeping bags work more efficiently as single units.

VARIATIONS AND INNOVATIONS

There is increasing interest in sleeping bags that adapt to changing needs – instead of having different bags for each season or activity you can adjust the warmth of an individual bag.

Some manufacturers offer a purpose-built insulated liner which integrates with one of their mainstream bags. The liner can be used as a light summer bag or to extend the operating range of the main bag, but it succeeds only if the two bags are tailored to fit together, and if there is some method of linking the bags with zips or ties. Other brands offer a variation on this by adding a layer of insulation in the form of a mantle that zips over the top of the bag.

If your bag doesn't have these options it's worth considering one of the specialised inner bags made from a lightweight polyester fleece or pile. Excellent liners are also now available in fabrics similar to those used for thermal underwear.

Some of the more contentious developments deal with heat loss by radiation and vapour transmission. Radiant heat barriers are made from reflective materials not unlike the space blanket, and are normally part of the bag's inner lining. The theory is that your body's radiant heat, which normally passes out through the bag, is reflected back to its source. It works, but often the increase in weight and loss of compactibility doesn't justify the warmth gained.

A vapour barrier liner is based on the idea that a lot of heat escapes as body moisture evaporates out through the sleeping bag. The answer is to sleep in a light waterproof nylon liner that traps a layer of humid air next to the skin, virtually eliminating the need for the body to keep on sweating. Heat loss is thus minimised, and body moisture can't reach your bag's insulation. In practice, vapour barriers perform best in conditions of extreme dry cold.

Other versatile ideas abound. Several makers design bags that can be opened flat and then zipped to a special bottom sheet to create a summer bag for two. This sheet is usually two-layered with pillow sleeves and openings to allow sleeping mats to be slipped inside. A related concept for a single sleeper is to dispense with the underside of the bag altogether, and to offer a variety of 'quilt' style tops that zip directly onto an integrated sleeping mat and sheet. Doubtless the future will see more such innovations.

NECESSARY ACCESSORIES

Inner sheets

A good inner sheet serves two purposes: it adds warmth to the bag

---

BUYING A SLEEPING BAG

- Where and when will you be using the bag? (Buy a bag for the conditions you'll most often encounter, not the 'worst case scenario'. For the occasional colder night use a liner or wear extra clothing.)
- What activities will you need the bag for? (For water pursuits favour synthetic bags. For any lightweight excursions consider compact down models.)
- What is your budget? (If funds are scarce, go for a good synthetic rather than a cheap down bag.)
- Are you a cold or restless sleeper? (Look at warmer and roomier bags respectively.)
- Shop around and do your research. Eye the loft and feel the fill quality of different bags. Look for good workmanship, even stitching and well finished seams. Every manufacturer has a method of grading their bag's performance. Be warned: temperature ratings are notoriously unreliable for judging a bag's potential.
- Does the bag fit? Kick off your shoes and crawl into the bag to see how it feels. Check that you're happy with the length, shoulder room and toe space. Ask whether the bag is available in extra large sizes. Test your normal sleeping positions, and try the hood.

and keeps it cleaner for longer periods (which is an excellent idea given the traumas of washing a down bag). Most inner sheets are made from cotton or polycottons and you can easily make up your own out of an old bedsheet. For the ultimate in sensuous comfort there are pure silk inner sheets which are lightweight and fast drying, but rather costly.

Stuffsack

It's hard to overstate the importance of this seemingly insignificant item. A stuffsack needs to be made from a robust, fully waterproof fabric, and impeccably sewn to cope with the stresses of repeated bag stuffing. The size will accommodate your particular sleeping bag, but only just, so you don't waste valuable rucksack space. The better stuffsacks have tape-sealed seams and a loop on the bottom to make removing the bag easier. A strong drawcord and cord grip are essential. Special compression stuffsacks are handy for cumbersome synthetic and down models. These use straps and buckles which pull corset-style across the outside of the stuffsack to dramatically reduce its volume.

Sleeping mats

It's imperative to have a barrier between your bag and the cold ground. The simplest and most dependable is a lightweight mat made from closed cell foam that insulates, and is impervious to moisture. Though hardly luxurious, the foam does offer some padding. These mats come in a myriad of sizes, thicknesses and qualities, so shop around.

Vastly more comfortable – and expensive – are the 'self-inflating' mats which have open cell foam enveloped in an airtight nylon shell bonded to the foam. These are very effective insulators but it's the soft cushioning they provide which makes them 'the cat's pyjamas'. In theory, when you open the valve the mat inflates as the foam inside expands and draws in air. This works but you may need to blow in a little extra air to make the mat firm. The only catch is that they can be punctured, but experience has shown that this is not hard to avoid.

Air-beds are only really suited to car camping. Although comfortable they are hard to inflate, heavy to carry, and cold air circulating inside the chambers draws warmth away from your bag and you. The exception is on leisurely river and canyon trips where the flotation is most welcome.

Bivvy bag

At one extreme a bivvy bag is a long tube of heavy duty plastic sealed at one end. At the other it's a mini-tent, made from Gore-Tex or a similar fabric, which has hoops, storage areas and peg out loops. (See Chapter 18, *Tents*.)

If you want a sleeping bag cover for the rare occasion when you're caught out in wild weather, carry a plastic bag. For more frequent tent-less nights, planned or otherwise, a bivvy bag is a good investment and will add several degrees of warmth to your sleeping bag.

TAKING CARE OF YOUR SLEEPING BAG

With the right treatment a good sleeping bag can last a lifetime. Regardless of the fill, never store a bag in its stuffsack for extended periods, as over time this will affect its ability to loft. Bags should be kept, instead, in a large storage sack.

In the field, use every opportunity to air the bag. When packing it into the stuffsack don't roll the bag but cram it firmly and evenly. Do your best to keep a bag clean and dry. The worst place for a sleeping bag is around a dusty campfire where there is the added peril of sparks melting holes in the shell fabric.

The best way to clean a down bag is to buy a proper down soap and hand wash it. Fill a bath with lukewarm water, immerse the bag and gently squeeze the soapy water through the bag for a while. Then empty the bath (leaving the bag in place) and refill with fresh water at least a couple of times to rinse the soap thoroughly from the bag. Drain the bath a final time and very gently press as much water from the bag as possible. Lift it with great care by cradling it in your arms, and take it to where it can be laid out on a flat but well-ventilated surface to air dry. This may take several days.

Washing a down bag should only be necessary every two or three years at the most. Much can be done to restore loft by washing an old bag, but bad handling of a wet bag can rupture the delicate baffle structures between each compartment. Likewise, harsh detergents will strip the down of its natural oils and destroy the bag's loft.

Synthetic bags can either be hand washed or carefully machine washed using any mild soap. Do not use detergents or dryclean.

17

PACKS

The legendary British climber Don Whillans defined a pack as 'a bag with two straps'. This is a welcome relief to the jargon of rucksack design that burdens prospective buyers even before they have anything on their backs. In essence, a pack is a bag which allows you to carry everything you need for a trip. The latest packs are certainly more comfortable to wear, but no pack can do the work of load carrying for you – and many models are over-engineered and overpriced. Regardless of design, the best thing about any pack is taking it off.

LOAD CARRYING

The evolution of the padded hip belt has been the most practical advance in large rucksacks. Early packs relied on shoulder straps to bear the weight of a load. This was crudely effective, but with enough equipment and provisions for a week or longer, the strain on shoulders was severe. Then came skimpy waist straps that helped keep the pack from swaying when walking on steep ground. Gradually this strap was refined into a wide padded belt shaped to fit over the hips. As a result around half the load could be transferred to the hip area, and rucksack users everywhere breathed a sigh of relief.

Such a distribution of weight can only succeed if the distance between the shoulder straps and hip belt corresponds to your back size. To cater for different torso heights manufacturers began to offer packs in a number of frame lengths. Shortly after this a new type of pack emerged with harnesses that could be adjusted for length by relocating the position of the shoulder straps or hip belt.

The problem with an adjustable harness is that it introduces a lot of unnecessary complication. Once you find a comfortable setting, the extra webbing, buckles, bells and whistles are of no benefit. Adjustable harnesses are usually either too flimsy at the precise points where most stress is applied, or too fussy with the added bits needed to make them stable and sturdy.

Thankfully there is a trend back to building packs in different lengths with securely mounted shoulder straps and hip belts. Many companies have turned their attention to more worthy innovations such as making packs more stable, better ventilated and more appropriate to different body types.

As well as the ability to share the load between shoulders and hips a pack needs to sit snugly against the back. Traditional external frame rucksacks forced the wearer to stoop forward in order to stay on balance, which was tiring and uncomfortable. The advent of the internal frame pack, with bendable aluminium stays, allows the pack to be contoured to an individual's back. The load is closer to the body's centre of gravity and the wearer can walk in a more upright fashion.

A pack that conforms to your back gives a smoother, more stable ride, but the shape of the frame is only part of the story. When walking on flat, even ground some independent movement between you and the pack is acceptable, but for scrambling off the track, skiing downhill, and any form of climbing, a pack needs to move with you. Modern harnesses have a series of adjustments so that you can fine tune the fit: top tensioners on the shoulder straps pull the upper part of the pack over your shoulders and can also be used to ease the downwards pressure by lifting the pack slightly off the shoulders. A chest or sternum strap holds the shoulder straps in place and minimises side to side movement. Hip belt stabilisers allow the base of the pack to be brought snug against the hips.

Stability is also governed by the profile of the sack and how the load is arranged. Some packs taper down to a narrower base so the load sits high on the back and weight is transferred directly to the hips, which is ideal for trail walking, but a top-heavy pack is precarious for climbing and skiing. Packs for these activities tend to be wider at the base, creating a lower centre of gravity. Even more important is the way in which gear is packed inside the sack. By positioning heavy items higher or lower you can adjust the feel of the pack. (See Chapter 1, *Packing up*.)

In the course of a trip one regularly adjusts the fit of a rucksack according to changes in terrain and activity. There is always a balance to be struck between the stability of a pack that hugs tight against the back, and the freedom to loosen straps and shift the load easily from shoulders to hips.

MATERIALS AND DESIGN

In the dim dark past, rucksack straps were made from a heavy leather which was strong but rather hard on tender flesh. Nowadays the weight of a pack is cushioned by straps padded with closed cell foam and covered by a nylon or wicking texturised fabric. Hip belts are often padded with two or three foams of different density for comfort and a snug fit. A more recent innovation on large packs is a lumber pad that sits in the small of the back. This cushions the load and keeps some separation between the pack and your back, which helps with ventilation. Lumber pads use a soft foam enclosed in a highly breathable mesh fabric.

The cut and shape of harness straps varies from brand to brand. Most have a slight taper and curve back under the arms and out of the way. Hip belts are usually contoured so as not to inhibit leg muscles. Needless to say no one shape will suit all physiques – only by trying different harness designs will you find out what feels comfortable.

Almost all manufacturers use light plastic buckles which are sturdy and simple to operate, even in the cold. Quick release buckles are essential for the hip belt, sternum strap and lid straps. Adjustable 'ladder' style

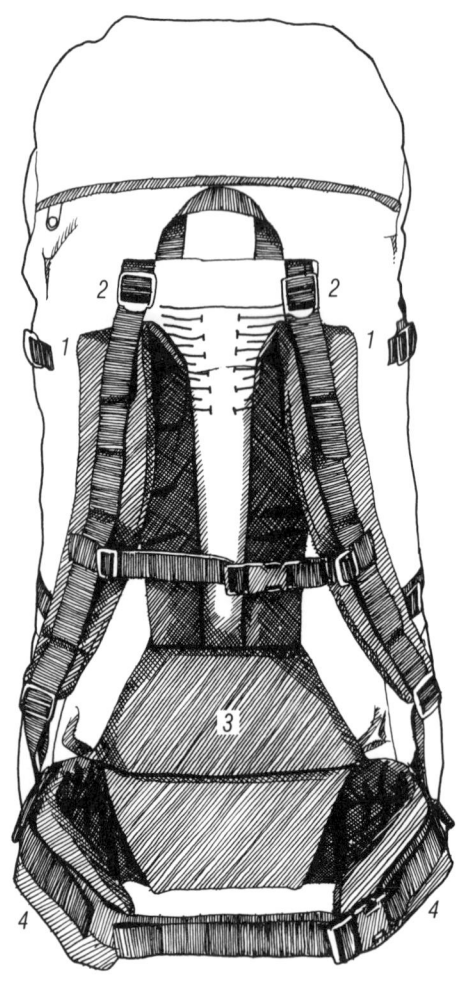

HARNESS DETAIL
1. Wide shoulder pads for more stability
2. Shoulder pads are easily adjusted to fit back length
3. Lumbar pad helps cushion the load
4. Adjustable hip belt

buckles are used on shoulder straps and any other strap which is not regularly unbuckled. The webbing used for straps must run smoothly through the buckle but hold under the load. Webbing that's too thin will slip; if it's too thick it won't feed properly.

Fabrics for the main body of the pack need to be rugged. The canvas commonly used these days is an excellent polyester/cotton blend which is often treated with a proofing compound to make the cloth even more water resistant. For wet environments and river trips a canvas pack is ideal. Cordura is a nylon fabric made from fibres which have been air blasted to give the cloth a rough, abrasion resistant finish. Even when the body of the pack is made from another fabric, Cordura is frequently used on the base and other wear points. Pack cloth has a finer weave that's smoother and lighter than Cordura but still surprisingly hard wearing. Like Cordura it needs to have a waterproof coating applied to keep out moisture.

Other fabrics found in pack manufacture include a tough bulky weave nylon known as ballistics cloth, lightweight ripstop nylons for summit packs, and some of the ultra-lightweight cloths using Kevlar and Mylar.

Each fabric has its merits but they are only as good as the pack construction. Stitching needs to be even and at the right tension. All exposed seams should be bound to prevent fraying. Stress points are best reinforced with additional fabric and then bartacked to take the strain of heavy loads.

DAYPACKS

The subtle nuances of pack design may seem less critical with small packs that are required only to tote lunch and spare clothes, yet a daypack has to be as sturdily built as an expedition rucksack. The loads carried may not be as heavy but away from the bush daypacks are frequently pressed into service as book bags and shopping carry-alls. The wear and tear of everyday use can be at least as punishing as anything meted out in the wild.

Bum bags

For brief outings lasting an hour or two a small bag that straps around the waist is ideal. Bum bags were originally made popular by skiers who needed to carry their gloves, goggles, suncream and ski waxes. Now bum bags have been adopted for general use, especially in activities such as cycling, mountain running and climbing, where shoulder straps would be a hindrance.

With this new-found popularity the choice of bum bags has widened to include everything from pouches barely big enough to hold car keys, to mini-packs with multiple compartments and padded waist belts. For most excursions a mid-size bum bag that can take a water bottle, windshell, compact camera and snack bar is sufficient. The latest designs are shaped to the hips and have compression straps to hold the contents snugly.

Teardrop daypacks

The classic small pack for trail walking and around town has a tapered teardrop shape. This keeps the bulk of the load comfortably in the middle of the back. Some larger teardrops also feature waist straps and sternum straps to hold the pack snug when required. The main compartment has a zip closure which gives the pack its clean lines.

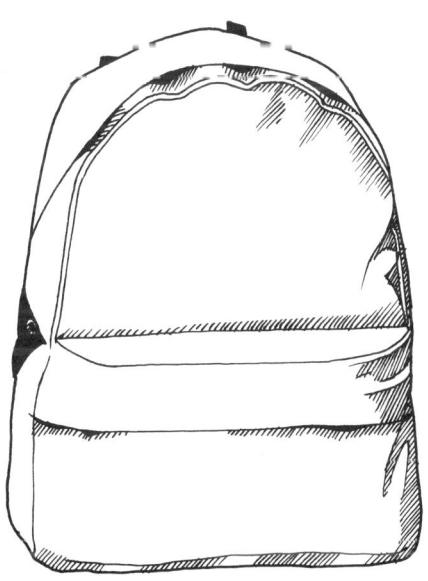

The teardrop pack is a daypack that keeps the load comfortably in the middle of the back

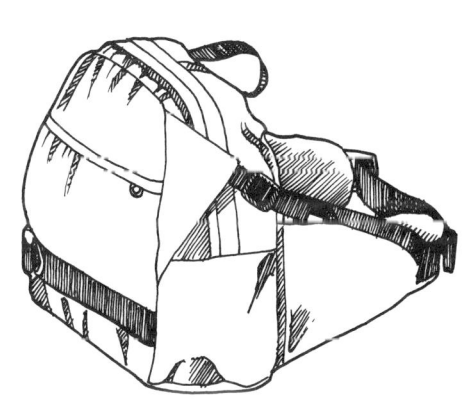

A bum bag is useful for short outings where shoulder straps would be a hindrance

Most teardrops have an external pocket for carrying small odds and ends. Models designed more for use around town can boast multiple compartments, coin wallets, document pouches and organisers for pen and pencils. With a capacity around 20-30 L (35-53 pt) the teardrop's customary role is transporting light loads over short distances: they are neat, versatile and simple to use.

Top-loading daypacks

Like scaled-down rucksacks these designs have a main sack with a drawcord closure and a top lid which is held down by straps. This is a more weatherproof arrangement than a zip, and adjustable straps allow extra gear like ropes and clothing to be stowed under the lid. Top-loaders have a slimmer profile and in some cases are tall enough for part of the load to be borne by a hip belt. Though access to the main compartment is limited to the top opening, most versions have a back pocket or lid pocket for storing smaller items.

Top-loading daypacks adapt better to bulky loads and the trials of heavy duty use in the bush. Most are of 25-45 L (44-79 pt) in capacity, and the larger of the species will serve for overnight walks or long winter day trips when extra equipment and supplies need to be carried. At the other extreme, a light nylon top-loader can be carried in your main pack as a stuffsack and then converted to a summit pack.

ALPINE PACKS

Climbers and ski tourers need a pack that fits like a glove. The load has to rest low down near the hips, and the sack's profile should be streamlined to eliminate any interference to arm or head movement.

Smaller than a full-sized rucksack, an alpine pack has to accommodate everything needed for an action-filled day trip when a bivouac is likely. The load can include the usual clothing and hardware plus spare provisions, a stove, bivvy bag and down jacket. Normally the capacity is around 40 L (70 pt) and weight is saved by dispensing with any internal frame. Instead, the sack shape is maintained by a foam back panel which can often also be removed for sitting on cold ledges.

The best alpine packs have clean, uncluttered lines with no extraneous compartments or gimmicks. They do, however, need external attachment points for equipment such as skis, ice climbing tools and snow shovels. Though designed for lightness and speed these packs have to be rugged enough to be hauled up rock pitches and survive unscheduled descents down icy slopes.

RUCKSACKS

A dependable rucksack gives you the freedom to go bush for a night, a week, or longer. Once you're in your stride a good-fitting pack seems as natural as the boots on your feet.

A pack, however, is nothing if it doesn't hold together. A burst seam or ripped shoulder strap poses a serious problem when you're deep in the wilderness. Simplicity of design and robust construction should take priority. Every zip, seam and attachment is a potential weak point on packs intended for hefty loads. Fancy straps and clever openings might make a good impression when buying a pack, but these features often don't stand up to the bump and grind of the bush.

Compartments

The basic pack is a big sack topped by a lid. Older sacks were made from a single piece of fabric, forming a sausage-shaped bag to which the harness was attached. This had the strength of simplicity but made it difficult to give the sack a body-hugging shape. Most single compartment packs now have separate contoured side panels. This construction also allows compression straps to be sewn into the side seams.

One drawback with a single compartment pack is the lack of easy access to items sunk deep in the sack. To get around this problem many bushwalking packs have two compartments. On most packs this is created by having a shelf (which can often be unzipped or removed) that separates the bottom third of the pack. This lower compartment has an outside zip allowing entry without having to undo and unpack the rest of the rucksack. As convenient as this may seem it's highly debatable whether a zip in a position so exposed to wear and water entry is justified. Given that sleeping bags invariably ride in the lower third of the pack, and they are only needed when you will be unloading the rest of your gear anyway, the advantage of two compartments seems negligible.

Capacity

The first law of large rucksacks is that gear will invariably accumulate to fill the available space. No matter how disciplined you may be there is always the temptation to carry a big pack fully laden. At the other extreme, a rucksack that's too small will mean having to lash important items onto the outside of the sack, where they swing about and are easily snagged, so it's worth buying a pack that will take just what you need and no more. For journeys lasting a week or so a pack with a capacity of 55-75 L (97-132 pt) is normally adequate. Rucksack manufacturers are notorious for overstating the capacity of their sacks, so compare any figure quoted in a catalogue with how big the pack looks against other brands.

Some rucksacks have features which allow the capacity of the sack to be adjusted according to the load. Most common are compression straps down either side of the pack which can be pulled tight to bring anything less than a full load in against the back, where it's most comfortably carried. Mountaineering rucksacks often have extendable lids and weatherproof throats sewn into the top of the sack, which can be extended to increase the volume of the pack.

Pockets and attachment points

Side pockets are another way to add space to a pack. Detachable pockets can usually be bought to fit on to compression straps or slotted patches. Packs with fixed side pockets are not popular as they catch scrub and impede your natural arm swing. A few packs have side pockets that lie flat when not in use and fold out if needed. Another option is a pocket which straps on to the back of the pack – these are permanently attached on some packs. Though unobtrusive, such pockets can place weight further away from your centre of gravity and cause the pack to drag back off the shoulders.

Bulky gear like sleeping mats, tent poles and wet flysheets, that are often best carried on the outside of the pack, need a different solution. Compression straps are effective for holding slender items, especially if there are pole pouches at the base of the side panels. Otherwise you need to use attachment points and accessory straps normally found on top of the lid and on the back of the sack. The latter is probably the best place for most items, and a lattice of thin shock cord is very handy for securing slippery mats or odd shaped articles. Even the packs that are most unlikely for alpine use seem to have specialised ice-axe loops. These are handy for carrying snow shovels and tripods, but many walkers cut them off.

For storing small items on the outside of the pack the lid pocket is best. On a full-sized pack this is usually roomy enough to take your water bottle and other items needed during the day. If not, you are better off buying a separate front-mounted waist pouch for holding odds and ends. As well as extendable lids some varieties detach completely and transform into small daypacks or bum bags.

No matter what tricks it can perform, the lid's main function is to keep out the elements. It should leave room for you to tilt your head back and fit snugly around the top of the sack. While in terms of weatherproofing the fewer seams and zips the better, no pack is truly waterproof. A good water resistant fabric, a double layer base, and sealing seams can all help, but in time water will find a way in. The best defence is a seam sealed liner and stuffsacks. (See Chapter 3, *Weather* and the section on *Rain*.)

Rucksacks have come a long way since the H-frames of 20 years ago. While it's questionable whether the new generation is any more durable, at least it's now possible to travel in less pain! Most good rucksacks are now sold in three or four different back lengths, which reflects the wide variation in torso shapes. Enlightened manufacturers also offer packs designed for the female figure, with

BUYING A PACK

- If possible try before you buy. Borrow a pack from a trusting friend, or hire a pack for a weekend to get the feel of load carrying.

- Pack capacity is dictated by the style of trip you regularly go on. If in doubt consider taking into the store your standard collection of clothing and equipment to see how it fits the sack you've chosen.

- Look for simplicity of design and sturdy 'bomb proof' construction. Beware of frills and features that add unnecessary weight, cost and complications.

- Packs with adjustable back lengths are useful only if the pack is to be shared by different sized individuals, or worn with extremely bulky clothing layers.

- Try several packs for a comparison of fit and features. (See *Fitting a pack*.) Buy the pack that is the most comfortable and best suits your body size.

narrower and shorter harnesses and better shaped hip belts. With a little experimentation and shopping around you can find that most essential feature of any pack – a comfortable fit.

External frame packs

These once-noble packs have become the social outcasts of the equipment world. An external frame pack has a rigid alloy frame to which the pack bag is attached.

The traditional H-frames made few concessions to user comfort. Both frame and pack had no body shape, and the load rode too high for any weight to be borne by the hips. Unfortunately the taller external frame designs that came onto the market extended so far above the head that they caught on every branch and bush. These high-rise versions often had so many compartments that they looked more like a chest of drawers with straps than a rucksack.

Accordingly, the external frame pack has disappeared from specialist bushwalking outlets, but in the United States these packs remain very popular and have evolved into worthy alternatives to the internal frame pack. For walking with heavy or awkward loads on prepared trails an external frame pack with a well-padded harness can give excellent weight transfer to the hips. The separation between the mesh back panel and the wearer also ensures better air circulation.

TRAVEL PACKS

If packs for the bush need to be tough, then travel packs should be doubly so. What happens to luggage in the time between checking it in, and then hopefully finding it on the luggage carousel at your destination, remains a mystery. All the evidence, however, suggests that your precious bag will not be accorded anything like the respect a rucksack would get on the roughest back-country voyage.

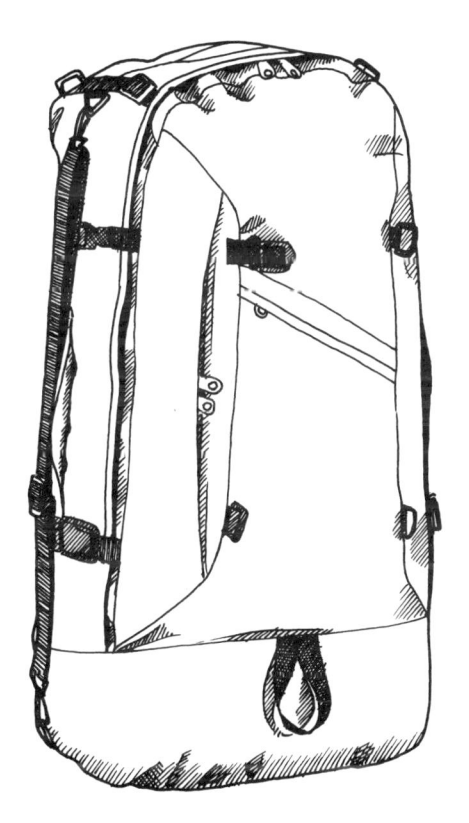

The travel pack doubles as a rucksack and a suitcase

Travel packs differ from conventional rucksacks in two ways. Firstly, instead of having a top opening there is a back panel which unzips, so the contents of the main compartment can be easily unpacked like a suitcase. Thankfully on

FITTING A PACK

- The only reliable way to judge a pack is to have at least 10–15 kg (22–33 lb) of weight on board. Before putting the pack on loosen off the harness straps.
- Start by tightening the hip belt so that the top of the belt sits near the top of the hip bone. Pull down on the shoulder straps to bring the pack snug against your back.
- If the shoulder straps sit too high or low, try a pack with a different back length, or on some packs you can adjust the distance between the shoulder straps and hip belt.
- When the pack is adjusted so that weight can be distributed between the hips and shoulders, tighten the top tension straps, hip belt stabilisers and sternum strap so the load rests firmly.
- Take time to walk with the pack on. Make sure the shoulder straps sit comfortably and don't chafe your neck. The hip belt should ride over the hips and not interfere with leg movement. For an optimum fit it's usually necessary to bend the internal frame to suit your back shape.
- Try accentuated body movements — knee bends, sharp turns, steep descents — to see how the pack responds.

---

modern travel packs this crucial zip is usually of the heavy duty coil variety, and the strain of the load is taken by compression straps. Secondly, whereas a rucksack harness is exposed for the world to see, the travel pack has a panel which zips over the harness and keeps loose straps and buckles away from hungry conveyer belts.

Most travel packs are also more square and squat than conventional packs. This makes them more compact and simpler to load. A capacity of around 60 L (105 pt) is best; anything more risks going over luggage limits and is too unwieldy to be carried by a shoulder belt or carry handle. Travel packs are legendary for their tricky compartments and add-on bags. These can be useful for keeping your clothing and possessions organised, but to survive rough baggage handling and accidental tumbles from buses, yaks and camels the simpler the design the better.

For serious bushwalking a travel pack is at best a compromise. The boxy shape tends to keep the load away from the back, and often the shoulder straps and hip belt are a 'bare bones' version of what you find on a true rucksack harness. For wandering strange towns in search of an inn or for short overnight walks in the hills nearby, this is ideal, but some companies are stretching the definition of travel packs with designs that use sophisticated harnesses and elegant body-hugging sack shapes. These rival mainstream rucksacks for carrying comfort, and are a good choice for the globetrotting skier, climber or trekker.

18
TENTS

A tent is a home away from home. At the end of a long day you can crawl inside, snuggle into your sleeping bag and dream about tomorrow. In storms and downpours a sturdy tent is a welcome refuge: a bubble of civilisation in the unruly wilderness. On clear nights you can peep out at the stars or watch the moonlight roam across the canopy. At such times a tent is your very own stately pleasure dome.

Of course there is another school of thought that regards tents as heavy bundles of nylon and alloy to be carried just because of some remote chance of rain; or to placate partners who are anxious about sharing their nights with creepy crawlies. The logic here is that a tent will most likely be the single heaviest item in your pack, and on a long climb there will be plenty of reminders of the extra kilograms.

Obviously there's no point in carrying around a fortress-like mountain dome if you only ever need an overnight shelter for summer walks. Conversely you might rue the decision to carry that skimpy flysheet if you get trapped on a windswept ridge during a three-day storm.

The truth about choosing the right tent is that you need to define not only where and when you will be using it, but also how much you like your comforts, or alternatively are prepared to improvise with more rudimentary shelters.

For generations backpacking tents were made of japara or canvas and used upright poles to give them their classic A-frame and pyramid shapes. These fine shelters are still very much in use, but they have some decided drawbacks. For a start their sloping side walls leave you with a lot of unusable nooks and corners. These same side walls are unsupported and are very vulnerable to wind gusts and snowfalls – many a night has been spent in A-frames with the occupants braced against flexing poles and billowing side walls.

These are also the same type of tents that weigh a tonne when they get wet, need an armoury of pegs and guy ropes just to keep their shape, and have all sorts of openings for mosquitoes. So, while you will see A-frames and their equally venerable owners ensconced in their favourite campsites, this style of tent has all but disappeared from the equipment stores.

Taking its place is a seemingly infinite array of curvaceous tunnel and dome structures. The last 20 years have seen remarkable innovations in these

> ## BUYING A TENT
>
> - Does it offer the weatherproofness and stability for the prevailing conditions it will be used in?
> - Is there adequate room inside for occupants and their gear? (Crawl inside, stretch out and make sure there is ample clearance for you and your sleeping bag.)
> - How easy is it to pitch? (Don't take the salesperson's word for it. Ask for a demonstration, or better still give it a go yourself.)
> - If required, is the vestibule area large enough? (Imagine what it will look like crammed with wet packs and a stove on the boil.)
> - Are there sufficient doors and windows for ventilation? Can they be sealed up if required?
> - Look closely at the fabrics used, the evenness and thickness of the waterproof coating.
> - Likewise, inspect the way in which the tent has been sewn. Look for even and straight stitching and whether seams have been tape-sealed.
> - Finally, if all else fails, ask whether any of the tents you are contemplating buying are available for hire. A night or two spent in the outdoors will almost always settle the issue.

designs – all made possible by developments with lightweight nylon fabrics, waterproof urethane coatings, and tent poles made from aircraft-grade 7075 aluminium.

For all the different configurations these tents share some common features. Firstly a framework of flexible poles that are sprung into arcs to give the tent its taut shape. With nearly vertical side walls, the interiors offer a lot more head and elbow room. At the same time their sleek profiles are highly efficient at shedding wind, rain and snow. With poles providing so much support for the tent, the need for pegs and guy ropes is minimised, and in the case of free-standing domes pegs are required only to hold down the tent in strong winds.

For the most part these tents have a breathable inner tent with a waterproof floor sewn in, bug-proof mesh doors and windows, and a waterproof flysheet over the top. This double wall arrangement allows condensation to pass through to the flysheet where it will mostly disperse or run off. On frosty nights the still air trapped between the flysheet and inner tent gives some added insulation.

All this ingenuity gives us tents which are lighter to carry for their capacity, faster to pitch, easier to ventilate, more stable, better defended against insects, and best of all more habitable in both fair and foul weather. Is there a downside? Well, generally speaking the materials and construction of the new generation tents are less robust and the designs more complicated. So for instance should you happen to break a pole, or more embarrassingly leave one at home, there is every chance that the tent will not go up at all!

Such risks, however, seem minor alongside the benefits of the new technology, and if the proliferation of futuristic tent designs is any guide they are here to stay. Finding your way through this maze of geometric structures, not to mention the jargon of wind tunnel tests and fabric specifications, is another matter. A good place to start is with your planned use for the tent.

THREE-SEASON TENTS

For general backpacking and lightweight trips you can get away with a simple one or two pole tent that sleeps two and weighs between 2 and 3 kg (4.5 and 6.5 lb). Assuming that you're not planning any winter forays into the mountains your criteria should be a tent that is easy to carry, quick to set up and capable of fending off moderate attacks of wind and rain.

If summer camping is on your agenda then good ventilation is essential. These days most tents have large mesh doors and windows. Some models include long mesh panels in the ceiling of the inner tent which also let in the fresh air. On fine nights you can dispense with the flysheet, lie back and study the constellations.

Aside from conventional A-frame tents, which still have a place in this category, the choice of tent designs include the following:

Hoop tents employ a single long pole which, depending on the design, arcs over either the length or breadth of the tent. With the former you sleep in line with the pole, which means you sit up into the highest point of the tent. In the latter format the pole spans across the sleeping area and often allows for a small vestibule area. These tents are lightweight and simple to pitch, but should the wind turn side-on during the night the large, unsupported side walls can be a problem.

Two-pole tunnel tents have a more streamlined shape and the support of the extra pole helps keep everything trim and taut in windy conditions. Most of these smaller tunnels are tapered and lowered at the foot end of the tent.

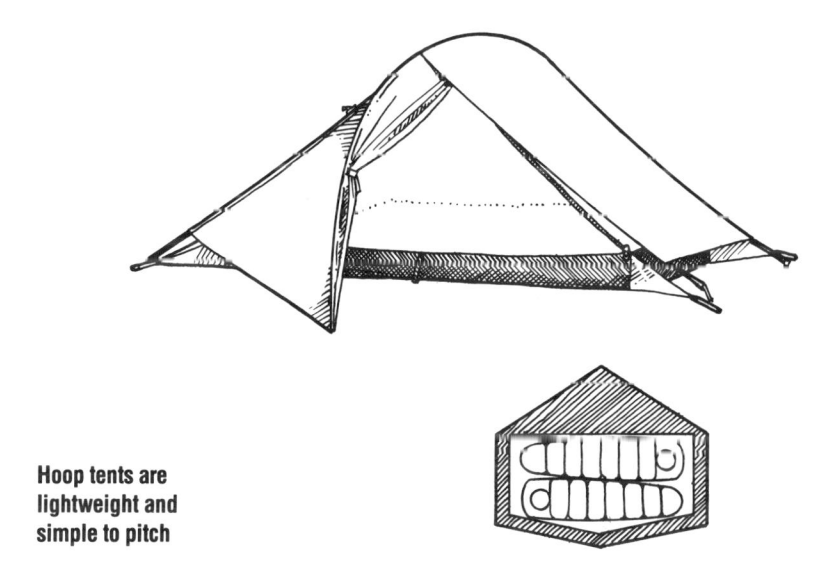

Hoop tents are lightweight and simple to pitch

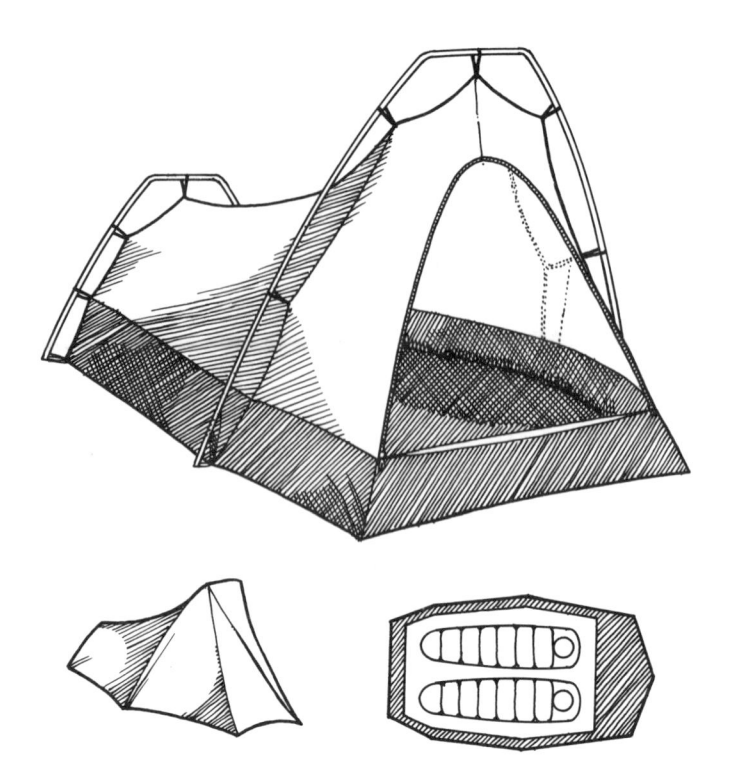

Two-pole tunnel tents are popular and economical all-rounders

Depending on the position of the front pole, headroom when sitting up can be tight. With some floor plans, just getting into the tent can expose the interior to the elements.

For most conditions, however, a two-pole tunnel is ideal and it is probably the most popular and economical all-round tent for the outdoors. In all but the most blustery weather it need only be pegged down front and back, and if it has sufficient peg-out points then, at a pinch, this is a tent you could take to the high country for a weekend ski trip.

Two- and three-pole domes are for those who cherish personal space or like the idea of being able to easily move their tent around at whim. Roomy and stable they are, and by virtue of their design, free-standing. This has real advantages when camping on sand, hard ground or a rock platform. These domes come in a host of different pole configurations which can create storage areas inside or entrance vestibules. If weight is not absolutely critical, then such tents offer spacious accommodation, good ventilation, and in many cases excellent windows on the world outside.

MOUNTAIN TENTS

A shelter for snowcamping or alpine extremes has many tasks to perform. Above all else it must be a sanctuary when conditions are at their worst. This includes withstanding raging winds and sudden dumps of snow. To do this the tent will need a substantial pole structure, a full-length flysheet, a

TENTS

steeply pitched roof to shed rain and snow, and well-designed guying out points which help take the strain on poles and fabrics – no matter from which point of the compass the wind is gusting.

Meanwhile, the occupants will need ample room for themselves and their gear: cramped quarters are no joy when tentbound in a two-day blizzard. An entrance vestibule is essential for stowing wet packs and iced up parkas as well as providing a place for cooking up the stew, well out of spilling range of your treasured down sleeping bag. Ventilation is still a factor, but not at the risk of waking up finding the tent full of swirling spindrift.

Another important point to consider is the ease of pitching the tent in an emergency or on your own. After all, feeding poles through sleeves in the dark is not easy when wearing mittens in sub-zero temperatures – nor is restraining a ballooning mass of fabric whose only ambition is to become airborne in a howling gale. Some designs, for instance, allow the inner tent and flysheet to be pitched in one operation which saves time and keeps the inner dry.

Three-pole tunnel tents are among the most efficient shelters for extreme winds in high places. Although not totally self-supporting, their low-slung shape makes them highly aerodynamic. The poles are usually graded in height with a tall middle hoop to ensure headroom and create a rakish structure that spills wind and snow. While not overgenerous with a living area these tunnels are the lightest option for winter travel. Having smaller floor areas they are also favoured by skiers and ice climbers heading into steep country where tent sites often have to be hacked out of the side of a snow ridge.

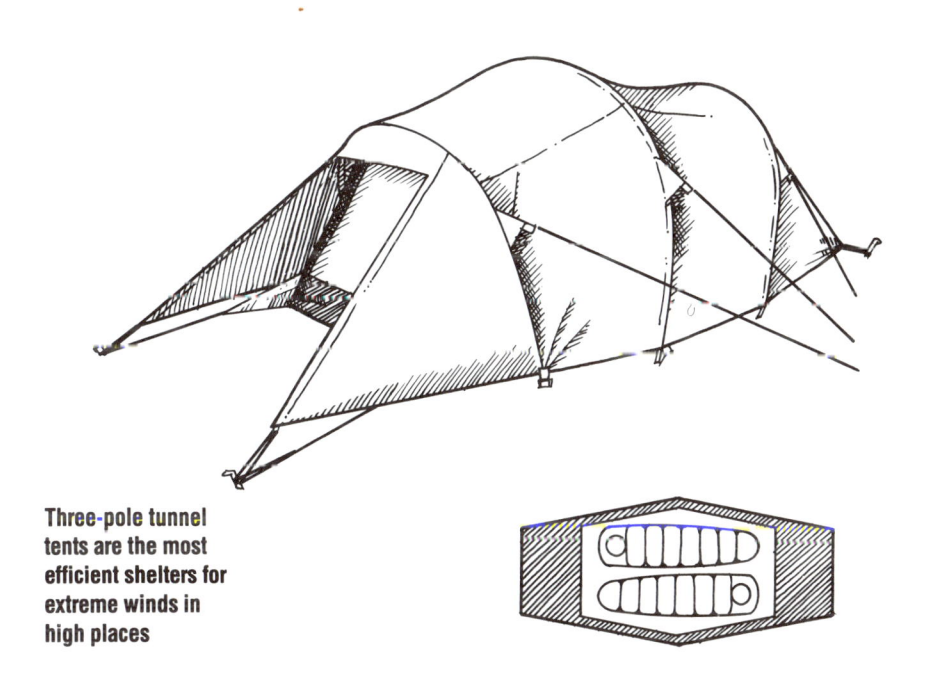

Three-pole tunnel tents are the most efficient shelters for extreme winds in high places

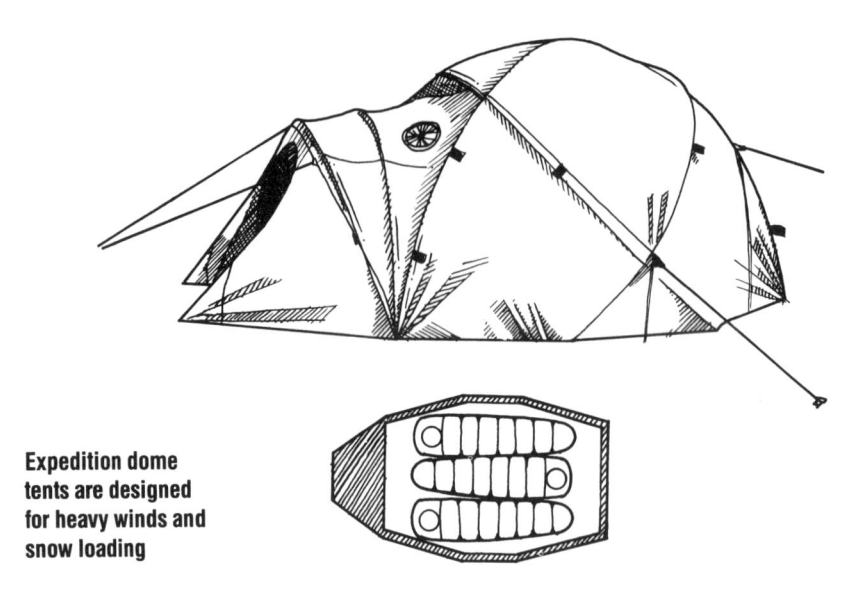

Expedition dome tents are designed for heavy winds and snow loading.

Multi-pole dome tents are engineered to endure heavy wind and snow loading. They use four or more poles that intersect and reinforce one another at crucial points. This forms a resilient structure that will by itself deflect most wild weather, but if things turn violent the addition of strategic guy ropes allow you to see out the night. Some domes also have the facility to run guy lines across the inside of the tent to bolster the corresponding external guys.

The larger of the domes are cosy for three, or palatial for two. Their spaciousness and dependability makes them ideal for extended winter excursions and base camping up high, and on a sunny dawn these airy, cathedral-like creations are a joy to wake up in.

LIGHTWEIGHT ALTERNATIVES

There are many purists and old hands who reject such weighty luxuries in favour of far simpler shelters, even for travel in the mountains. Their contention is that you can move faster with a basic canopy that is easier to erect and keeps you in better touch with the outdoors you've come to see.

Flysheets or 'tarps', are the most spartan and traditional of these alternatives. A simple sheet of waterproof nylon with guy ropes securely attached can be strung between trees as a roof over your head to keep off dew and light rain. Should the winds blow you can peg the sides to the ground to form a makeshift A-frame. Ventilation is rarely a problem but your 'tent' site needs to be chosen with care and adaptable to quick changes in climate.

Pyramid-style flysheets with a sturdy central pole offer more reliable protection. They stand up well in windy conditions and with a full groundsheet they perform admirably. For the last word in lightweight snowcamping a pyramid's side walls can be buried and the floor packed down to create a hybrid tent-cum-snowcave.

Bivvy bags made from a waterproof and breathable fabric like Gore-Tex are an excellent alternative for solo trips and lightweight specialists like cycle tourers and alpine climbers. The simplest versions are little more than an envelope into which you and your sleeping bag slide. More refined styles have room to store gear, mesh entrances for ventilation and insect proofing with hoops over the head area to stave off claustrophobia. Bivvy bags are very popular both for summer outings and for keeping sleeping bags dry in snowcaves. The better constructed brands have taped seams and tough, waterproof bases.

Single skin tents using the same waterproof/breathable fabric technology are also available in simple tunnel and dome designs. Extremely light to carry, they are popular as high altitude mountain tents, but given the limitations of these fabrics to transmit moisture vapour they need, under certain conditions, to be used carefully and well-ventilated.

TENTS OF THE FUTURE

The future for tents will doubtless see new, lighter and stronger fabrics and other components. Given the money invested in fabric research there will also be more progress with single skin tents for general backpacking applications. In terms of design there will be more 'modular' options. This means tents that function happily on their own for one or two people, and that will also have the capacity to be linked together to create a much larger dwelling should the need or mood arise. Additionally, tents of the future will do more to make their owners comfortable. There will be better ways of storing and drying gear inside, and cooking areas will be more defined and ventilated.

TAKING CARE OF YOUR TENT

Before going bush to test out your new tent there are a few preliminaries. Firstly make sure all the components have been supplied: most better brands will have an instruction sheet and a list of what parts, including spares, come with the tent. Inspect the tent to make sure that all the seams are evenly sewn, the zippers work, and the proofed panels are well-covered.

To make a tent weatherproof it's essential to seal all seams that are vulnerable to water entry. Many tents come with a tube of liquid seam sealer which is applied along the seam on the coated surface of the fabric. The aim is to fill the needle holes, so a few thin applications work better than one heavy coat. Pitch the inner tent and seal the floor and lower side wall seams. To seal the fly it's a good idea to put it upside down on the inner tent so you can access the seams. On some models the floor and flysheet seams come tape-sealed from the manufacturer. It's worth taking a close look in case the tape has not sealed properly in corners or at seam crossover points.

Looking after your tent in the field is mostly a matter of commonsense. Protect the tent floor from sharp sticks and stones – a lightweight groundsheet helps. If weight and space permit, a sheet of thin 3 mm ($1/10$ in) closed cell foam can be used to protect the tent floor, as well as providing an extra margin of insulation when on snow or cold ground.

A wet tent is heavy to carry, not to mention damp and uninviting, so make an effort to dry it out before night-time rolls around again. Nylon tents dry quickly but a small sponge is handy for removing excess water and mopping up spills indoors.

Some fabrics will deteriorate after prolonged exposure to UV light. If base camping in the wilds for several weeks or months it pays to give your tent some shelter from direct sunlight.

After returning from a trip resist the temptation to fling your tent into a cupboard and forget about it. Tents should be dried and aired before storing, unless you like the idea of a mouldy tent. If you've been camping near the sea, the poles and perhaps the tent too should be given a sluice with fresh water. It is not a good idea to machine wash tents.

Finally, to protect the proofing tents should be rolled rather than folded.

19

STOVES AND COOKING EQUIPMENT

A light, compact stove is now an essential item of equipment for wilderness travel. Even in places where campfires are not out of the question there is still a compelling case for having a stove. It allows you to camp and cook where you please; it gives you a more controlled flame to work with; it can be used for quick lunchtime brews and emergency meals. Most of all, a stove reduces the need for large, wasteful cooking fires. If you hanker after flickering flames purely for warmth and contentment, it is remarkable how effective a small, well-managed fire can be.

The best stove is the one you know. Like any piece of apparatus they have their idiosyncracies. After several trips with a particular stove you know instinctively how to coax it alight, how long a pot will take to boil, and just how to tweak the flame adjustment to cook a meal to perfection. With the more cantankerous ones you will probably also learn how to pull the thing to bits when it gets temperamental.

Apart from a couple of notable exceptions the design of backpacking stoves has remained surprisingly constant. The wilderness is a severe testing ground, particularly when rumbling stomachs are involved, so you can be reasonably sure that the stoves which have survived will do the job. These include some timeless classics that have purred away in every far-flung part of the globe.

A stove for rucksack travel has to be lightweight and easy to pack. The longer the excursion, the more critical is fuel efficiency and reliability. Stoves are vulnerable to wind and clumsy handling so stability and some form of windshield are important. A powerful burner is needed in extreme cold and at high altitudes. Stove safety has be considered when travelling with young or inexperienced companions. Above all else a stove should be simple to use and suited to your style of cooking, whether that be boiling up bulk or the sauté-and-savour approach.

The objective criteria of stove performance – like the boiling rate and the burn time of a full tank – are less important than how comfortable you feel handling the unit. Some stoves are better suited to mechanical wizards and inveterate tinkerers, but if you value convenience or are intimidated by priming procedures and volatile fuels, choose a model that's easy to operate.

The type of fuel a burner runs on largely determines a stove's personality. Butane gas delivers clean, instant heat at the flick of a switch, but gas is expensive and the spent cartridges cannot be recycled and are a chore to carry out. Cartridges with an 80:20 mix of butane and propane are becoming increasingly popular for their superior performance in cold weather. Methylated spirits (alcohol) is safe, simple to use and more environmentally sound than petroleum-derived fuels. Shellite or white spirits is basically petrol without additives – it generates nearly twice as much heat as metho for a given weight, but is highly combustible and often difficult to obtain. Kerosene is a less flammable alternative. It is also the only fuel you can buy in some foreign countries. Like Shellite however, kerosene needs to be primed and any kero spilt in a pack leaves a foul stench and can render food inedible.

No single fuel will suit everyone's needs, or excel in all circumstances. Until the perfect solar cooker is invented it's a case of burning fossil fuels or expensive substitutes – unless of course you're happy with cold meals.

STOVE TYPES

Butane stoves

For brief forays, and for anyone overwhelmed by fiddly mechanics, a butane powered stove has real appeal. In its natural state butane is a gas but when pressurised inside a canister it's in liquid form. Simple butane stoves enclose the fuel canister in the wire frame which is topped by control valve, burner ring and wire pot supports.

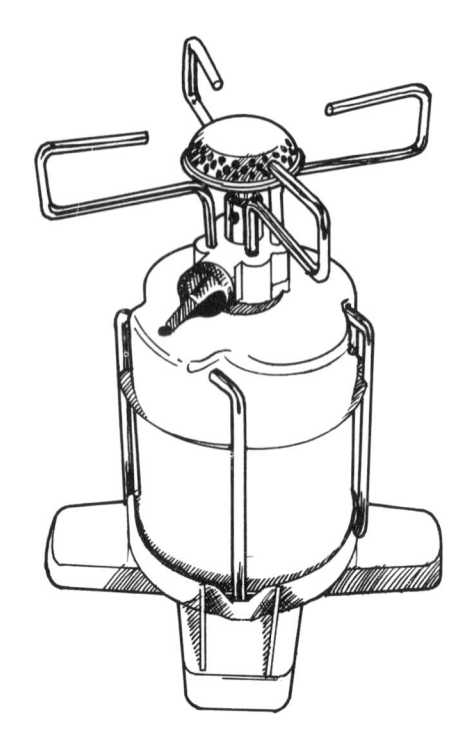

The butane stove is best used on short, summer trips

When the valve is opened the butane vaporises and is ready to set alight. It's quick, reliable and easily controlled for simmering. Unfortunately, such stoves tend to be inefficient in high winds and for heavy-duty use. They are also easily toppled by stray boots and elbows.

The *Camping Gaz Bluet* 206, with its distinctive blue colour scheme, is the classic butane stove; the cartridges are sold worldwide. The big problem is that at low temperatures, and when the canister is less than full, the pressure drops inside the canister and the flame dwindles. Propane helps solve the problem of cold, but otherwise these stoves are best employed on short, summer jaunts. The exception is at high altitude where the outside air

STOVES AND COOKING EQUIPMENT

pressure is much less, and the differential with the pressure inside the canister keeps the butane vaporising happily. Hence the popularity of these stoves on Himalayan expeditions.

Methylated spirits stoves

In its most rudimentary form a metho burner is hardly a star performer in the back-country. The fuel is costly and doesn't burn hot enough for anything more than taking the chill off a fondue, but the smart Swedes applied some lateral thinking and came up with the *Trangia Storm Cooker*. At the heart of the unit is a simple burner cup that wicks the fuel to a ring of flame holes. The real innovation was to enclose this burner in a two-part windscreen. This makes the stove extremely stable and maximises the otherwise modest output of the burner. To complete the story the stove comes with pots that nestle snugly on arms inside the upper half of the windscreen. There is also a frying pan that doubles as a lid for faster boiling. Trangias come in two sizes: the 27, which is big enough for one or two people, and the larger Trangia 25 for three to four.

The result is a very complete stove and cookset that is easy to light and uses a safe non-pressurised fuel. It packs away into a tidy package for carrying and needs minimal maintenance. Counting against the Trangias however is the short running time of the burner — only about half an hour — which means having to refill the burner if you're rustling up a full-blown feast. Also, to adjust the flame you have to reach into the stove and slide a metal disc over the burner, which is tricky unless you have a pair of welder's gloves.

This is not the stove for expedition use or melting buckets of snow, but for trouble-free camping and bushwalking it's a quiet, good-natured unit, and you can always put it into service for your next fondue party.

Shellite stoves

Affectionately known as 'choofers', these are the traditional lightweight stoves for the back-country. They are fuel-efficient and generally very reliable, if somewhat noisy — hence the nickname.

In their basic formats Shellite stoves have a wick that feeds fuel from the tank through a tube, which, if hot, converts the fuel to a stream of vapour. This mixes with air and when ignited strikes the burner plate. The trick is to get the vaporising tube hot to begin with; this requires priming the stove

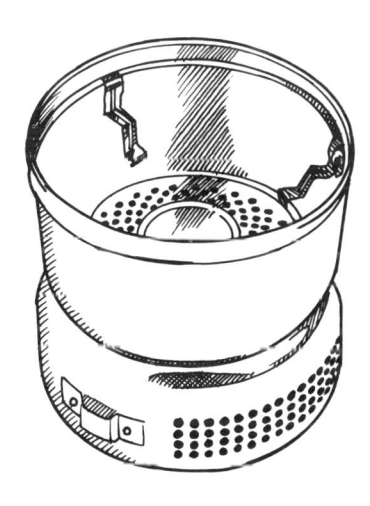

The methylated spirits stove is easy to light and pack away neatly, but they are expensive to run and have a short running time

(see *Lighting a Stove*). Once up and running they punch out a lot of heat, albeit at one point – the burner plate.

The *Optimus 123 Climber* is the classic 'choofer' (formerly made by Seva). Weighing a paltry 510 g (18 oz) and no bigger than a tin of beans, this stove has given mountain travellers faithful service for more than a generation. Never mind that it's easily tipped over, or that the pot-supports and windscreen are rather 'dinky' – this is a gutsy little stove that can bring a pot to the boil in less than six minutes. Its cousin the *Optimus Hunter 8R* is more stable and robust but functions in much the same way. With both models the optional mini-pump is a necessary addition in cold weather to raise the pressure inside the fuel tank.

There are thousands of these stoves in operation all around the world, but, inevitably, given the highly flammable nature of the fuel, accidents do happen. Old-timers delight in recounting tales of flaming choofers being drop-kicked out of tents and mountain huts. These incidents are almost always the result of spilt fuel and sloppy priming. All choofers have a safety valve which releases a spout of fuel should the stove become excessively hot. This is spectacular but not as serious as an exploding stove.

Such displays are less likely on the newer stoves that burn Shellite. The *Coleman Peak 1* is a solid, upright unit that performs well, even in sub-zero temperatures. Though not much better at holding pots than the 123R, the burner on the Peak 1 does deliver a more even, dispersed flame which is easily adjusted by an accessible throttle lever. The crown prince of Shellite cookers, however, is the MSR

The Shellite stove is fuel-efficient and reliable

Whisperlite. With its insect-like legs and distinctive fuel bottle/pump this stove is a radical departure from the old boxy choofer. The Whisperlite is a bare bones unit that weighs less than 350 g (12 oz) but can boil 1 L (1¾ pt) of water in under five minutes. As with the Peak 1 the fuel passes through a tube over the top of the stove to ensure good vaporisation as it exits the burner. Both stoves have a built-in pump to allow tank pressure to be improved, but unlike the Peak 1, which is easy to start, the Whisperlite can require some skill at priming and flame control. It's now the most efficient stove in its class, if you don't mind taking the trouble to get to know its quirks.

Kerosene stoves

A stove running on kerosene is inherently safer than a Shellite burner.

Kerosene has a much higher flash point, so spilt fuel doesn't easily erupt into flame and there's less risk if overheated or pressurised. This does mean that a kero stove needs to be cajoled into action with careful priming, but once going it generates an impressive amount of heat, albeit with some smoky fumes.

The veteran kerosene stove is the *Optimus* 00. It looks like a museum piece with its spindly legs and polished brass fuel tank, yet this appearance belies a powerful performance in the field.

Multi-fuel stoves

A stove that can burn a variety of fuels is a distinct advantage when travelling and for expedition cooking.

The first multi-fuel stove, and still one of the best, is the MSR XGK. The original brief was for a stove to melt snow, and lots of it. This resulted in a design that the Spartans would have been proud of. It boasts an ingenious pump that fits into the standard Sigg fuel bottle, thus eliminating the need for its own fuel tank – the set-up that MSR handed down to the Whisperlite. Fuel is pumped down a rigid tube and through the pre-heating loop. At the business end is a conventional burner plate that gives the XGK its ferocious heat output and unmistakable roar. One of the best features of the stove is also the simplest: a heavy-gauge aluminium foil windscreen that traps and reflects heat around the cooking pot. The long fuel line, however, causes a delay in throttle adjustment and simmering is a fine art – basically the XGK prefers to run at full blast, which is why it has become the standard stove for expeditions and serious snowcamping.

MSR also produces a multi-fuel version of the Whisperlite called the *Internationale*. Like the XGK it will run on Shellite or kerosene. Both units are described as 'field maintainable'. This means that you can clean and repair them using the tools supplied and optional spares; a real advantage if using dirty fuels in remote places.

There are other options too. Coleman makes a *Peak 1 Multi-fuel* stove with similar attributes to the Shellite-only model. The *Optimus* 199 looks much like the 8R but will run on Shellite or kerosene, and unlike other multi-fuel stoves it can also burn methylated spirits.

Other options

Solid fuel stoves that burn Hexamine or Esbit heat tablets are of little use for extended cooking. Their only real value is for heating a brew in an emergency.

Small wood-burning stoves that efficiently consume small twigs and sticks are a more practical, if somewhat rustic, alternative. Such stoves are very popular in the United States.

The conventional Primus stove that runs on LPG is only suited to car camping and canoe touring. The weight of the fuel bottle and their awkward bulk rule them out for any backpacking use.

STOVE ACCESSORIES

To safely transport fuel in a pack it is essential to have a strong, leakproof container. The best fuel bottles are made by Sigg from spun aluminium, which is light but still robust enough to take most knocks. They are available in 1 L (1¾ pt) and 0.5 L (⅞ pt) sizes with a sturdy plastic cap. MSR makes similar bottles, and like the Sigg versions, these are suitable for use with the XGK and Whisperlite stoves. Beware of cheap imitations that may not be strong enough to handle the pressurisation that these stoves require.

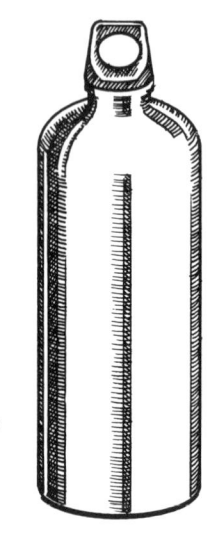

Aluminium bottles are ideal containers for fuel as they are strong and leakproof

Sigg bottles are also commonly used as drink bottles. It's imperative that anything containing fuel be boldly marked. There are plenty of horror stories of people emptying the contents of unmarked fuel containers onto plates of muesli or into billies over raging campfires, in the mistaken belief that the bottle contained water. Better still, use the silver Sigg bottles only for fuel and the red Sigg bottles for drinking purposes. (The red variety also has a lining which prevents acidic fluids like fruit juices from reacting with the aluminium.)

Most spillages occur when transferring fuel from the bottle to the stove fuel tank. The caps on Sigg bottles have two small holes located part-way down the thread. The larger hole dispenses the fuel, the other one is an air inlet. These work, but a small funnel or a special accessory spout that threads into the bottle are better options.

For any stove that requires priming it is a good idea to use a small squirt bottle or eyedropper for placing accurate measures of priming fluid where they have the most effect. Methylated spirits is the most popular priming fluid, although Shellite can also be used.

Any stove benefits from a windscreen. The MSR windscreens are also sold separately and can be adapted to suit most other stoves. You can also improvise your own crude windscreen by shaping and stapling several layers of kitchen foil. If running a Shellite burner take care that the windscreen does not cause the stove to overheat.

Stoves should be insulated from cold ground, and especially snow. At the same time the base of many stoves can become hot enough to melt tent fabrics. A small sheet of plywood or some other insulating material should be used under the stove for protection and efficient running.

Whether you take matches or lighters to start your stove make sure they are stored in a waterproof bag or container. Lighters are probably the most popular method, but waterproof matches stored in an old 35 mm film canister travel well, and a lit match can reach places that a lighter flame can't. Windproof matches are expensive and not especially useful.

LIGHTING A STOVE

- Find a flat, sheltered place out of the way of traffic. Some ventilation is essential to avoid a dangerous build-up of carbon monoxide.

- If using a liquid fuel make sure that the tank is topped up but not full to the brim. Shellite stoves should only ever be three-quarters full. Any fuel spilt should be mopped up or allowed time to evaporate.

- Pressure stoves have a safety release valve that will in extreme circumstances send out a stream of flame. Orientate the stove so that the valve is directed where it will do the least damage in the event of a blow out.

- If the stove requires priming the safest method is to pour a little priming fluid into the priming cup. Make sure that the caps on the fuel tank and any fuel bottles are screwed tight. Close the fuel control valve on the stove. Light the priming fluid and allow it to burn for a few seconds. Just before the priming flame dies, gradually open the stove's fuel control valve. You should have an even, blue flame. Any sputtering or flaring may indicate insufficient priming.

- Stoves should be manned at all times. If a stove runs out of fuel it should be left to cool before refilling the tank. In the unlikely case of a safety valve blow out or any stove flare-ups carefully attempt to shut down the fuel supply to the burner.

- Ensure that the stove is well clear of anything flammable, including equipment and undergrowth. Stoves should be a good distance from any other flame such as candles, campfires and other stoves.

COOKWARE AND UTENSILS

For most outdoor cooking you need at least two good billies and a frying pan. Some hardened types make do with a single pot, but this severely limits the kind of meals that can be prepared and means that the pot is forever being cleaned to boil a brew. The traditional billy is tall and narrow with a wire handle. This is fine for hanging over a campfire, but a wider, squat billy is more easily brought to the boil and better suited to most stoves. The exact size will depend on the numbers being catered for. Most people choose a nesting pair of pots which are about 2 L (3½ pt) and 1 L (1¾ pt) in size respectively.

Such billies are usually bought as a set. Trangia makes nesting cooksets similar to those included with their Stormcookers. They also have well-designed kettles that fit inside the pots, and offer pans with a non-stick surface. For lightness and strength billies have been conventionally made from aluminium. Stainless steel is also now popular for cookware – Sigg offers nesting pots and frying pans made from light, sturdy steel.

Not all the pots in these combination sets have handles. A pair of billy grippers is thus essential for pot handling, and they are always useful for lifting any pot off a hot campfire. The grippers supplied with cooksets often only grip well the pots in the particular kit. All-purpose wire grippers are more versatile and have longer handles for safer manoeuvring over campfires.

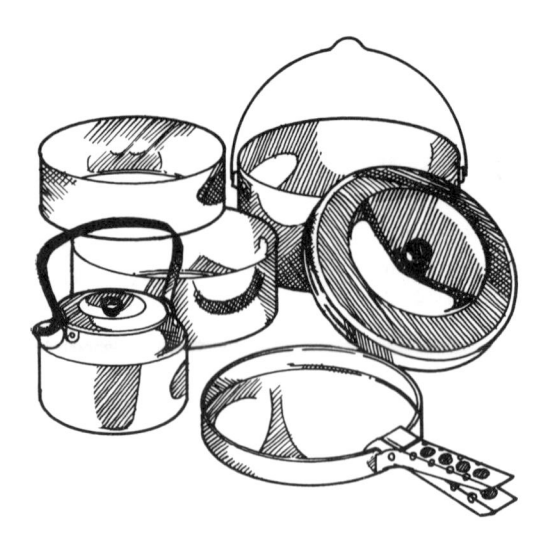

Nesting billies with billy grippers

Your choice of cookware need not be dictated by tradition. If inclined towards Asian cooking then a small, lightweight wok can reasonably be carried in place of a frying pan on all but the most arduous trips. Items like jaffle irons and cast-iron camp ovens, while very useful, are probably only practical for standing camps and canoeing trips. At the other extreme, don't underestimate the usefulness of aluminium foil for outdoor cooking, but don't leave it behind as rubbish.

When travelling light the only utensils you probably need are a spoon and your pocket knife, but if cooking with a large group a few carefully chosen implements will make life much more civilised. A compact wooden cutting board and a decent-sized sharp knife are invaluable for chopping fresh ingredients. Opinel makes a classic knife with a blade that folds away into the wooden handle. Other useful items to consider include a wooden spoon, light plastic egg flip and a small bowl scraper. The latter is very handy for extracting the last morsels from the cooking billy and simplifying washing up.

Personal eating items can be kept to a minimum. Many people survive with

---

BUYING A STOVE

- Try to become familiar with different stoves. Some equipment stores have stoves for rent, others run stove demonstrations.
- Decide whether you need a fast, fuel-efficient stove or are better served by something that's safe and easy to run.
- Consider the cost and availability of particular fuels in the areas where you will be using the stove.
- Buy the simplest stove that suits your style of cooking.

a high-sided plastic bowl which also functions as their mug: a bit tricky if you like to have a drink with the evening meal. If you fall into this category take a sturdy plastic mug as well. Knife, fork and spoon sets, and pocket knives with cutlery attached can be left at home. A spoon and knife are all you need unless you're carrying a wok, in which case only chopsticks will do!

Nobody should venture into the outdoors without a personal water bottle. The Sigg aluminium drink bottles are very popular but even more robust are the plastic Nalgene bottles made from high-density polyethylene. The Nalgene bottles have leak-proof lids and are less affected by food flavours than the cheaper containers. Whatever bottle you choose it should be of at least 1 L (1¾ pt) in capacity.

For transporting water in bulk the best option is to recycle wine cask inners. Several companies sell strong carry bags designed to take these inners, but it's simple enough to sew your own. The classic canvas water bucket is another alternative for carrying water short distances to your camp.

20

CLIMBING, MOUNTAINEERING AND CROSS-COUNTRY SKI GEAR

Rock climbing, mountaineering and cross-country skiing are all sophisticated, active ways of interacting with the outdoors, and in most instances they take people into potentially dangerous environments. In each of these activities the proper use of the right equipment can make the difference between a safe, enjoyable outing or a disaster. Where one's life may depend on an item of gear such as a rope, harness, or ice-axe it is foolish to skimp on quality. This chapter will give you the basis of what to look for when purchasing many of these items, but it's always best to buy from a specialty store where you can get good advice on the sizes and items to suit your physique, and knowledge about gear that is appropriate to where you wish to climb or ski.

The sport of climbing and mountaineering is governed internationally by the UIAA, the International Union of Alpine Associations. This body has a sub-committee that has established a set of standards to which climbing gear should conform with regard to strength and materials. Many manufacturers conduct tests on their own gear, and those that conform to the UIAA standards are entitled to carry a UIAA stamp of approval. Like many standards, however, those of the UIAA are not universal and some manufacturers do not participate in this programme. Despite this, their own products are usually tested and rated well above the UIAA standards.

In conjunction with the growing popularity of climbing and skiing there has been a proliferation of innovative designs in the items of gear used in these activities. This has been aided by the development and introduction of stronger, lighter materials such as chrome moly steel, aircraft grade aluminium alloys, Gore-Tex, Kevlar and carbon fibre. The gear has also become highly specialised to the point where items are now tailored to the particular needs of each facet of the activity. A telemark ski, for instance, is very different to a touring ski, and mountaineering rope is quite different to free rock climbing rope.

ROCK CLIMBING

Ropes

Ropes made for climbing are highly specialised, and nothing but a proper climbing rope should be used whenever this sport is practised. The earliest climbing ropes used in the Victorian era were hawser-laid in construction (three strands wound together) and made of natural hemp fibre. These were not very strong and gave rise to the maxim 'the leader never falls'. Nylon was invented in 1938 but laid ropes of this material were not introduced to climbing until after the Second World War. Nylon-laid ropes are still available today, mostly for fixed ropes and handlines, but they are seldom used for rock climbing as they kink badly and give a lot of friction as the ridges drag over rock edges. Goldline is the main brand of laid nylon climbing rope. The most popular style of climbing ropes used today are known as kernmantle. They have an inner core or kern that gives the rope its major strength, stretch and load-bearing properties, and an outer braided sheath (mantle) that protects the core from abrasion and gives the rope its handling characteristics.

Climbing ropes are constructed of a type of nylon called perlon and are extremely strong — most have almost a 3.06 tonne (3 ton) breaking strain. There are different ropes for different styles of climbing (free climbing, mountaineering, glacier travel) and varying diameters for different techniques of protection: (single rope protection – usually 11 mm in diameter; double ropes – usually 9 mm diameter, and twin ropes). Climbing ropes also vary in length, but the accepted standard length for free rock climbing is now 50 m (165 ft). New developments in rope technology are making it possible to have smaller diameter single ropes (10 mm) that are as strong as the thicker (11 mm).

Climbing ropes, also known as dynamic ropes, are designed to stretch under the shock loading of a leader's fall, but under the static weight of a climber (up to 80 kg [175 lb]) have minimal extension. This stretch under the fall of a leader may be up to 50 per cent of the length of the rope over which the load is spread. The ropes are rated according to the number of factor one falls they can safely hold – usually between seven and 12. A factor one fall is where the leader falls twice the distance of the rope that has been paid out. It is extremely rare for a climber to make such a plummet, and ropes are usually discarded because they become furry or frayed, rather than having absorbed too many serious falls. A good climbing rope will handle well. It should not be too stiff, or kink easily. It is a good idea to mark the midpoint of a climbing rope in some way that will not damage the rope. This is useful when setting up abseils and will make coiling the rope faster.

Most rope manufacturers now offer a type of rope that is impregnated with a

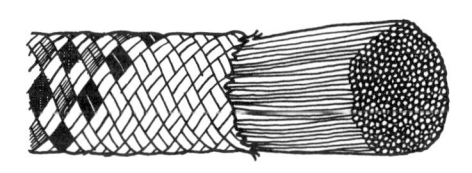

Kernmantle rope has an inner core that gives the rope its strength, stretch and load-bearing properties

water-repellent treatment, both on the core and sheath filaments. In mountaineering situations, where it is quite possible to be caught out in rain or snow, a rope that will not freeze up and is easily handled, even if wet, is a distinct advantage. Dry treatment, as some manufacturers refer to it, also reduces the friction and drag properties and gives the rope added resistance to abrasion.

The other main type of rope used in climbing is known as a static rope. These ropes have very low elongation and high resistance to abrasion, and are used only for ascending and descending — in situations such as caving, abseiling and rescue work where hauling is required.

All climbing ropes have to be treated with the utmost care to ensure their continued strength and good condition. It is not advisable to either borrow a rope, or climb on a rope whose history is unknown. Secondhand ropes should be used only for sack hauling or towing cars — any use where failure would not be life-threatening. Climbing ropes should be stored out of direct sunlight and washed occasionally in warm soapy water to remove any grit or dirt. They should also be kept well away from batteries that could leak acid or any corrosive materials. Inspect the rope regularly for any damage to the sheath, and run your fingers over the inner core to ensure that there are no hidden thin spots. When climbing, avoid treading on your rope, especially if mountaineering and wearing crampons, and ensure when abseiling or climbing that the rope does not run over any sharp edges.

Friction boots

Specialised rock-climbing boots are known as friction boots. Most people start out climbing in tennis or running shoes, as friction boots are expensive; but if you are convinced you want to take up rock climbing a pair of proper boots will probably be your first purchase. Friction boots have smooth soles of soft, even sticky, rubber with leather or synthetic uppers. The reason for the smooth soles rather than a lug or vibram pattern, as is common on most walking or mountaineering boots, is to get as much rubber in contact with the rock as possible. As

Friction boots have smooth rubber soles to achieve as much contact with the rock as possible

with many modern trekking boots cambrelle is often used as the lining in friction boots. For many years the most popular friction boots were EBs; these were quickly overtaken by a Spanish-made style with softer rubber called 'Fire' pronounced 'Feeray'. In recent years there has been a boom in different brands and styles so that now there is a wealth – almost a confusion – of choice in what to buy.

The main techniques required of climbing friction boots are edging, jamming and smearing. Stiff-soled boots are better for the former, while very soft flexible boots are best for smearing. The softer the sole the more quickly it will wear out but resoling is possible. There are now two main styles of boot: low-cut ballet-type slippers that are recommended for thin cracks, overhangs, bouldering and competitions, and the more traditional style of high-cut boots which are better for all-round climbing. Things to look for when buying a friction shoe or boot are comfort, edging, stiffness, breathability and the stickiness of the rubber sole; the boots should be a firm fit but not to the point of being painful. The more serious the climbing, the more the quality of boot will make a difference. High grade climbers do not usually wear socks with friction boots as this gives them a tighter fit and sense of 'feel'.

Harnesses

The forces involved in a climbing fall are sometimes very large, and if these are not distributed over the body they can result in it being pulled up very painfully. There is even the possibility of being injured or asphyxiated from a big leader fall if only a waist tie is being used. Most harnesses today are a form of sit harness which involve the load being taken by waist and leg loops. When starting out in climbing and only top-roping or seconding, many people will find a waist harness, or 'swami

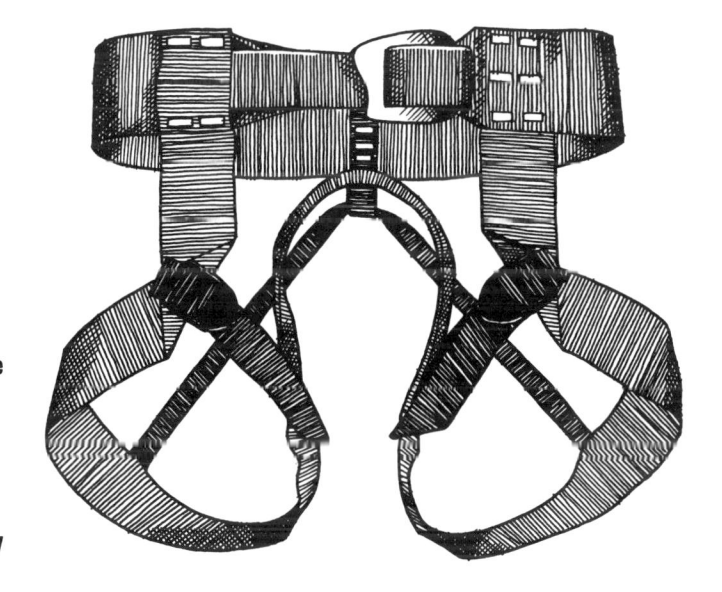

A harness should be comfortable for walking in as well as climbing, and it should distribute the force of a fall over the whole body

belt' as they are sometimes known, adequate. These can be improvised from a long length of broad seatbelt webbing wrapped several times around the waist and tied with a proper tape knot. When abseiling, however, leg loops should also be added or a proper sit harness worn.

Free-climbing harnesses may have some padding on the waist and leg loops, but where weight is a consideration this is usually omitted. The ideal harness will be comfortable for walking in as well as climbing, and spread the load in the case of a fall. A good harness will not rely on the holding power of a buckle on the waist belt to hold to be safe, and often there will also be different adjustments to ensure that the harness fits properly. If it is not a snug fit, it is possible to come out of a harness if turned upside down in a fall. The potential for this to happen is greatly reduced by wearing a combination waist and chest harness, or full body harness. These, however, are not very popular with rock climbers as they are more complicated to put on and take off especially if adding or removing clothing. Some climbers carry their rack of protection equipment (karabiners, stoppers, etc) on gear loops attached to the waistband of their sit harness. Others prefer to use a gear sling over the shoulder and across the chest.

BUYING ROCK CLIMBING GEAR

- The first purchase for a budding rock climber will probably be a pair of high cut friction boots which are the best for all-round climbing. They should be a firm fit but not to the point of being painful. Try them on with a pair of thin socks and wear them around the shop for a while. The main things to look for in boots are, comfort, edging ability, stiffness, breathability and the stickiness of the rubber sole.

- A harness will be the second purchase. When starting out and only top-roping or seconding, many will find just a waist harness adequate which can be improvised from a long length of broad seat belt webbing. When abseiling and leading, however, leg loops should also be added. A proper sit harness with waist and leg loops is the best. Good free climbing harnesses may have some padding on the waist and adjustable leg loops. The harness should be comfortable for walking in as well as climbing and spread the load in the case of a fall. A good harness will not rely on a buckle on the waist belt to hold in order to be safe. Only screw gate karabiners should be used in conjunction with the harness.

- An 11 mm diameter dynamic climbing rope 50 metres in length, which handles well and does not kink is the single rope to start out with for free rock climbing. If using double ropes then two 9 mm diameter ropes will be needed. Single 10 mm ropes that are as strong as the thicker 11 mm are available but they are more expensive.

- A rack of climbing protection gear is the next item to be purchased. This can take years to assemble and be very expensive. Start out with a dozen modified D Karabiners, several quickdraw slings, several 2·5 cm tape slings and a selection of small wires, medium stoppers and several Friends. Add to this according to the needs of where you climb.

Karabiners

Like giant metal safety pins karabiners are the vital link in the climbers' protection chain. They are used to clip the rope to protection points, slings, belay anchors and harnesses, and for carrying and organising protection gear. They are mostly made of aluminium alloy and are extremely strong – lengthways with the gate (opening) closed they can hold loads of over 2000 kg (4400 lb). The 'gate open' strength is usually of the order of 600 kg (1320 lb). There are two main styles of karabiner – the screw or locking gate, and the standard gate. Screw gates are used in belaying and abseiling, and for attaching to one's harness – any situation where it is crucial that the karabiner should not be opened unintentionally. Standard gate karabiners are usually used for clipping protection points to the rope. A lead climber may be carrying anywhere from 20 to 30 of these when carrying a full rack (selection) of protection (stoppers, slings, cams, etc) gear.

There are a great variety of shapes, colours and weights of modern karabiners – from oval to D-shaped and curved gate, and even offset openings. Some steel screw gate karabiners are still made, but because of their weight they are used mostly in rescue work.

Protection

Lead climbing is the most challenging, and also one of the most potentially dangerous, aspects of rock climbing. As the lead climber moves up a rock face they carry a selection of protection devices that are left wedged, jammed or driven into the rock to shorten any possible fall. In the very early days of rock climbing there were only soft metal pitons (a special type of metal nail pioneered in Italy) that could be hammered into cracks in the rock. An American climber, Yvon Chouinard, introduced hardened steel pitons in the 1950s but these caused serious damage to rock face.

The 'clean climbing' revolution in the 1960s was made possible through the development of artificial chockstones. The very first of these were made by British climbers and were drilled-out machine nuts threaded onto hemp slings. Clean climbing was pioneered by the American, Royal Robbins, in an attempt to prevent the damage of rock faces through repeated placement and removal of hardened pitons. Gradually, aluminium wedges of all shape and sizes were developed, which were either large enough to be threaded with a nylon cord, or through a swagged wire loop. A myriad of these, variously known as wedges, wires, rocks, hexentrics and stoppers, came into being.

The next revolution came with the invention of 'Friends' by a Californian climber, Ray Jardine. These are ingenious spring-loaded camming devices that can be inserted into cracks through a syringe-like trigger action that pulls back the cams. They are quick to place and usually easy to remove. 'Friends' revolutionised free climbing by enabling leaders to protect previously impossible situations such as ice cracks, vertical or flaring cracks, and rotten pockets. There are now many second generation camming devices that fit thinner or wider cracks, or are stronger, cheaper or more fashionable. These include Black

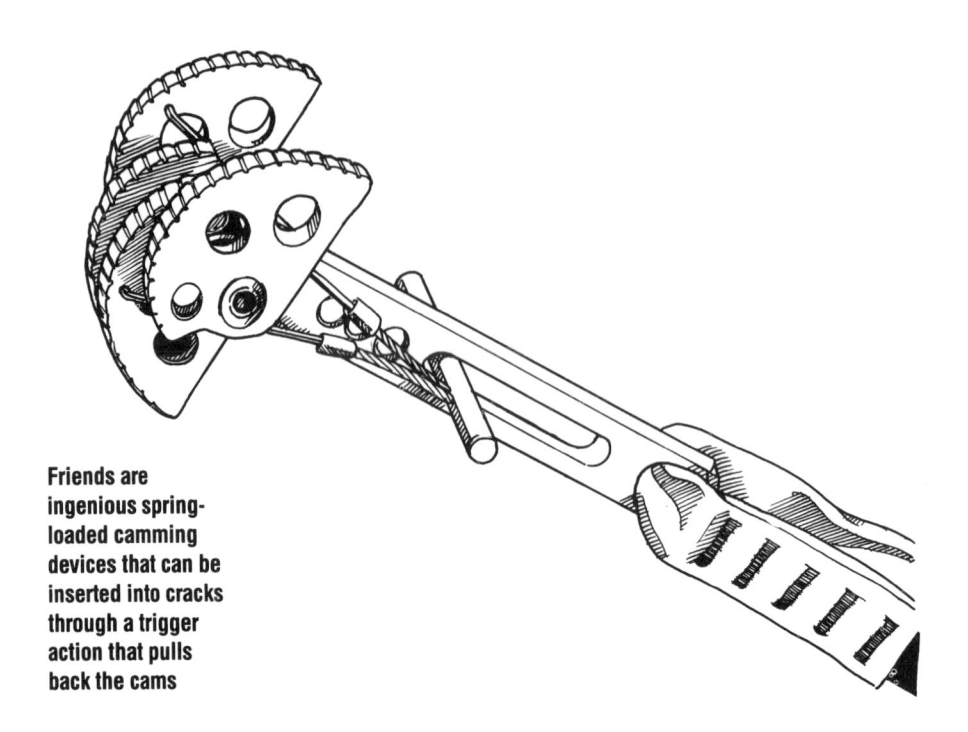

Friends are ingenious spring-loaded camming devices that can be inserted into cracks through a trigger action that pulls back the cams

Diamond Camalots (which come in four colour-coded sizes), HB Quad Cams (five colour-coded sizes of four cam units), HB Micromates (five colour-coded sizes of a three cam device), the HB Fix series, and The Joker. There have also been many variations and improvements in wedges – examples being: HB Cobra Slide Nut, HB Offsetts, HB Anchors, Bi Caps, four sizes of Go Pro Rock N Rollers, Black Diamond Steels, and the fifth generation of stoppers (sizes 1 to 13 on swagged wire loops and sizes 10 to 13 drilled to accept 5.5 mm Gemini Cord). Where will it all end?

Slings and tapes

Webbing slings are an integral part of belaying and climbing protection equipment. Short slings, known as 'quick draws', are used to extend wire stoppers or any piece of protection (running belay) so that the climbing rope runs in as direct a line as possible. Longer tape or webbing slings are also used for the same purpose, as well as for threading around boulders, through holes in the rock, and as an aid in setting belays. Sewn slings are much stronger than knotted ones.

Accessory cords are made in the same way as static rope, having low stretch characteristics. These come in varying diameters from 3 to 9 mm and are sold off the reel so that you can choose the preferred length. Several new types of cord using either Kevlar or Spectra or a combination of both have recently been introduced to climbing. While Kevlar is very strong it is not particularly durable, and Spectra has a relatively low heat resistance.

One brand called Gemini, marketed by Black Diamond, is a combination of Kevlar and Spectra and has the advantages of both. In 5.5 mm diameter a knotted loop of Gemini has a strength of nearly 1800 kg (4000 lb). Because of its heat and cutting resistance, however, Gemini cord has to be cut with bolt cutters. Webbing tape is now also available in Spectra material.

Accessory cords are used mainly to thread aluminium wedges and for prusik loops or safety lines. It is often a good idea for a bushwalking party to carry 20 m (65 ft) of 7 mm or 8 mm climbing cord for emergencies.

Bolt plates

On many difficult rock climbs hexagonal headed bolts have been placed into the rock by the first ascendants for protection or belays. Special bolt plates are available to slip over the head of the bolt, and these are then twisted about to accept a karabiner.

Belay devices

In the early days of rock climbing belaying was practised with the rope wrapped around the belayer's body and held in a gloved hand. A fall sometimes meant that the belayer suffered more than the leader. Being able to hold a long leader fall without being hurt is now possible through the use of a specialised device such as a belay plate or 'Sticht plate'. These are available with two different-sized apertures — one for 11 mm ropes and some for use with double 9 mm ropes. Figure of eight descenders are also often used for belaying.

Descenders

Most climbers use a figure of eight descender, or occasionally a belay plate, to abseil. In long descents the latter can become too hot, however, as there is insufficient metal to dissipate the heat generated by friction. The simplest ways to abseil are with crossed crabs or an angle piton across a screw gate karabiner. Cavers who regularly rappel long pitches use more specialised devices such as a Rappel Rack, Whaletail, or a Petzel Simple or Stop.

Ascenders

These devices slide along a rope in one direction only and lock when weight is applied to them in the other direction. They do the same job as the prusik knot which is often used in emergencies or in glacier travel as a light, inexpensive alternative. The name of the most well known ascender, the Jumar, is now used generically (jumaring) to describe climbing fixed ropes with an ascending device. Ascenders are used extensively in big wall climbing, mountaineering and SRT style caving; and also in self-belaying, rescue and hauling systems. Ascenders are generally used in pairs, one for each leg, although some SRT techniques used by cavers will involve a third ascender attached at the chest or waist.

There are two main styles of ascender: the larger expedition models favoured mostly by climbers have a handle incorporated (Jumar Petzel Expedition and CMI). Smaller ascenders (Gibbs, Petzel Basic, Petzel Croll and CMI Shorti) are often part of ascending systems used by cavers, where the ascender is attached to the harness at the chest or waist. The Gibbs variety work best on icy or muddy ropes.

Chalk bags and chalk

Originally first used by American gymnast and pioneer of bouldering, John Gill, today most serious rock climbers often use 'chalk' to help keep their hands dry during a climb. This can be especially valuable in hot weather and on slippery, greasy rock. For some time the use of chalk was regarded as cheating, and the white marks that are left on the holds are unsightly. Because of both its real and psychological value chalk, however, has become almost universally accepted by rock climbers and boulderers. Chalk is in fact light magnesium carbonate – it is usually purchased in block form and then crushed to a powder and carried in a small nylon pouch-shaped bag that is worn on a belt around the waist or clipped onto one's harness. There are now several different-coloured chalks available (red, grey and ash colour) that are designed to blend in with the surrounding rock. The possibility now exists where a climber could carry three different chalk bags on a climb to cope with changes in the colours of the rock.

Nut extractor tools

Wedges, wires and camming devices often 'walk' or become inextricably stuck in cracks. Apart from the obvious financial loss of having to leave an expensive 'Friend' or similar item behind, this is also not good ethics.

Many climbers carry a nut extractor device which they can use to dislodge firmly placed or difficult to reach pieces of protection. These can be as simple as a length of stiff wire, or a sophisticated Wild Country nut key or Black Diamond Nut Tool – the latter has a hook that also doubles as a bottle opener.

Pitons

There are four main styles of pitons: horizontals – the best known example of which are the Black Diamond Lost Arrows; angles – these have a V cross section; offsetts or knife blades with the eye at 90º to the blade of the piton; and rurps – miniature knife blades that come with a swagged wire cable. Most pitons in use today are forged from chrome moly steel; they are heat treated to give the greatest hardness and stiffness without being brittle. The use of pitons is now mostly restricted to big wall climbs and mountaineering.

MOUNTAINEERING

Boots

Mountaineering boots were once all-leather in construction. In the very early days, they also had patterns of triconi nails on their soles to give the necessary grip on rock and ice. The next major improvement was the substitution of a Vibram rubber lug sole for the nails. The problem of keeping warm when snow and ice climbing was originally taken care of by wearing countless pairs of socks, but double boots were the next advance that helped to conquer the cold. These have a removable leather inner boot, which makes drying easier. The most recent advance, which solved the problems of waterproofness and insulation, came with the transfer of ski boot technology to mountaineering boot construction. Many single and double technical climbing boots are now made of injection moulded plastics or other similar polymeric compounds. The 'plastic' outer shells of double boots are very stiff and often uncomfortable when worn off snow and ice, but the advantages are that they require very little maintenance and are completely waterproof. Double boots are very expensive and there may be many climbing situations where they are not necessary, but what price do you put on your toes — frostbite is the ultimate price to pay. Many double boots for extreme high altitude climbing have inner boots made of a closed cell foam called Alveolite, which, while being extremely warm, breaks down easily. Some mountaineers still prefer the 'give' of leather boots for alpine climbing, but for Himalayan or winter climbing the plastic boots have almost universal acceptance. The more popular plastic mountaineering double boots today include the Koflac Ultra, the Asolo AFS101 and the Scarpa Inverno.

Crampons

Crampons are an arrangement of metal spikes worn on the sole of mountaineering boots to give grip on glaciers, snow and ice slopes, or for ascending steep ice faces or waterfalls. There are a number of styles: instep or heel crampons for occasional glacier travel and emergencies; 10 point crampons (with points projecting downwards) for more serious glacier travel and general mountaineering, and 12 point crampons — where two additional points project forwards at the toe. The latter style are for climbing

Mountain boots consist of two pairs of boots — double boots — which are technical climbing boots usually made of plastic, and removable inner boots

steeper ice walls using what is called front point technique. Most front point technique crampons are rigid, and as a result must be worn with rigid boots. Crampons were originally held on to one's boot with leather and later with neoprene rubber straps. These sometimes come loose, usually at the most inappropriate time. Straps can also often constrict blood flow in the foot which can cause cold feet and hasten frostbite.

Today, 12 point crampons for serious ice climbing have a step-in binding attachment that incorporates a toe-bale and a heel clamp like a downhill ski binding. This heel piece also has a nylon or neoprene safety strap that fastens around the ankle – a type of binding which will work only with boots that have a deep welt or lip on the toe for the binding to grab onto. The high tech crampons that heralded a new era in ice climbing and mountaineering were the Lowe Foot Fangs, but the all-purpose crampon for mixed climbing and glacier travel is still the hinged variety, with either the step-in or strap-on style of attachment. Most styles of crampons are adjustable in length and width.

Crampons for technical mountaineering should be kept sharp and checked regularly for cracks. It is also important to make sure that all nuts or screws are always tight, and that the straps are in good condition. Many climbing accidents have been caused by problem crampons. Crampons, especially the 12 point style, are also potentially dangerous and great care should be taken when wearing these, even at level ground. It is extremely easy to trip by catching a point of one's clothing or gaiters, or even stab your calf with a front point.

Harnesses

Harnesses for mountaineering are generally lightweight sit harnesses which are capable of holding several ice tools in holsters on the waist band. The best model is one which allows the

Crampons are metal spikes worn on the sole of mountaineering boots to provide grip on glaciers, snow and ice slopes

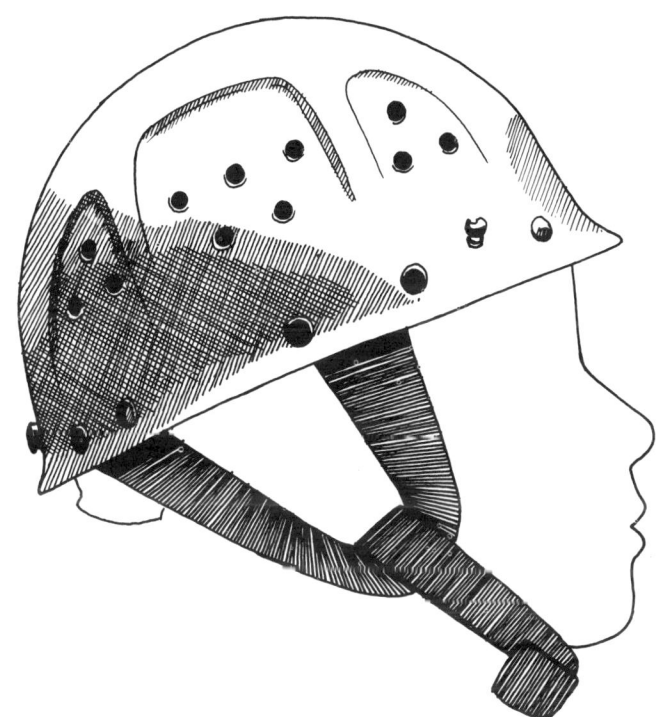

Climbing helmets are used by most mountaineers as protection from falling objects such as rocks and ice

leg loops to be unclipped, so that it is possible to relieve yourself without having to unrope.

Helmets

Today helmets are seldom worn by the higher grade free rock climbers, but they are advisable if somewhat unfashionable. They tend to make one feel off-balance and are rather cumbersome, but helmets should be used in any teaching situation, or where beginners are involved. Climbing helmets are used by most mountaineers, more for protection from falling objects such as rocks, ice, etc, rather than for protection in a fall. There are two main styles of climbing helmets – the 'Joe Brown' bonded-shell/urethane lined model preferred by many rock climbers, and the Edelrid bonded-fibre reinforced model that is popular with mountaineers.

Ice protection

Snow and ice each require different types of equipment and techniques to establish good anchors and belays. On soft snow the best type of belay is with a dead boy or dead man (a flat or dished piece of aluminium plate that has a 1 m (3 ft) wire cable swagged into the middle) – these are dug into the surface of the snow like a ship's anchor. If placed correctly, the more the load the further the dead man buries itself. In firm snow, a snow stake – a 40-90 cm (16-35 in) length of aluminium with a tape tie at the top – can be driven into the snow and used as an anchor. In firm snow, in some situations, it is possible to construct a snow bollard.

An ice-axe is the most important piece of ice climbing and mountaineering equipment. A dead man is the best type of belay on soft snow

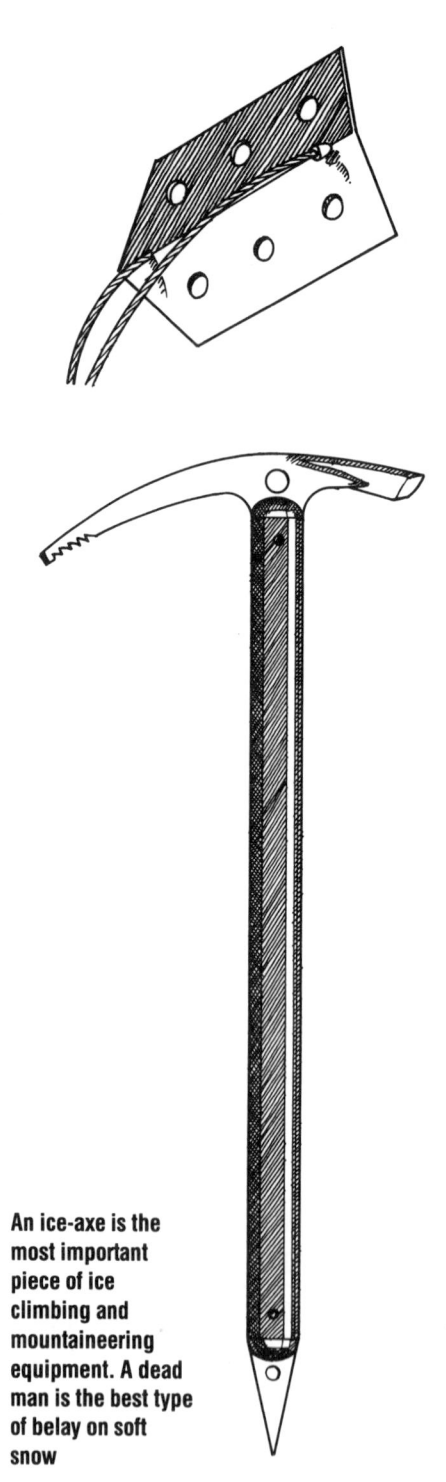

On water ice the only secure anchor is an ice screw or ice piton. There are two main styles of ice screw – 'drive in's' or ice pitons as they are also known, which are hammered in like a piton; and regular tubular ice screws that have a prominent thread, a series of sharp teeth and have to be wound in with turns like a screw. The security of any ice screw depends on the quality of the ice, but in good water ice tubular ice screws can hold 600-2000 kg (1320-4400 lb). The most popular 'drive-in' is the Lowe Snarg, although there are now many copies of this model. These are of a tubular construction. The second style of ice piton, known as the 'wart hog', has a solid cross section and tends to work well in softer ice conditions. Drive-in's have the advantage of being fast to place, but they do not have as great a holding power as the regular ice screw.

Ice tools

An ice-axe is the single most important item of ice climbing and mountaineering equipment. A good ice-axe is a joy to own, and no mountaineer would be without one on any snow or ice route – ice-axes are the first line of defence in a fall. The standard ice-axe has a serrated, drooped pick on one side of the head, and an adze or flat blade on the other. The pick is used for driving into steep ice or self-arresting, while the adze is for chopping steps. The spike at the end of the shaft is used for driving into snow or ice to keep balance, or for belaying. The best ice-axes are light, strong and well-balanced, and come in varying lengths with either metal, fibreglass, carbon fibre or wooden shafts. A classic

BUYING MOUNTAINEERING GEAR

- Good boots are an important early specialised purchase for mountaineering. Leather or plastic shell single boots are adequate for alpine climbing but for Himalayan or winter climbing the plastic double boots are recommended. Plastic boots do not have any 'give' and should be big enough to wear a thick and a thin pair of socks from the outset.

- An ice-axe is one of the most important single items of mountaineering kit. For general snow and ice climbing for a person of average height then a 70 cm metal-shafted axe with a drooped pick is the best style to start out with. If you are shorter 60 cm may be a better length, but if tall or travelling on glaciers where the axe is used mostly as a walking stick, then an 80 cm shaft would be appropriate.

- Crampons for glacier travel and general mountaineering should have 12 points and depending on the style of boots, be flexible or rigid. The attachments can be either a step-in binding or neoprene straps. Most styles of better 12 point crampons are adjustable in length and width.

- Harnesses for mountaineering are generally lightweight sit harnesses capable of having several ice tools in holsters on the waist band. The best model is one which allows the leg loops to be unclipped so that one can relieve one's self without having to un-rope.

- For general protection on mixed alpine routes it is best to start out with a dead boy or dead man, an aluminium snow stake, two or three pitons of varying styles and several ice screws and ice pitons.

---

modern general mountaineering ice-axe, such as the Black Diamond Allpamayo, has a metal shaft and is available in lengths of 60, 70, 75, 80 and 85 cm. Metal shafts are very strong but cold to handle.

. Many models of technical ice tools now have interchangeable heads. These can be varied from curved picks, to reverse curved picks, to tubular picks according to the needs of the climber and seriousness of the route or climb. Most ice tools should have some sort of strap connected to the head, or a sliding ring on the shaft. The other end is usually a loop that goes over the wrist or connects with a shoulder sling. These straps are to prevent the tool from being lost if it is dropped accidentally, or to help support the climber's weight if on steep ice.

Ice hammers, or North Wall hammers, are the second ice tool carried by mountaineers on serious ice routes. The latter are like short ice-axes but the adze is replaced by a hammer head. They are the preferred second tool for ice climbers and mountaineers to carry, and can be used for self arresting and belaying if an ice-axe becomes lost or damaged. The ice hammer is not as versatile as the North Wall hammer but is preferred by many for front pointing and placing ice screws. The ice hammer has an ice-axe style pick and a hammer head, but a short hammer handle. There is a profusion of styles of picks and axes for more technical ice climbing, and anyone contemplating such a purchase should consult a specialty store.

CROSS-COUNTRY SKI GEAR

Twenty years ago cross-country ski gear was all much the same. Most skis were soft, parallel-sided boards best suited to ambling across gentle terrain. The boots consisted of lightweight uppers and sloppy soles and as a result, they had an alarming tendency to twist sideways off the ski the moment you tried to execute the turn.

With the resurgence in telemark skiing and the growth in back-country touring, track skiing and skating, the range of ski hardware has become increasingly specialised. There are now models designed for every branch of the sport, with some even catering for subtle changes in snow conditions.

Skis

Cross-country skis are much longer and thinner than their downhill counterpart. They also have a more pronounced camber (the upward curve in the ski that makes kick and glide movement possible). When one ski bears all your weight the middle section of the ski, where the patterned base or wax is located, flattens to grip the snow when you 'kick' off in the diagonal stride. On the other hand when your weight is distributed between both skis the stiffness of the camber keeps the gripping section off the snow, allowing you to glide freely on the skis' tips and tails.

For driving forward in a straight track a parallel-sided ski is fine, but for turning it's much easier if the ski has some sidecut. This means the ski is shaped so it's widest at the tip, waisted in at the middle and then flared out again at the tail. When weight is applied to the edge of the ski it creates a smooth arc and the ski naturally wants to turn.

The flex of the ski also governs its behaviour when turning. A stiffer flexing ski that's torsionally rigid has more chance of retaining its edge on hard surfaces. In powder and variable snow, a ski with a softer flex is more responsive and easier to turn. Most general touring models strive for a compromise between these extremes with an even flexing ski.

These days the majority of skis have a foam core sandwiched between the top sheet and base. This makes for a light and inexpensive ski. Models with more performance in mind usually have a laminated wood core which is stronger and livelier. There are still devotees who use wax on the base of their skis to provide the necessary grip. Waxing is not as traumatic as some people make out, but in changeable snow conditions it can be time-consuming. Not surprisingly, most back-country tourers, who have enough to worry about with navigation, pack-carrying and steep terrain, choose to use skis with a patterned base or removeable skins. Refinements in the waxless patterns have reached a point where they give excellent grip for only a small loss of glide and downhill speed.

For cross-country racing and skating, where the emphasis is on speed and control in prepared tracks, the critical factors are weight and camber. The skis are narrow and straight-sided with a stiff camber, and demand precise

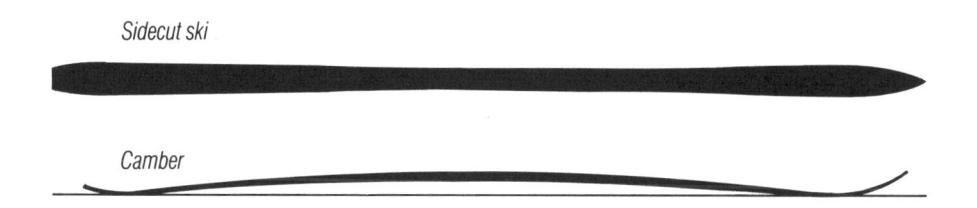

CLIMBING, MOUNTAINEERING AND CROSS-COUNTRY SKI GEAR

Sidecut ski

Camber

Cross-country skis are longer and thinner with a more pronounced camber than downhill skis

technique to flatten the ski when grip is required. Light touring skis are wider and have some sidecut for stability in more mixed snow types but the focus is still on performance across undulating terrain.

Back-country touring skis need to be sturdier to cope with the stresses of skiing with a pack. Some camber is essential for covering long distances, but the likelihood of long descents on unreliable snow requires back-country skis to have additional width and sidecut, with good torsional rigidity to handle bumps and turns. These skis typically have metal edges to help carve turns on icy surfaces.

When the priority becomes control for serious telemarking and other more advanced downhill manoeuvres, the ski needs to have ample sidecut (up to 20 mm [¾ in]) and a smooth flex with minimal camber. The construction has to be stronger to cope with heavy bindings and boots. Mobility on level ground is sacrificed for stability and carving performance on steep, packed slopes.

Boots and bindings

A ski can only deliver the goods if you have a successful combination of the right boots and bindings. Boot styles are largely dictated by the weight and characteristics of the ski and the specific linkage with the binding. Yet, in each category, there are some innovative choices now on the market.

For skating and racing two of the most popular binding systems are Salomon's SNS Profil and the New Nordic Norm (NNN)-II from Rottefella. Both are strong, compact bindings that transfer power smoothly to the ski. Skating boots are higher cut than classic racing models. There is normally a plastic cuff to support the ankle and give control in the dynamic side-to-side motion of the skating.

The traditional choice for touring has been a 75 mm (3 in) three pin binding. This is still very popular and three pin

Skating boots are high cut with a plastic cuff to support the ankle and give control

boots are widely available. For efficient diagonal striding and occasional downhill runs, a boot with a light, flexible upper but torsionally rigid sole is best. If turning control is more critical, then there are boots with increasing degrees of stiffness and ankle support.

Competition boots for telemarking have plastic cuffs and buckles that firmly hold the ankle in place

Touring boots have a light, flexible upper with a torsionally rigid sole

The challenge to this orthodox set up has come from Rottefella's NNN-BC system. This is a development of the lighter NNN bindings. It secures boots with a wider, thicker bail in the toe section to a strong clamp-like binding. This gives an efficient pivoting action for striding, and slots in the binding plate, and lugs in the sole of the boot make the combination very stable on the ski when edging in turns. Manufacturers have risen to the challenge with boots that offer excellent performance for touring and telemarking.

Yet for extreme skiing on free-heel gear you still need heavier three pin boots that give lateral control and have a stiff high cuff for ankle support. These can be used in beefed up 75 mm (3 in) bindings but many skiers prefer the security and added torsional rigidity of a cable binding. Boots for resort and competition telemarking usually have plastic cuffs and buckles that hold the ankle firmly in place.

Poles

The classic touring pole was made of bamboo with a simple grip and a wide basket for soft snow. Now poles are commonly made of lightweight aluminium or fibreglass. For racing, the poles employ exotic carbon fibres to save weight and have compact baskets. Skaters need poles that are stiffer and longer with radically different t-shaped grips.

Versatility is essential in the backcountry: one moment you need a long pole for driving power in the diagonal stride, and the next you want a shorter pole that swings easily and helps initiate turns. The solution is an adjustable pole that can be extended for level country and then shortened

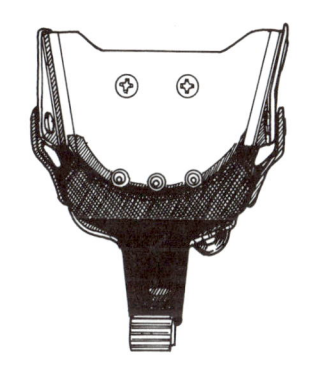

CLIMBING, MOUNTAINEERING AND CROSS-COUNTRY SKI GEAR

75 mm bindings

Cable bindings give added security and torsional rigidity.

for descents. Adjustable poles come in two and three piece versions with a cam, which can be undone and then locked to set the pole at the desired length.

Accessories

For skis that require waxing you need a small armoury of accessories including scrapers, corks, waxing irons and, of course, a selection of waxes and klisters. Even with waxless skis it's important to use a base wax or glider wax.

Many of the wider telemark skis have smooth alpine style bases and minimal camber. For steep ascents with a pack, climbing skins are best used on the base of such skis. Traditionally, skins are made from natural mohair, but nylon fibres are also now used. The principle is simple – the hairs point backwards allowing for smooth forward gliding, but they grip the snow when the ski is pushed back. The better skins have a re-usable adhesive backing.

A small but essential item is a leash which attaches the ski to the boot. This prevents the potentially serious loss of a ski down steep slopes in the event of a binding failure. There are also a host of different ski straps designed to keep your skis together when the snow runs out and you have to carry them.

A broken binding or a bent pole is common enough in the back-country to warrant carrying a repair kit. This can include a small screwdriver, needle-nose pliers, epoxy glue, duct tape, wire, spare bindings, spare pole baskets, pole splints and emergency plastic ski tips.

If snowcamping, then a sturdy snow shovel is essential. Most are made

BUYING CROSS-COUNTRY SKI GEAR

- Start by deciding whether you want light, responsive gear for mobility on trails, or something sturdier with metal edges for the back-country. If possible, rent or borrow before you buy. Some stores have on-snow demonstration days, which allow you to test out a batch of skis, others offer to take the price of ski rental off a subsequent purchase.

- Some people buy skis first, then they select a compatible boot and binding combination. But if you have trouble finding footwear, start by finding a comfortable pair of boots.

- Specific boot/binding systems like the SNS Profil and NNN-BC work well but limit you to that particular set up. This is not a problem for racers, but 75 mm (3 in) gear often makes it easier to try a variety of skis, including ones with cable bindings.

- The correct ski length is critical. A longer ski will give you greater speed on the flat and more support on deep snow. Slightly shorter skis are easier to turn on packed surfaces. The rule for touring skis is that the top of the ski should reach your wrist when your arm is upraised. These days many skiers prefer a slightly shorter ski for telemarking and tight turning. The guide here is your height plus 25 cm (10 in).

- A ski has to have the right camber for your weight if it is to glide properly. One simple test is to stand on the skis where the bindings would be mounted and have someone slide a piece of paper under the skis. With your weight evenly distributed between both skis you should be able to pull the paper out easily from underneath them. If not, the camber is too soft and the skis won't glide. Then, try the same test with your weight on one ski. The ski should be flattened and the paper held in place. If the paper can be pulled out easily, the the ski won't grip.

- Unless you're an expert it is not possible to tell much about a ski's performance by flexing or twisting it in a shop. For those characteristics you need to be guided by the manufacturer's specifications and the advice of the shop salesperson.

from tough aluminium alloy but there are also some excellent models in tough Lexan. A snow shovel is also an indispensable item in locations where there is any risk of avalanches. If the risk is extremely high then carrying avalanche beacons is one way to improve the chances of rescue.

When the snow melts many people keep up their skiing skills by using roller skis or rollerblades. The former is fine for practising diagonal stride on level terrain but the blades are better for skating training and are more manoeuvrable. They behave like ice skates, except you have to turn uphill, or use the rubber brake behind the heel to stop.

21

ACCESSORIES

At the top of the list of outdoor accessories are a bright light, a sharp blade and a good compass. Then come kits for survival and first aid (see Chapter 7, *First Aid and Survival*), toiletries, and repairing gear in the field. A camera, bird book and pair of binoculars seem like a good idea, and what about a novel or two, a frisbee, chess set, notebook, hacky sack, pack of cards and a Walkman. Then of course there are spare clothes, food, fuel, batteries . . .

The inventory of possible odds and ends to carry in the outdoors is endless. Equipment stores are crammed with handy knickknacks to tempt the wilderness traveller, but if you're not careful your pack can become so laden with extras that you may never reach your destination, let alone have the energy to put these items to good use. So be ruthless in defining what accessories are luxuries and what are essentials.

MAPS AND COMPASSES

A simple compass mounted on a base plate with a clear sighting arrow and a scale for measuring map distances is all you need. Silva and Suunto are the most common brands. The more expensive models, with multiple scales, mirrors and other gadgets don't necessarily make navigation any easier.

Having selected the right map for a trip, give some thought to how the map can best be folded (if it isn't already) for your particular itinerary, and how you plan to carry your map. Laminating maps with a thin film of plastic is one solution, but a good map case that protects the map and allows you to carry it close at hand is probably the best answer.

KNIVES

Unless you plan on wrestling crocodiles, Tarzan-style sheath knives are not necessary. The most elegant and functional choice is a Swiss Army pocket knife. These come in a bewildering array of combinations, but the simpler models with a couple of blades, tin opener, corkscrew and a pair of scissors are sufficient. Models with mini-saws, magnifying glasses, etc are strictly for the poser. Victorinox and Wegner are the brands to consider.

If you want a longer blade for cooking or eating, the Opinel knives with blades that fold into a wooden handle are quite useful.

The 'Mountaineer' Swiss Army knife features: a large blade, small blade, corkscrew, can opener with small screwdriver, cap lifter with screwdriver and wire stripper, reamer, scissors, nail file with metal file, nail cleaner and metal saw, key ring, tweezers and tooth pick

LIGHTS

Torches – even the most expensive models – have the unfailing ability to let you down when you need them most. Accordingly, some people use cheap throw-away flashlights on the grounds that they are as good as any, but for most occasions something more robust and reliable is called for.

Weight and size are important in a torch. Bulky models that run on D-cells are generally too heavy for pack travel. A torch is usually needed only on the odd occasion when you want to find your way to a campsite at dusk, or to get out of the tent in the middle of the night.

The most popular hand torches use two or three AA size batteries and are made from rugged ABS plastic or a lightweight alloy. In many instances the switch is built into the lens housing or end cap, so they are less likely to switch on in your pack. The lens housing also serves to focus the beam to give a spread of light or a pinpoint beam. Most are highly water and impact resistant but none is infallible. Their neat size and low weight makes them ideal for backpacking – if anything, they can be too small and many users attach a leash to these torches so they are not as easily lost. Common brands include Tekna, Maglite and Legend.

Mountaineers need a hands-free light for early morning alpine starts and evening descents – head torches are also ideal for preparing meals in the dark, night walking and reading in bed. Lightweight versions include the battery pack as part of the headband. Other styles have a separate battery unit that can be carried on your waistbelt or in a jacket pocket. It's important to try a head torch on before

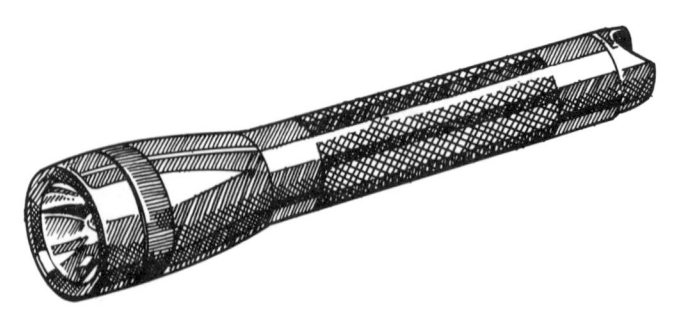

A hand torch is useful for finding your way around the campsite in the dark

ACCESSORIES

A head torch is useful if you need a hands-free light

buying to ensure it fits comfortably. Petzel make a good range of head torches but there are many other brands.

Most long-life batteries will do the job. A few torches also function with lithium cells which have the advantage of being lighter, longer lasting and more efficient in low temperatures, but lithium batteries are very expensive and not readily available. Rechargeable nickel-cadmium batteries are good for short yet frequent use. The light generated by a torch can be increased by using special krypton or halogen bulbs, but these cost more and can handle only certain voltages.

One way to bypass such arcane considerations is to carry a candle or two. They work wonderfully in snow caves and in the tent if you take care. Candle lanterns protect the flame from the wind and are more efficient. Though hardly the cutting edge of technology, the glow of a candle adds a certain romance to any campsite and they also contribute welcome warmth in winter.

REPAIR KITS

When you're in the middle of nowhere it's good to have the tools at hand to sew up a hole in the tent or mend a pack strap. A variety of needle and threads is the basis of most repair kits. Heavy duty sewing awls are worthwhile for expedition groups; assorted spare buckles, buttons, straps and webbing can also come in handy. For major surgery, seasoned back-country types carry some heavy-duty duct tape, a length of strong wire and a small tube of 'super' glue. Ski tourers add to this spare bindings, ski tips, Phillips head screwdrivers and a small pair of pliers.

SUNGLASSES

A good pair of sunglasses is essential to any activity where reflected light becomes a concern, and that includes skiing, mountaineering, canoeing and most things apart from caving.

Glacier glasses are fashionable, but the leather side pieces limit airflow and vision, and are not necessary unless you are actually wearing them in the snow. Much more important is the ability of the lenses to filter both ultraviolet and infrared light; good brands eliminate 100 per cent of both. Glacier glasses are also often too dark for general wear.

Choose glasses that feel comfortable on and have sturdy plastic frames that will cope with the abuse of outdoor activity. Arms that loop behind the ears are good, but a retaining strap is worth using with any glasses to prevent losing them overboard or down an icy gully.

TOILET KIT

This is mostly a personal matter. Many people get by happily with only a toothbrush and paste, a small cake of soap, a towel and an appropriate supply of toilet paper. Anything else like shampoo and cosmetics either shouldn't be used anywhere near back-country water supplies, or is simply not worth carrying.

ENTERTAINMENT

The scope here is unlimited. On many trips nothing at all is needed, and the nights are spent either in simply recovering or in happy reflection on the day's events.

If, however, you've planned a leisurely trip, or long tentbound days are likely, a pack of cards or a chess or Scrabble set can help while away the hours. Musical types have been known to trek into the back-country with their guitars but instruments like harmonicas and flutes are more practical. 'Walkperson' tape players make an occasional appearance, especially on climbing and ski trips.

At some point though you need to call a halt to added paraphernalia. Beyond considerations of weight there are also ample reasons for enjoying the bush as it is, and for what it is.

GLOSSARY

abseiling a means of descent using ropes and usually a descending device.

anchor any point to which a climbing rope can be attached. An anchor judged to be totally safe is called bombproof.

anorak pullover-style weatherproof top, usually with a hood.

bivouac unplanned night spent in the outdoors without a tent and the usual camping comforts.

bivvy bag waterproof sleeping bag cover for use in bivouacs.

bouldering unroped climbing close to the ground on boulders or crags, usually as training for rock climbing.

bridging climbing technique where the hands and feet are splayed out with the right and left sides on the opposing rock surfaces of a very wide crack or chimney-like feature.

bum bag small waist pack.

chimneying climbing technique where upward progress in a very wide crack or chimney-like feature is accomplished by having one's back against one side of a rock face and one's feet on the opposite side.

choofer compact Shellite stove.

crack climbing hand- or foothold using a fissure or crevice in the rock.

crampons spikes that can be attached to the underside of mountaineering boots for grip in ice and snow.

crux the most difficult section or part of a rock climbing route.

dead boy a small dead man — a plate that is used as a belay anchor when buried in the snow.

dead man a small alloy plate that can be buried in snow as an anchor.

edge climbing hand- or foothold using a small lip or ledge of rock.

fall-line the steepest, most direct path down a slope.

fibrepile fluffy, polyester pile fabric.

fingerlocks a strenuous climbing technique where the fingers are placed into a vertical crack just wide enough to take them. When the wrist is rotated downwards this locks the fingers in place and creates a handhold.

gaiters fabric covers to keep snow, stones etc out of boots.

head torch battery-powered torch worn around the head for hands-free operations.

hexes hexentric-shaped pieces of alloy used for wedging in cracks as rock climbing anchors.

hypothermia serious lowering of the body's core temperature.

inner sheet sleeping bag liner.

jamming climbing technique where the hands, fist or fingers are wedged into a vertical crack in the rock to provide a secure grip.

jug a very secure climbing handhold where there is a good wide lip to hang onto.

karabiner oval-shaped snap links widely used by climbers. Screw gate karabiners have sleeves that lock over the gate to prevent accidental opening.

klister honey-like ski wax.

mantle shelving climbing technique where one has to pull up and stand on a small ledge, like a mantle shelf, because there are no holds on the wall above.

offwidthing climbing technique used to ascend a crack that is too wide to jam and too narrow to bridge or chimney. It involves strenuous shimmying movements with one hand and one leg inside the crack.

papoose carrier for transporting a baby on the back.

peak bagging accumulating mountain ascents.

pinch grip climbing handhold where a protruding nose of rock is gripped between thumb and fingers.

pocket a hole or recess in a rock face that makes a good hand- or foothold.

portaging procedure for carrying canoes or rafts etc down or around stretches of river that are unsafe or unnavigable.

prusik knot a knot tied with a thin cord around a climbing rope that will slide up when pushed up by hand, then grip when loaded with a climber's weight. This is used for ascending ropes in an emergency.

rappelling see abseiling.

salopettes high-cut pants, usually with a bib front, held up by braces.

sidehold climbing handhold using a sideways grip.

smearing climbing technique used where there are little or no footholds. The friction of one's boots is used to maximum advantage to stay on the rock face.

spray deck a waterproof skirt that effectively seals the gap between the canoe and the occupant to keep out spray.

sternum strap adjustable strap to keep rucksack shoulder straps in place.

stoppers various sized alloy wedges placed in cracks by climbers as anchors.

stuffsack storage bag, usually made from a waterproof fabric.

swag assorted sleeping gear.

undercut climbing handhold using an upturned hand.

white-out combination of low, dense cloud and snow-covered terrain that confounds perception of space and distance.

wind chill the combined cooling effect of low temperatures and high winds.

windshell outer garment made from light, windproof fabric.

wires small pieces of rock-climbing protection, for example hexes or stoppers, threaded with wire.

BIBLIOGRAPHY

OUTDOOR SKILLS

Abbot & Mullins, **Bushcraft,** New Zealand Mountain Safety Council, Wellington, New Zealand, 1984.

Hart, J., **Walking Softly in the Wilderness,** Sierra Club Books, San Francisco, USA, 1984.

Lamble, T., **Paddy Pallin's Bushwalking and Camping,** Paddy Pallin, Sydney, Australia, 1988.

Rankin, R., **Australian Wilderness Skills,** Rankin Publishing, Brisbane, Australia, 1983.

NAVIGATION

Disley, J., **Tackle Orienteering,** Stanley Paul, Sydney, Australia, 1984.

Gatty, H., **Nature is Your Guide,** Fontana Books, Sydney, Australia, 1977.

Kals, W., **Land Navigation Handbook,** Sierra Club Books, San Francisco, USA, 1983.

Phillips, N. & P., **Rogaining — Cross Country Navigation,** Outdoor Recreation in Australia, Australia, 1982.

FOOD

Axcell, C., Cooke, D., Kinmont, V., **Simple Foods for the Pack,** Sierra Club Books, San Francisco, USA, 1986.

Cribb, A. & J., **Wild Food in Australia,** Collins, Melbourne, Australia, 1974.

Low, T., **Wild Food Plants,** Angus & Robertson, Sydney, Australia, 1988.

FIRST AID AND SURVIVAL

Dawood, R., **Travellers' Health,** Oxford University Press, Oxford, UK, 1986.

Dunleavy, M., **Stay Alive,** Australian Government Publishing Service, Canberra, Australia, 1981.

Hackett, P., **Mountain Sickness,** The American Alpine Club Inc., New York, USA, 1987

Mitchell, D., **Mountaineers First Aid and Accident Response,** The Mountaineers, Seattle, USA, 1978.

Pressley, M. & Macdonald, L. (eds), **Australian First Aid,** St John Ambulance Association, Australia, 1984.

Setnicka, T., **Wilderness Search and Rescue,** Appalachian Mountain Club, USA, 1980.

Turner, Dr A., **The Traveller's Health Guide,** Roger Lascelles, Middlesex, UK, 1985.

Wilkerson, J. (ed.), **Medicine For Mountaineering,** The Mountaineers, Seattle, USA, 1975.

BUSHWALKING

Blay, J., **Trek Though the Back-Country,** Methuen, Sydney, Australia, 1987.

Bonython, W., **Walking The Flinders Ranges,** Rigby, Adelaide, Australia, 1969.

Butler, D., **The Barefoot Bushwalker,** ABC, Sydney, Australia, 1991.

Pallin, P., **Never Truly Lost,** University of New South Wales Press, Sydney, Australia, 1987.

Rankin, R., **Classic Wild Walks of Australia,** Rankin Publications, Brisbane, Australia, 1989.

Smith, R. (ed.), **The Winding Trail,** Diadem Books, UK, 1981.

Fletcher, C., **The Thousand-mile Summer,** Vintage Books, New York, USA, 1989.

ENJOYING THE OUTDOORS

Costermans, L., **Native Trees and Shrubs of South-eastern Australia,** Rigby, Adelaide, Australia, 1981.

Cronin, L., **Key Guide to Australian Wildflowers,** Reed Books, Sydney, Australia, 1987.

Pizzey, G., **A Field Guide to the Birds of Australia,** Collins, Melbourne, Australia, 1980.

Simpson, K. & Day, N., **The Birds of Australia,** Lloyd O'Neill, Sydney, Australia, 1984.

Triggs, B., **Mammal Tracks and Signs,** Oxford University Press, Melbourne, Australia, 1984.

Rowell, **Mountain Light,** Sierra Club Books, San Francisco, USA, 1988.

CROSS-COUNTRY SKIING

Gillette, N., **Cross-Country Skiing,** The Mountaineers, Seattle, USA, 1979.

Parker, P., **Free-Heel Skiing,** Diadem Books, UK, 1988.

Siseman, J., Peck, W. & Brownlie, J., **Ski Touring in Australia,** Algona Publications, Melbourne, Australia, 1986.

Tejada-Flores, L., **Backcountry Skiing,** Sierra Club Books, San Francisco, USA, 1981.

TREKKING

Armington, S., **Trekking in the Nepal Himalaya,** Lonely Planet, Melbourne, Australia, 1985.

Chester, J., **The Himalayan Experience,** Simon & Schuster, Sydney, Australia, 1989.

Swift, H., **The Trekker's Guide to the Himalaya and the Karakorum,** Sierra Club Books, San Francisco, USA, 1982.

Rowell, G., **Many People Come Looking, Looking,** George Allen & Unwin, London, UK, 1980.

CLIMBING & MOUNTAINEERING

Barry, J. & Mear, R., **Climbing School,** Simon & Schuster, Sydney, Australia, 1988.

Chouinard, Y., **Climbing Ice,** Sierra Club Books, San Francisco, USA, 1981.

Langmuir, E., **Mountaincraft & Leadership,** Scottish Sports Council and the Mountain Leader Training Board, UK, 1984.

Livesey, P., **Rock Climbing,** Springfield Walker, UK, 1978.

Long, J., **How To Rockclimb!,** Chockstone Press, Colorado, USA, 1989.

Main, L., **Mountaincraft,** New Zealand Mountain Safety Council, New Zealand, 1980.

Peters, E. (ed.), **Mountaineering The Freedom of the Hills,** The Mountaineers, Seattle, USA, 1982.

Robbins, R., **Basic Rockcraft,** La Siesta Press, USA, 1971.

Wilson, K. (ed.), **Games Climbers Play,** Diadem Books, UK, 1978.

OTHER ACTIVITIES

Ferguson, S., **Canoeing for Beginners,** A. H. & A. W. Reed, Sydney, Australia, 1976.

Tejada-Flores, L., **Wildwater,** Sierra Club Books, San Francisco, USA, 1978.

Judson, J. (ed.), **Caving Practice and Equipment,** David & Charles, UK, 1984.

Montgomery, N., **Single Rope Techniques,** Sydney Speleological Society, Sydney, Australia, 1977.

OUTINGS WITH CHILDREN

Doan, M., **Starting Small in the Wilderness,** Sierra Club Books, San Francisco, USA, 1979.

NATURE, WILDERNESS & ADVENTURE NARRATIVES

Abbey, E., **Desert Solitaire,** Ballantine Books, New York, USA, 1980.

Bode, C. (ed.), **The Portable Thoreau,** Penguin, New York, USA, 1980.

Cahill, T., **Jaguars Ripped My Flesh,** Bantam Books, New York, USA, 1987.

Chatwin, B., **The Songlines,** Jonathan Cape, London, UK, 1987.

Craig, D., **Native Stones,** Collins, London, UK, 1987.

Davidson, R., **Tracks,** Jonathan Cape, London, UK, 1980.

Dillard, A., **Pilgrim at Tinker Creek,** Pan Books, London, UK, 1976.

Dunphy, M., **Selected Writings,** Ballagirin, Sydney, Australia, 1986.

Lopez, B., **Arctic Dreams,** Macmillan, London, UK, 1986.

Mathiessen, P., **The Snow Leopard,** Bantam Books, New York, USA, 1978.

McDonald, R. (ed.), **Gone Bush,** Bantam Books, Sydney, Australia, 1990.

McPhee, J., **Coming into the Country,** Bantam Books, New York, USA, 1979.

Muir, J., **The Mountains of California,** Ten Speed Press, USA, 1977.

MOUNTAINEERING & EXPEDITION BOOKS

Bonington, C., **Annapurna South Face,** Cassell & Company Ltd, London, UK, 1971.

Boardman, P., **Sacred Summits,** Hodder and Stoughton, London, UK, 1982.

Bowman, E. W., **The Ascent of Rum Doodle,** Dark Peak Books, UK, 1979.

Cherry-Garrard, A., **The Worst Journey in the World,** Penguin Books, Middlesex, UK, 1970.

Child, G., **Thin Air,** Patrick Stephens, London, UK, 1988.

Hall, L., **White Limbo,** Weldons, Sydney, Australia, 1985.

Shipton, E., **The Six Mountain Travel Books,** Diadem, UK, 1985.

Tilman, W., **The Seven Mountain Travel Books,** Diadem, UK, 1983.

CONSERVATION

Bell, C., **Beyond the Reach: Cradle Mountain-Lake St Clair National Park,** Laurel Press, Hobart, Australia, 1990.

Brown, B., **Wild Rivers,** Peter Dombrovskis, Hobart, Australia, 1983.

Hutton, G., **Australia's Natural Heritage,** Australian Conservation Foundation, Australia, 1981.

Mosley, J. & Messer, J., **Fighting for Wilderness,** Fontana Books and The Australian Conservation Foundation, Melbourne, Australia, 1984.

Prineas, P. & Gold, H., **Wild Places,** Kalinna, Sydney, Australia, 1983.

Russell, R., **Daintree,** Kevin Weldon and Australian Conservation Foundation, Sydney, Australia, 1985.

MAGAZINES

Australian Geographic, Australian Geographic, Australia.

Australian Wild, Wild Publications, Australia.

Ascent, Sierra Club, USA.

Backpacker, Rodale Press, USA.

Climbing, Elk Mountain Press, USA.

Cross Country Skier, Ehlert Publishing, USA.

Geo, Weldon International and Fairfax Magazines, Australia.

Habitat, Australian Conservation Foundation, Australia.

Mountain, Mountain Magazine, UK.

Outside, Mariah Publications, USA.

Rock, Wild Publications, Australia.

Summit, Summit Publications, USA.

OUTDOOR CLUBS AND ASSOCIATIONS

This listing is by no means comprehensive, but the addresses given are generally good starting points. Other organisations which have active outdoor clubs include tertiary institutions, such as universities, Youth Hostels Associations and National Parks Associations.

BUSHWALKING

Adelaide Bushwalkers Inc.
PO Box 178
Unley SA 5061

Canberra Bushwalking Club Inc.
PO Box 160
Canberra ACT 2601

Darwin Bushwalking Club
PO Box 1938
Darwin NT 5794

Federation of Victorian Walking Clubs
GPO Box 815F
Melbourne Vic 3001

Federation of Tasmanian Bushwalking Clubs
PO Box 1090
Launceston Tas 7250

New South Wales Federation of Bushwalking Clubs
GPO Box 2090
Sydney NSW 2001

Perth Bushwalkers
2 Pearl Parade
Scarborough WA 6091

Queensland Federation of Bushwalking Clubs
GPO BOX 1573
Brisbane Qld 4001

ROCK CLIMBING

Brisbane Rock Climbing Club
PO Box 495
Toowong Qld 4066

Climbing Association of Western Australia
C/- 862 Hay Street
Perth WA 6000

Sydney Rock Climbing Club
Box A592
Sydney South NSW 2000

The Climb Club of South Australia
C/- Thor
228 Rundle Street
Adelaide SA 5000

The Victorian Climbing Club
GPO Box 175P
Melbourne Vic 3001

MOUNTAINEERING

New Zealand Alpine Club Inc.
PO Box 41
038 Eastbourne Wellington New Zealand

SKI TOURING

New South Wales Nordic Ski Club
PO Box A683
Sydney South NSW 2001

Victorian Ski Association
PO Box 210
South Melbourne Vic 3205

CANOEING

Australian Canoe Federation
Box A98
Sydney South NSW 2001

CAVING

Australian Speleological Federation
PO Box 388
Bradbury NSW 2560

PARAGLIDING

Hang Gliding Federation of Australia
157 Gloucester Street
Sydney NSW 2000

ORIENTEERING

Orienteering Federation of Australia
PO Box 16
Abbotsford Vic 3067

CONSERVATION

See your local telephone directory for the address of the following associations in your state.

Australian Conservation Foundation
340 Gore Street
Fitzroy Vic 3065

Greenpeace
PO Box 51
Balmain NSW 2041

Wilderness Society
130 Davey Street
Hobart Tas 7000

ADVENTURE COMPANIES

AUSTRALIAN CAPITAL TERRITORY

Wildrivers Adventure
River Trips
PO Box 140
Dickson 2602
Ph (06) 247 4899

NEW SOUTH WALES

Australian School of
    Mountaineering
182 Katoomba Street
Katoomba 2780
Ph (047) 82 2014

Blue Mountains
Climbing School
PO Box 242
Katoomba 2780
Ph (047) 82 1271

Exodus Overland
73 Walker Street
North Sydney 2060
Ph (02) 956 7766

Explore Worldwide
73 Walker Street
North Sydney 2060
Ph (02) 956 7766

Future Wings Paragliding
46 George Avenue
Bulli 2516
Ph (042) 67 4570

Guerba Expeditions
73 Walker Street
North Sydney 2060
Ph (02) 956 7766

Hi Himalaya
17/89 Broome Street
Maroubra 2035
Ph (02) 661 8928

Kosciusko Adventures
Private Mail Bag no 5
Jindabyne 2627
Ph (064) 56 2922

Out 'n' About
Adventure School
PO Box 417
Unanderra 2526
Ph (02) 963 2370

Outward Bound
GPO Box 4213
Sydney 2001
Ph (008) 26 7999

Peak Experience
PO Box 64
Thredbo Village 2627
Ph (064) 57 6366

Rockcraft Climbing School
    and Mountain Guides
182 Katoomba Street
Katoomba 2780
Ph (047) 82 2014

Somerset Outdoor
    Education
Centre (Colo River)
18 Hunter Street
Hornsby 2077
Ph (02) 476 5566

Wilderness Expeditions
73 Walker Street
North Sydney 2060
Ph (02) 956 8099

Wilderness Sports
Shop 7
Nuggets Crossing
Jindabyne 2627
Ph (064) 56 2966

Wildwise Adventures
for Women
PO Box 63
Gerringong 2534
Ph (042) 34 2563

World Expeditions
3rd Floor
377 Sussex Street
Sydney 2000
Ph (02) 264 3366

NORTHERN TERRITORY

Willis's Walkabouts
12 Carrington Street
Millner 0810
Ph (089) 85 2134

QUEENSLAND

International Parktours
c/- Binna Burra Lodge
Beechmont
via Nerang 4211
Ph (075) 33 3583

Peregrine Adventures
Back Track Adventures
226 Given Terrace
Paddington 4064
Ph (07) 368 4987

World Expeditions
6th Floor
131 Elizabeth Street
Brisbane 4000
Ph (07) 229 5355

SOUTH AUSTRALIA

Peregrine Travel
Scout Outdoor Centre
192 Rundle Street
Adelaide 5000
Ph (08) 223 5905

Thor Adventure Travel
228 Rundle Street
Adelaide 5000
Ph (08) 232 3155

TASMANIA

Craclair Tours
PO Box 516
Devonport 7310
Ph (004) 24 3971

Maxwell's Cradle Mtn – Lake
St Clair Charter Bus Service
Wilmot 7310
Ph (004) 92 1431

Paddy Pallin
Adventure Travel
32 Criterion Street
Hobart 7000
Ph (002) 31 0777

Tasmanian Expeditions
59 Brisbane Street
Launceston 7250
Ph (003) 34 3477

Tasmanian Highland Tours
PO Box 168
LaTrobe 7307
Ph (004) 26 9312

Tasmanian Wilderness
Transport & Tours
12 Edward Street
Devonport 7310
Ph (004) 24 9599

Tasmanian Wilderness
Transport & Tours
28 Criterion Street
Hobart 7000
Ph (002) 34 2226

Wild Cave Tours
RSD 708
Caveside 7304
Ph (003) 63 8142

Wilderness Tours
c/- Robert H Geeves
Arve Road
Geeveston 7116
Ph (002) 97 1384

VICTORIA

Alpine Paragliding
PO Box 3
Bright 3741
Ph (057) 55 1753

Bogong Jack Adventures
PO Box 221
Oxley 3678
Ph (057) 27 3382

Kaykaze Recreation
& Adventure Consultants
GPO Box 141B
Melbourne 3001
Ph (03) 670 4829

Snowy River Expeditions
Orbost Road
Buchan 3885
Ph (051) 55 9353

Victorian Board
of Canoe Education
332 Banyule Road
View Bank 3084
Ph (03) 459 4251

World Expeditions
1st Floor
393 Little Bourke Street
Melbourne 3000
Ph (03) 670 8400

WESTERN AUSTRALIA

Adventure Out
862 Hay Street
Perth 6000
Ph (09) 322 4555

Blackwood Expeditions
PO Box 64
Nannup 6275
Ph (097) 56 1081

Merribrook Adventure
Pursuits
PO Box 27
Cowaramup 6284
Ph (097) 55 5490

Peregrine Adventures
Summit Travel
1st Floor
862 Hay Street
Perth 6000
(09) 321 1259

World Expeditions
Bench International
445 Ventnor Avenue
West Perth 6005
Ph (09) 321 3930

NEW ZEALAND

Alpine Guides Mt Cook Ltd
PO Box 20
Mt Cook National Park
Ph (Mt Cook) 834

Alpine Recreation
Canterbury Ltd
PO Box 75
Lake Tekapo
Ph (05056) 736

High Country Expeditions
21 Godley Street
Twizel
Fax 00 64 5620 765

Mountain Works
PO Box 647
Queenstown
Ph (03) 442 7329

EQUIPMENT SUPPLIERS

AUSTRALIAN CAPITAL TERRITORY

Jurkiewicz Adventure Sports
47 Wollongong Street
Fyshwick 2609
Ph (06) 280 6519

Kathmandu Pty Ltd
Shop 1
BMI Building
City Walk
Canberra 2600
Ph (06) 257 5926

Mountain Designs
7 Londsdale Street
Braddon 2601
Ph (06) 247 7488

Paddy Pallin Pty Ltd
11 Lonsdale Street
Braddon 2601
Ph (06) 257 3883

Scout Outdoor Centre
Unit 12
24 Mort Street
Braddon 2601
Ph (06) 257 2251

Wild Country
59 Woolley Street
Dickson 2602
Ph (06) 247 4899

NEW SOUTH WALES

Alpsport
Ski and Camping Centre
1045 Victoria Road
West Ryde 2114
Ph (02) 858 5844

Bush & Paddle Sports
226D Princes Highway
Kogarah Bay 2217
Ph (02) 546 5455

Bushcraft Equipment
29 Stewart Street
Wollongong 2500
Ph (042) 29 6748

Canoe & Camping Supplies
265A Victoria Road
Gladesville 2111
Ph (02) 817 5590

Canoe Specialists
5 Wongala Crescent
Beecroft 2119
Ph (02) 484 3934

Eastwood Camping Centre Pty Ltd
3 Trelawney Street
Eastwood 2122
Ph (02) 858 3833

Kathmandu Pty Ltd
Shop 34A
Town Hall Arcade
Cnr Kent & Bathurst Streets
Sydney 2000
Ph (02) 261 8901

Mountain Designs
494 Kent Street
Sydney 2000
Ph (02) 267 8238

Mountain Equipment Pty Ltd
272 Victoria Avenue
Chatswood 2067
Ph (02) 419 6955

Mountain Equipment Pty Ltd
291 Sussex Street
Sydney 2000
Ph (02) 264 3146

Paddy Pallin
Opposite Thredbo Turn-off
Jindabyne 2627
Ph (064) 56 2922

Paddy Pallin Pty Ltd
527 Kingsway
Miranda 2228
Ph (02) 525 6829

Paddy Pallin Pty Ltd
507 Kent Street
Sydney 2000
Ph (02) 264 2685

Rockcraft
182 Katoomba Street
Katoomba 2780
Ph (047) 82 2014

Scout Outdoor Centre
Carrington Avenue
Hurstville 2220
Ph (02) 57 7842

Single Rope Technique
54 Blackshaw Avenue
Mortdale 2223
Ph (02) 580 6420

Southern Cross Equipment Pty Ltd
66 Archer Street
Chatswood 2067
Ph (02) 412 3372

Southern Cross Equipment
  Pty Ltd
18 Hunter Street
Hornsby 2077
Ph (02) 476 5566

Southern Cross Equipment
  Pty Ltd
493 Kent Street
Sydney 2000
Ph (02) 261 3435

Summit Gear
(In laneway)
88 Katoomba Street
Katoomba 2780
Ph (047) 82 3467

The Outdoor Experience
518 Macauley Street
Albury 2640
Ph (060) 21 5755

Wildsports
327 Sussex Street
Sydney 2000
Ph (02) 264 2095

NORTHERN TERRITORY

NT General Store Pty Ltd
42 Cavenagh Street
Darwin 0800
Ph (089) 81 8242

QUEENSLAND

Adventure Camping
  Equipment
11 Ross River Road
Townsville 4812
Ph (077) 75 6116

Adventure Equipment Cairns
69 Grafton Street
Cairns 4870
Ph (070) 31 2669

Caloundra Camping Centre
63 Bulcock Street
Caloundra 4551
Ph (071) 91 7177

Jim the Backpacker
138 Wickham Street
Fortitude Valley 4006
Ph (07) 252 4408

K2 Base Camp
140 Wickham Street
Fortitude Valley 4006
Ph (07) 854 1340

Mountain Designs
105 Albert Street
Brisbane 4000
Ph (07) 221 6756

Scout Outdoor Centre
132 Wickham Street
Fortitude Valley 4006
Ph (07) 252 4745

Torre Mountain Craft Pty Ltd
40 High Street
Toowong 4066
Ph (07) 870 2699

SOUTH AUSTRALIA

Canoes Plus
30 Avenue Road
Highgate 5063
Ph (08) 272 9998

Flinders Camping
102 Gawler Place
Adelaide 5000
Ph (08) 223 1913

Mountain Designs
76 Pirie Street
Adelaide 5000
Ph (08) 232 0690

Scout Outdoor Centre
192 Rundle Street
Adelaide 5000
Ph (08) 223 5544

Thor/Paddy Pallin
Adventure Equipment
228 Rundle Street
Adelaide 5000
Ph (08) 232 3155

TASMANIA

Allgoods Pty Ltd
71 York Street
Launceston 7250
Ph (003) 31 3644

Jolly Swagman
107 Elizabeth Street
Hobart 7000
Ph (002) 34 3999

Mountain Creek Camping
and Clothing
71 Murray Street
Hobart 7000
Ph (002) 34 4395

Paddy Pallin Pty Ltd
76 Elizabeth Street
Hobart 7000
Ph (002) 31 0777

Paddy Pallin Pty Ltd
59 Brisbane Street
Launceston 7250
Ph (003) 31 4240

Scout Outdoor Centre
107 Murray Street
Hobart 7000
Ph (002) 34 3885

VICTORIA

Ajays Snow Country Sports
115 Canterbury Road
Heathmont 3135
Ph (03) 729 7844

Aussie Disposals
283 Elizbeth Street
Melbourne 3000
Ph (03) 670 4057

Bogong Equipment
55 Hardware Street
Melbourne 3000
Ph (03) 600 0599

Bush & Mountain Sports
  Pty Ltd
360 Lonsdale Street
Melbourne 3000
Ph (03) 670 1177

EQUIPMENT SUPPLIERS

Canoes Plus Pty Ltd
140 Cotham Road
Kew 3101
Ph (03) 817 5934

Eastern Mountain Centre
401 Riversdale Road
Camperwell Junction 3123
Ph (03) 882 7229

Kathmandu Pty Ltd
13 Market Street
Box Hill 3128
Ph (03) 890 1130

Kathmandu Pty Ltd
78 Hardware Street
Melbourne 3000
Ph (03) 642 1942

Kathmandu Pty Ltd
Warehouse/Mail Order
52 Smith Street
Collingwood 3066
Ph (03) 417 6411

Mountain Designs
654 Glenferrie Road
Hawthorn 3122
Ph (03) 818 1544

Mountain Designs
377 Little Bourke Street
Melbourne 3000
Ph (03) 670 3354

Mountain Designs
20 Tarwin Street
Morwell 3840
Ph (051) 34 3411

Mountain Sports Wodonga
25 South Street
Wodonga 3690
Ph (060) 24 5488

Outbound Camping
83 Mitchell Street
Bendigo 3550
Ph (054) 43 0070

Outdoor Gear
1213A Sturt Street
Ballarat 3350
Ph (008) 03 4213

Outgear Pty Ltd
11 Mephan Street
Footscray 3011
Ph (03) 318 3244

Outsports
340B Hawthorn Road
Caulfield South 3162
Ph (03) 523 5727

Outsports
36 Young Street
Frankston 3199
Ph (03) 783 2079

Outwardly Mobile
34 Waltham Street
Sandringham 3191
Ph (03) 521 0393

Paddy Pallin Pty Ltd
8 Market Street
Box Hill 3128
Ph (03) 898 8596

Paddy Pallin Pty Ltd
360 Little Bourke Street
Melbourne 3000
Ph (03) 670 4845

Sam Bear Outdoor Gear
225 Russell Street
Melbourne 3000
Ph (03) 663 2191

Scout Outdoor Centre
172 Moorabool Street
Geelong 3220
Ph (052) 21 6618

Scout Outdoor Centre
523 Whitehorse Road
Mitcham 3132
Ph (03) 873 5061

The Wilderness Shop Pty Ltd
1 Carrington Road
Box Hill 3128
Ph (03) 898 3742

WESTERN AUSTRALIA

Mountain Designs
31 Jarrad Street
Cottesloe 6011
Ph (09) 385 1689

Mountain Designs
862 Hay Street
Perth 6000
Ph (09) 322 4774

Paddy Pallin
1/891 Hay Street
Perth 6000
Ph (09) 321 2666

Scout Outdoor Centre
581 Murray Street
Perth 6005
Ph (09) 321 5259

Wilderness Equipment
29 Jewell Parade
North Fremantle 6159
Ph (09) 335 2813

USA

Recreational Equipment,
 Inc (REI)
International Mail Order
PO Box 88125
Seattle
WA 98138-0125
Ph (01) 206 575 3287

INDEX

Aboriginal culture, 49
Abseiling
  Cavers, 92, 93
  Children, 120
  Single rope technique, 92
Accidents, 59, 106
Acute mountain sickness, 105–106
Adventure companies, 215–216
Alpinism, see Mountaineering
Aurora Australis, 44

Birdwatching, 42
Bleeding, 56
Blisters, 57, 67
Books, 4, 48
Botany, 41
Bowline knot, 14
Breakfast, 36
Burns, 57
Bushfires, 54
Bush tucker, 34
Bushwalking
  Climbing hills, 66–67
  Clubs and Associations, 213
  Day walk checklist, 73
  Descending hills, 67
  Native flora, 42
  Pack carrying, 67–68
  Path ahead, 74
  Rest stops, 66
  River crossings, 71
  Rock scrambles, 73–74
  Route finding, 68–69
  Setting the pace, 65–66
  Sleeping bags, 150
  Slippery surfaces, 70
  Snow underfoot, 70
  Stone country, 69
  Thick scrub, 69–70
  Wildlife, 43

Cameras, see Photography
Campfires
  Control, 13
  Cooking, 15, 39
  Extinguishing, 16
  Lighting, 40
Camp, setting up, 13–15
Camping out with children, 120–121
Campsite, choosing
  Campfires, 13
  Cleaning up, 13
  Cold, 22
  Heat, 23
  Leaving, 16
  Plan ahead, 13
  Sleep and shelter, 12
  Snow, 23
  Water, 12
  Wet weather, 20
  Windbreaks, 12
Canoeing
  Canadian canoes, 109–110
  Canoe styles, 109
  Children, 120
  Clubs and Associations, 214
  Courses, 4
  Equipment, 110
  Kayak, 109–110
  Native flora, 42
  Paddling techniques, 110
  Sleeping bags, 149

Training, 8
Utensils, 39
Canyoning, 111
Cardio-pulmonary resuscitation CPR, 55–56
Cave archaeology, 112
Caving, 111–112, 120
  Clubs and Associations, 214
Children, outings, see Outings with children
Climbing
  Aid climbing, 93–94
  Artificial climbing walls, 93
  Big wall climbing, 94
  Bouldering, 87, 88
  Children, 120
  Climbing routes, 87
  Free climbing, 87
  Mountaineering, see Mountaineering
  Packing gear, 9–10
  Rock climbing, 86, see also Rock climbing
  Rock grading systems, 87–88
  Ropes, 86, 87
  Rules and regulations, 87
  Safety, 94
  Solo climbing, 87, 88
  Sport climbing, 87, 93
  Training, 8
Clothing
  Bush shirts, 146–147
  Buying clothing, 145
  Checklist for clothing, 147
  Dachsteins, 145
  Fibrepile jacket, 140–141
  Functional layering, 137
  Gloves, 145–146
  Hats, 144–146
  Insulation, 140–141
  Long pants, 146
  Micro-fibre insulation, 141
  Mittens, 145–146
  Natural fibres, 138
  Neck gaiters, 144–145
  Padded vests, 141
  Pullovers, 147
  Rainwear, 141–144
  Shorts, 146
  Socks, 146
  Synthetics, 138–139
  Underwear, 139–140
  Wool breeches, 146
  Wool garments, 141
Cloud formations, 19
Clubs, 3–4, see also Outdoor Clubs and Associations
Cold, 20–22
Colds and sore throats, 57
Comets, 44
Compass, using
  Back bearings, 31
  Cardinal points, 27
  Land bearings, 29–31
  Magnetic declinations, 28
  Magnetic needle, 27
  Map bearings, 29
  Orienteering, 27
  Orienting map and compass, 28
  Setting a map, 29
  Taking bearings from a map, 30
Compasses, 203

Cooking see Food
Cookware and utensils, 181–183
Courses
  Canoeing, 4
  Skiing, 4
Cross-country journey
  Topographic maps, 5
Cross-country ski gear
  Boots and bindings, 199–201
  Buying gear, 202
  Climbing skins, 201
  Leash, 201
  Poles, 200
  Repair kit, 201
  Rollerblades, 202
  Skis, 198–199
  Snow shovel, 201
  Waxes, 201
Cross-country skiing
  Basic skills, 75, 76
  Diagonal stride, 76
  Downhills, 78
  Equipment, 75
  Free-heel skiing, 75
  Skating, 77
  Snowcamping, 83–85
  Snowplough turns, 78–79
  Snowsense, 82–83
  Techniques, 76
  Telemarking, 79-80
  Touring, 80-82
  Uphills, 77
Cycle touring, 120

Day walk checklist, 73
Dehydration, 23, 53, 82
Diaries, 48
Dinner, 37
Dishwashing, 16
Distress signals, 61–62
Double fisherman's knot, 14
Drinks, 38
Dry skin, 58

Emergencies
  Accidents, 51
  Bushfires, 54
  Dehydration, 53
  Exposure, 52–53
  Floods, 54
  Heat exhaustion, 53
  Lightning, 53
Emergency rations, 35
Entertainment, 216
Equipment suppliers, 217–219
Exposure
  Exhaustion, 53
  Hypothermia, 52–53
  Treatment, 53
  Wind chill, 52

Feet, taking care of, 136
Fell running, 115–116
Figure of eight knot, 14
First aid, 8
  Checking kit, 9
  First aid kit, 50–51, 52
  Preparation, 50
  Training, 50
First aid kit checklist, 51
Fish, 34
Fitness, 8
Fleas, 59

220

INDEX

Flooded rivers, 54
Floods, 54
Food
  Basic requirements, 33
  Breakfast, 36
  Bushfire restrictions, 35
  Buying food, 35
  Cooking, 39–40
  Dinner, 37
  Drinks, 38
  Emergency rations, 35
  Food types, 34
  Lunch, 37
  Menu planning, 34–35
  Packaging and carrying, 36
  Snacks, 39
  Snowcamping, 85
Footwear
  Buying footwear, 135
  Comfort, 128–129
  Design and construction, 129–131
  Gaiters, 134–135
  Leather boots, 133–134
  Lightweight fabric boots, 132–133
  Other footwear, 135
  Shoes, 131–132
  Socks, 134
  Styles, 128
  Taking care of, 136
Fractures and dislocations, 58
Frostbite, 22

Gear for kids
  Baby carriers, 122
  Clothing, 121
  Footwear, 121
  Rucksacks, 121
Gear preparation
  Assembling gear, 9
  Checks and tests, 9
  Final gear check, 11
  Making a list, 8
  Packing up, 9–10
Geology, 43
Glacier travel, 97, 98
Glossary, 207–208
Guides, 4

Hang-gliding Federation of Australia, 113
Heading off, 11
Health considerations, 103–106
Heat, 23
Heat exhaustion, 23, 53
Heat stroke, 23
Hiking
  Training, 8
Himalaya
  Religion, 102
  Trekking, 99, 101
History, 49
Home contacts, 6, 11
Hygiene, 15–16
Hyperthermia, 52
Hypothermia, 13, 21, 52, 53, 59, 82

Injuries, see Trauma and injuries
International Union of Alpine Associations (UIAA), 184

Journeys, 10

Knives, 203–204
Knots, 14

Leeches, 58
Lice, 59
Lightning, 23–24, 53
Lights
  Hand torch, 204

Head torch, 205
Lunch, 37

Magazines, 4
Manuals, 4
Map-reading
  Being lost, 32
  Contours, 26
  Grid lines, 26
  Land bearings, 29–31
  Map bearings, 29
  Orienting map and compass, 28
  Scales, 25
  Setting a map, 29
  Symbols, 26
  Taking bearings from, 30
  Topographic maps, 25–26
Maps, 203
Menu planning, 35
Meteors, 44
Minor ailments, 57–58
Moon, 44
Mosquito bites, 59
Mountain biking
  Clothing, 114
  Mountain bikes, 113–114
Mountain marathon, 115–116
Mountaineering, 86, 95
  Abseiling, 92–93
  Alpine climbing, 95
  Alpinism, 87
  Clubs and Associations, 213
  Dangers, 98
  Gear, see Mountaineering gear
  Glacier travel, 97–98
  High altitude climbing, 87
  Mixed climbing, 95
  Rock climbing, 95
  Snow climbing, 95
  Techniques, 95–97
Mountaineering gear
  Boots, 192–193
  Buying gear, 197
  Crampons, 193–194
  Harnesses, 194–195
  Helmets, 195
  Ice-axe, 196
  Ice hammers, 197–198
  Ice protection, 195–196
  Ice tools, 196
  UIAA standards, 184
Mountaineering techniques
  Boot ice-axe belay, 97
  Crampons, 95–97
  Equipment, 97
  Feet-first fall, 96
  French technique, 96
  Ice-axe, 95–97
  Self arrest, 95
  Moving on, 16–17

Navigation
  Alternative navigation, 31–32
  Compass, using, 27–31
  Errors in navigation, 32
  Essential skills, 25
  Getting lost, 25, 32
  Map-reading, 25–26
Night sky, 43–44

Orienteering
  Clubs and Associations, 214
  Compass, 27
  Course, 114–115
  Equipment, 115
  Events, 115
  Rogaining, 115

Outdoor Clubs and Associations
  Bushwalking, 213
  Canoeing, 214
  Caving, 214
  Conservation, 214
  Mountaineering, 213
  Orienteering, 214
  Paragliding, 214
  Rock climbing, 213
  Ski touring, 213
Outdoor gear
  Cost, 126–127
  Criteria, 127
  Hiring, 125
  Mail order, 125–126
  Purchasing, 125
  Quality brands, 126
  Second-hand gear, 126
  Shops, 125
Outings with children, 117–118
  Activities, 119–120
  Camping out, 120–121
  Child carrier, 118
  Gear for kids, 121–122
  Ground rules, 119
  Preparation, 119
Overexposure, 23

Packs
  Alpine packs, 162
  Buying a pack, 164
  Daypacks, 160–162
  Fitting a pack, 166
  Load carrying, 158–159
  Materials and design, 159–160
  Rucksacks, 162–165
  Travel packs, 165–166
Paragliding
  Clubs and Associations, 214
  Equipment, 112–113
Permits, 6
Photography
  Accessories, 45–46
  Camera bags, 46
  Cameras, 44
  Documentary, 47
  Equipment care, 46
  Film, 45
  Taking photographs, 47–48
Physical preparation
  Fitness, 8
  Specific training, 8
Planning a trip, 5–7
Plotting the trip, 6

Rafting, 110–111, 120
Rain, 20–21
Rainforests, 41, 42
Rainwear
  Selecting shellwear, 143
  Shellwear design, 143
  Waterproof fabrics, 142–143
Reading, 48
Record of trip, 41
Repair kits, 205
Resuscitation, 55
River crossings, 71–72
Rock climbing
  Abseiling, 92–93
  Climbing technique, 91
  Clubs and Associations, 213
  Equipment, 89
  Gear, see Rock climbing gear
  Ropework, 89–90
Rock climbing gear
  Ascenders, 191–192
  Belay devices, 191
  Bolt plates, 191

Buying gear, 188
Chalk bags and chalk, 192
Descenders, 191
Harnesses, 188
Karabiners, 189
Nut extractor tools, 192
Pitons, 189, 192
Protection, 189–190
Ropes, 185–186
  UIAA standards, 184
Rolling hitch knot, 14
Ropes, 185–186
Ropework, 89–90
Round turn and two half hitches knot, 14
Route finding, 68–69
Rucksacks, *see also* Packs
  Capacity, 163
  Children, 121
  Compartments, 163
  External frame packs, 165
  Pack carrying, 67–68
  Packing, 9–10
  Pockets and attachment points, 163–164
  Skiing, 82
  Waterproof, 20

Schussing, 78
Search and rescue, 61–62
Shock, 56
Skiing, *see also* Cross-country skiing
  Children, 120
  Courses, 4
  Native flora, 42
  Training, 8
Skies, 198–199
Ski touring
  Clubs and Associations, 213
Sleeping bags
  Accessories, 156
  Buying a sleeping bag, 155
  Construction, 152–153
  Design details, 153–154
  Down bags, 148
  Filling, 150–151
  Human element, 148–149
  Intended uses, 149–150
  Materials, 154
  Shape, 151–152
  Taking care of, 156–157
  Variations and innovations, 154–155
Snacks, 39
Snake bite, 57
Snow
  Ailments, 22
  Bushwalking, 70
  Clothing, 22
  Finding your way, 22
  Hazards, 23
Snowblindness, 22, 58, 82
Snow boarding, 115

Snowcamping
  Cooking, 85
  Igloos, 94
  Mountain tent, 170–171
  Shelter, 83–84
  Sleeping, 85
  Sleeping bags, 150
  Snowcaves, 84
Snow shoes, 115
Solar still, 60
Solo trip, 7
Southern Cross
  Navigation, 31
Stars, 44
Stomach upset, 58
Storms, 59
Stoves
  Accessories, 179–180
  Butane stoves, 176
  Buying a stove, 182
  Criteria, 175
  Design, 175
  Fuel, 176
  Kerosene stoves, 178
  Lighting a stove, 182
  Methylated spirits stoves, 177
  Primus stoves, 179
  Rucksack travel, 175
  Safety, 174
  Shellite stove, 177–178
  Small wood-burning stoves, 179
  Solid fuel stoves, 179
  Multi-fuel stoves, 179
Stuffsacks, 9, 20, 156
Sun
  Navigation, 32
Sunburn, 22, 23, 58, 82
Sunglasses, 205
Survival kit checklist, 8, 62
Survival skills
  Search and rescue, 61
  Seriously lost, 59, 62
  Water, 59–60
Survival training
  Books, 50
  Emergencies, *see* Emergencies
  First aid, *see* First aid
  Preparation, 50
Synthetic fabrics
  Chlorofibre, 138
  Nylon, 139
  Polyester, 138
  Polypropylene, 138
  Taffeta, 139

Talus running, 155
Tents
  A-frame, 167
  Buying a tent, 168
  Choice, 167
  Designs, 167
  Lightweight alternatives, 172–173

Mountain tents, 170–172
Pitching, 14–15
Snow, 23
Snowcamping, 83–84
Taking care of, 173–174
Taking down, 16
Tents of the future, 173
Three-season tents, 169–170
Wet weather, 20
Ticks, 59
Three Peaks Race, 116
Thunderstorms, 23–24
Toilet kit, 206
Toilet matters, 16
Touring
  Day tour checklist, 81
  Day tours, 81
  Longer tours, 81
  Skiing with a pack, 82
Training, 8
Trauma and injuries
  Bleeding, 55–56
  Burns, 57
  Coma position, 56
  Consciousness, 55
  Dislocations, 56
  External bleeding, 56
  Fractures, 56
  Resuscitation, 55–56
  Shock, 56
  Snake bite, 57
Trekking
  Cultural considerations, 100–102
  Gear, *see* Trekking gear
  Health considerations, 103–106
  Options and planning, 99–100
Trekking gear
  Clothing, 107–108
  Equipment, 108
  Equipment checklist, 107
Trip planning, *see* Planning a trip

Vehicles, 10–12

Water
  Choosing campsite, 12
  Collection, 15
  Contamination, 12, 60
  Filtering, 12
  Hot weather, 23
  Survival skills, 59–60
Weather
  Cloud formations, 19
  Cold, 21–22
  Forecasting, 18–19
  Heat, 23
  Rain, 20–21
  Reading the signs, 18
  Snow, 22–23
  Synoptic chart, 18
  Thunderstorms, 23
  Weather map, 18
Wildlife, 43